The
Last Tear

a memoir

The
Last Tear

a memoir

To John and Barbara
with love

Jean Alice Rowcliffe

Library of Congress Control Number: 2013912134
ISBN: Hardcover   978-1-4836-6468-2
                Softcover   978-1-4836-6467-5
                Ebook   978-1-4836-6469-9

This book was printed in the United States of America.

Author can be contacted at www.jeanalicerowcliffe.com

Rev. date: 08/17/2013

To order additional copies of this book, contact:
Xlibris LLC
1-888-795-4274
www.Xlibris.com
Orders@Xlibris.com
135982

Contents

SECTION 3

Slow Descent into Madness

SECTION 4

Retreat from the Precipice

SECTION 5

James's Legacy

SECTION 6

In Conclusion

SECTION 7

Reading List

For James

Acknowledgments

An overwhelming list of family and friends stood strong and faithfully by our sides during James's illness and death and my grieving. As with anything of this magnitude, I fear names might unintentionally be left off the roll, but this is due solely to the sweeping scope of numbers. So many were generous with their resources, energies, and unconditional love, and these gifts sustained and allowed James the best end of life possible. They also saved me from plunging over the edge while grieving his death. My gratitude runs deep.

Specific communities must be acknowledged. Without them, this journey would have been a debacle. The plethora of doctors, nurses, technicians, and social workers involved with James's care was remarkable. Among these, I wish to thank the team at UCSF: doctors Steven DuBois, Richard O'Donnell, Ashley Ward, John Goldberg, and William Wara; the nurses in the various clinics and hospitals; social workers Beattie, Anne, Mark, and Anu; the technicians who performed the countless PET scans, MRIs, and blood draws and who made what were very difficult days somehow bearable; all those on the hospital wards who understood James's desire to get out of there as quickly as possible and responded with patience and professionalism; Robin and Compass Care, the UCSF Palliative coordinators, who not only showed us the path but also helped us to walk it.

Their grace and wisdom were transformative. My gratitude goes out to the pediatric and orthopedic doctors at CPMC for their endless devotion, even when James transferred under the care of UCSF.

Hospice by the Bay guided us through the maze of letting go and surrendering to the unknown. Rowena, Jeanne, Jim, Stephen, Chris, Patrick, and Carol are just a few of the many in that organization who became the columns propping up the pediment so that we were not crushed by the weight, and Nancy who taught me to value, "of course".

The Make-a-Wish Foundation, whose team, under Patricia's bold leadership, worked tirelessly to provide the magical indulgence of a wish that excited the larger community as well as providing James much needed hope. A special thank you to President Barack Obama and Speaker of the House Nancy Pelosi, who willingly joined in the whimsy of bringing James's wish to fruition. You brought us all great joy. My gratitude also to Thom Yorke and Lewis Black who shared their gift of time with James.

Many thanks to the school communities that welcomed James wholeheartedly and helped him grow to be a young man of great compassion and wisdom. They nurtured the relationships that would be sustained throughout his life and after his death. Many of James's long-lasting friendships evolved at his elementary schools, Cathedral School for Boys and Notre Dame des Victoires. Thank you to the youngsters who honoured his story.

Stuart Hall for Boys and the Schools of the Sacred Heart community became the anchor not only for James but also for me, especially during those final months. The remarkable faculty, families, and deeply loved students gave James an opportunity to flourish and find his voice while encouraging his playfulness and zest for life. You were there with us through illness and remained strong while confronting death.

James's legacy will not be forgotten in the "Hall," and that is my *greatest* solace as the years pass.

The Village Well and St. Mary the Virgin provided refuge and work that sustained.

Even when I was broken and unable to articulate my needs, you stepped in and made sure the days would unfold with ease. Thank you to the many young men and women who volunteered to work alongside me. Offering much-appreciated support during those sad long months of illness, the community of St. Mary the Virgin have now become the stewards of James's final resting place.

Reverends Jason Parkin and Jennifer Hornbeck, you provided solace and a safe place to put my rage when I felt God had abandoned and most failed us. James found comfort in your presence, and he died knowing he was deeply loved.

To my family and countless friends who supported us from both near and far, you reached out and continued to do so even when I could not receive. My brokenness may have left you feeling banished, but nothing could be further from the truth. As I was unravelling, your largesse prevailed. I am especially grateful for the steadfast loyalty of Emma, Pat, and Marc, who were there from day one and never abandoned the ship, even when sailing in the roughest of waters.

To those who have been in my life for decades waiting in the wings to pick up the shattered pieces and to my new friends who came at the right time, I say a special thank you. Through your nurturing, I have allowed myself to receive and welcome love once again.

*   *   *

During the final months of James's life, I became committed to writing this book in hopes that it might help others walking the same path. I needed space and time to gather all the threads, and I thank my dearest mother who provided a peaceful harbour when I was finally willing to step off the grid and Jeffery, who reminded me to trust. I am indebted to Elizabeth Gooden for bringing fresh eyes and thoughtful guidance to this project. To Danielle Steel who graciously read the final manuscript and Her Royal Highness Princess Michael of Kent for her faithful and unflinching support, I will be forever indebted.

In honour of my loving parents and the memory of my beloved James, I dedicate this book.

Preface

Your death is a part of the order of the universe, 'tis a part of the life of the world . . . Give place to others, as others have given place to you.
—Michel de Montaigne

This book should never have been written.

If I had been told fifteen, eight, or even four years ago that I would need to record this tale, everyone, including James, would have said it was madness. I would be creating a story that would be so overtly fictitious that it would reek of hollow sentiments and be hailed an obvious lie. Yet here I am, tasked with this chronicle.

It is not a work of fiction, dug out of any overly stimulated imagination but tragically is very real. There is great urgency for me to capture all the threads while the memories remain fresh. I am warned that one day, they will start to fade.

With each key I strike, there is a hushed wish that my hands, lungs, or any body part could have been traded to give James life. I am told that mothers who lose a child to terminal illness often express that Faustian desire to make a trade. Whatever the universe might want in return would be fine. My death would be a fair exchange. Just let my child live. But that is not how it works.

Living with cancer and coming to terms with the fact that a mutant gene—perhaps not so unlike the miraculous one that created life—is the seed that will yank your child from your arms prematurely becomes one of the cruellest twists of fate imaginable. It will leave you broken, exposed, and completely vulnerable.

*   *   *

Over thirty years of my professional life has revolved around the care and nurturing of other people's families. Starting with their early years through teaching parenting skills and helping to organize their lives, I have guided families along the complex, often difficult, path of growing into a cohesive and loving unit. This work has been my life's calling. In 1979, I graduated Head Nurse from the prestigious Norland College in England and embarked on my career as a nanny, maternity nurse, household manager, and personal assistant that would take me from the British royal family at Kensington Palace to varied (often high-profile) households in California. The breadth of my vast experience has included working for the very privileged to those in homeless shelters in San Francisco, and it has been an incredible gift to follow the lives of my many children and families over the decades. In 2007, I founded and was executive director of the Village Well Inc., a community resource centre in San Francisco that provides daily programs to support, nurture, and educate families with young children.

My only child, James, was conceived when I was almost thirty-six years old, and I knew that my age was a deciding factor when stating that "one would be enough." The pregnancy was straightforward but for some preterm labour, which relegated me to bed rest. Yet it was ironic that James ended up being almost three weeks overdue, causing me to think that he did not want to be born and maybe knew something we didn't; perhaps it was better to remain safe and warm in the womb. Nothing made me happier or more proud than to be James's mother, and we had a special bond from the beginning. After all the years of dedicating my life to others' children, I had a marvellous sense of coming full circle in finally giving birth to my own child.

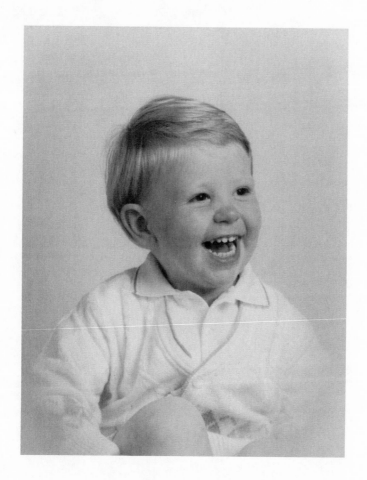

James, two years old

Named after both his grandfathers, James Walter Rowcliffe Kessler was born after a prolonged and difficult delivery on June 13, 1991, in San Francisco. He was ebullient and bouncy, truly relishing every moment that he had on this earth. Like us all, he suffered moments of profound frustration and weariness, but at his core was a tenacity and a deep sense of gratitude that sustained him through troubled moments. James did not complain about small things. He rarely cried or whined and, with a spirit of otherworldliness about him, had a grasp of the big picture. Even as a babe in arms, he had the air of an old soul. That said, he embraced the present with unbridled vigour and playfulness and was a born leader especially when great mischief needed to be exploited. He adored getting mucky; and we would tease that he could find mud in the desert.

Two year old Puddles

James was constantly inquisitive and pushed the envelope to see how far an idea might go, much to the chagrin sometimes of his teachers and peers. Yet even though he would nudge, he remained polite and respectful and could pull back if he knew he had gone too far. Confident in his ability to explore, he also had an innate ability to set boundaries, which was one of his greatest assets and gifts to me. His humour and giggle were infectious and would become one of his treasured legacies.

A voracious consumer of all things relating to skateboarding and alternative music, James also subscribed to *Fine Cooking* magazine and would spend hours in the kitchen happily concocting specialties; his guacamole and breakfasts were legendary.

James's ability to dissect musical trends was amazing, and he had over five thousand songs on his computer when he died. An external hard drive held another five thousand. From some unknown place, he had acquired the ear and discipline, as well as a self-taught knowledge, to be a wonderful critic, and he often said that he'd enjoy exploring that profession as an adult.

Teachers and friends would ask James to download music onto their MP3 players or iPods knowing they'd be assured of an eclectic selection. Being a quiet observer and thoughtful teacher, he would influence the tastes of those around him, often just by example. He was not proud or verbose, and if he shared a thought, you knew it would be astute.

However, James was by no stretch of the imagination a saint, and he possessed a colourful vocabulary that more than once landed him in hot water at school. I accept responsibility for that as I fear my ability to edit was lost decades ago. When his eighth-grade class prepared individual books to go on display for their graduation and they were asked to include a page of gratitude for their parents, James's opening sentence was to thank his mother for teaching him how to swear. He knew that he could share anything with me, and in hindsight, that was an incredible gift.

We christened our charcoal-grey diesel Volkswagen Beetle "Putters," and all of James's friends knew the car by that name. I made a rule (not unlike Las Vegas) that whatever was said in Putters stayed in Putters; hence, it became a safe place to vent. James and I often used Putters for that purpose, and even his friends would invite themselves over to sit in the garage for what would be affectionately known as a Putters moment. I often wonder what stories Putters would share had he been given a voice. Needless to say, I can never part with that beloved car.

What has taken me decades to acquire, the ability to be comfortable in one's own skin, James seemed to possess instinctively; and he never worried about what others thought of him. Choosing his wardrobe with flair, he unwittingly set many trends among his friends. Weekends spent scrounging about in second-hand stores, James happily introduced vintage waistcoats, hats, shirts, ties, and neon sunglasses to his closet. He so looked forward to developing his own style as an adult, and I often wonder what his "look" might have become. These unanswered questions haunt me now.

At the ocean, Half Moon Bay

Even with all his playful goofiness, James somehow maintained a deep sense of wonder. Nature and the human condition provided constant fascination, and in his final year, not a day went by that he did not articulate his amazement that we could create such marvellous things. Science and discovery programs on television became his viewing diet (along with the comedy channel), and he was filled with wonderment, exclaiming more often than not, "How did we figure that out?" He was amazed that humans, who once dragged around clubs in a cave, had miraculously evolved enough to design a machine that could construct a car, guitar strings, or endless rolls of tape without a hand being involved in the process. He never ceased to be mesmerized by our ever-expanding creativity.

Equally stunning to James was the notion that we are all stardust connected to one cosmic source, a belief that nurtured his willingness to embrace spiritual contemplation and eventually helped guide him in his final months. I miss his questioning mind and encouragement to look at things differently. The adult world gets so bogged down in the petty struggles of the daily minutiae that we forget to remind ourselves to be grateful.

Having permission and encouragement from my son to be in awe was one of his greatest gifts to me.

In hindsight, it does not surprise me that during James's last Christmas, armed with a $50 gift certificate from Best Buy, he chose the BBC boxed documentary *Planet Earth*. We spent many evenings in his room watching the magnificent images unfold, and as his nights became more troubled with horrible nausea and insomnia, *Planet Earth* was the lullaby that settled rattled nerves and allowed him to sleep, if even just for a few hours.

Mother Earth became the bosom of peace that James craved.

How James managed to hold on to gratitude, even as his disease progressed, still amazes those who knew him. This vile and rare cancer ravaged every part of his body, and yet in his final writings he talks of its gifts. He openly acknowledged the joy he felt when recalling how he once moved easily and without pain. Moments of satori were attainable even in the depths of his suffering. The closing line of James's final essay states that he would take more away from cancer than cancer could take from him.

So now, sadly, this tragic narrative must be written, in part as a cathartic exercise for me but also in an attempt to put at least a part of his story and legacy in a safe place.

James at Hyde Street Pier, Fisherman's Wharf

James did not have the luxury of a long and complete life in which to leave his mark on the world. Seventeen short years, with only a few in which to articulate his message, is not enough. Yet somehow, he managed to find his voice through essays, poetry, music, and his lively wit. James lives on through his friendships and the lives of those he touched. One of his close friends told me recently that he lives for two now.

James was the greatest blessing in my life, and I miss him more than feeble words can articulate. Hopefully, my journal entries and poems, along with some of James's writings, will help to capture, with honesty, the essence of those desperate days when we had to let him go. Sharing terminal illness and death with your child is a parent's worst nightmare, and when I started to write *The Last Tear*, I was convinced my life would never be more than enduring the acute suffering that plagued me every day. Yet as the years progress, I have discovered that there is a lightness of being that visits from time to time, reminding me that perhaps the story of our intersection *is* greater than the separation.

Section 1

My Leg Hurts

Chapter 1

Discovery

In my happier days I used to remark on the aptitude of the saying, "When in life we are in the midst of death." I have since learnt that it's more apt to say, "When in death we are in the midst of life."
—*Bergen Belsen survivor*

There have been few regrets in my life. Prior to this story, any sadness or longing seemed to be based on issues of the heart. Why did I not say what I meant? Why did I let go so willingly? What could have been the outcome had I stayed? Did they know I loved them? Why did the words become so elusive?

Through that wonderful gift of perfect hindsight, they were small and insignificant worries, and with confidence, I could say that, no, I really did not have any major regrets. I was at peace with decisions and outcomes. It all had to be. My life had played out as intended, and for this I would be grateful.

Now a very real regret sits heavily, and I will be forever haunted by three words—"My leg hurts"—which have become my albatross; perhaps I did not act soon enough.

*   *   *

The San Francisco spring of 2008 started much the same as every other year. As the air turned warmer, the sun appeared with greater frequency. Days lengthened, and the school baseball season began with the prerequisite laps around the field at the University of San Francisco. Leg lifts and stretching in the gym after school, hours of batting practice in the evening light of Moscone Park, and oiling the gloves became de rigueur. These were the start-of-season rituals James and I had experienced for a number of years. His school's baseball team, the Stuart Hall Knights, had been strong a few years prior, but the graduation of a particularly forceful group of classmates in 2006 had left the team struggling to find their footing.

In past seasons, James had been a pitcher and also played third base for the team. Not an avid sportsman, certainly not a jock, James's passion was skateboarding first, with baseball second. He had played autumn basketball and soccer when younger but struggled with asthma that was triggered by that season's foliage. Inhalers had been a part of his life since he was a toddler. The fall sports seemed to take their toll on him, but he continued to participate even if not with unbridled enthusiasm. Spring and summer were certainly his stronger seasons.

James as a toddler in vintage NY baseball outfit

As many parents know, the choice of team jersey numbers is a big deal for their children, and James picked them carefully. Funny now, since he was not an avid athlete, I am not quite sure why the number choice held such significance. James's number for his various activities while in elementary school was 10, and I now have a plethora of number 10 soccer, basketball, and baseball jerseys boxed away. The plan was for him to share them with his children one day. James's teammates all knew the reason behind his choice for number 10, but sadly I was never made privy to this. Perhaps one day someone from a team will share its significance with me.

Once at his secondary school, Stuart Hall for Boys, James chose a new number, 26, that stayed with him throughout the four years. Again, I am not aware of the significance. He wore it with pride, and it became a rally cry for the team in his senior year at the Hall. His final baseball jersey now hangs in a place of honour in the school's athletic department office. During the 2009 season, all the team painted *26*, using white ink, inside their caps in hopes of it bringing them good luck.

Number 26 on the pitcher's mound

James was affectionately known as the gentle giant by his teammates. His body size was big and powerful, but his humourous spirit was calm, gentle, and unassuming. This title had followed him from elementary school. He never bothered about winning or losing; having fun on the field with the team was his primary goal. Competitions at who could spit sunflower seed casings the furthest was the main focus of the teammates sitting on the bench in the dugout. He could hold his own with the best of them and never wanted a fuss to be made when he pitched a good inning or whacked a winning run into centre field. When focused and well trained, James could pitch a mean ball that was notorious for getting strikeouts, but he lacked the incentive to fight. As a result, he had very little attachment to outcome. Just getting out on the field to play and be with the team was enough for him. Deep down I am sure many coaches were frustrated at this lack of athletic ambition, but James was a staunch and supportive team member with a great wit and ability to mimic, therefore the games were always more fun just having him around. One coach shared with me that he had never seen a young man with so little ego regarding his performance. Win or lose, it was all good.

For the 2008 season, James was scheduled to play first and third bases and also pitch. Being robust, James was not a fast runner, but he had great strength in his thighs from years of skateboarding. The Knights' practice season began as usual in early February when daylight lasts a bit longer; and George, the lovable retired driver, turned up behind the wheel of his Mercury Tour bus to pick the team up from the front of the school. They waited at the Octavia Street gate for his arrival; and once on board, George would shuffle them to their practice fields, waiting there patiently to drop them back at school afterwards. Over the years, George had become a surrogate grandfather figure for many of the young men. Some practice fields were close by, but others were across the Bay Bridge on Treasure Island or in the far-flung Sunset district near the Pacific Ocean. Practices often ran until well after sundown, making it a late start for homework and dinner.

There was great enthusiasm for the upcoming 2008 season; and James, while in good form, expressed concern about the workload and how he would manage the necessary juggling to keep his grades up.

The junior year is an important one for students in American secondary schools as grades from this year are entered on university and college applications. Determined to do well and keep options open, James displayed a new focus and commitment that had been underdeveloped in the prior years. As we often said at the time, "his lights came on." Maturing later than girls, sixteen and seventeen-year-old boys seem to grasp the bigger picture at this age and become more willing to develop a discipline regarding time management and study skills.

As the practice season got into full swing, James complained about being more tired; and by the end of the week, he was exhausted, sleeping in on Saturdays until noon or later. It seemed the norm for many of his chums to be overly tired, so I thought this was just to be expected teen behaviour. He still made time, however, every weekend to skateboard and factored his schoolwork around precious time on the board.

Skateboarding at Wallenburg school

*   *   *

Skateboarding had become a passion for James since he was a youngster. His godmother gave him his first board when he was ten years old, much to my chagrin as I was convinced he was too young and unstable. I was wrong. He stepped on to it and flew down the street with unbelievable confidence and ease. Even when falling, he instinctively knew to tumble and roll, avoiding major injury. I have no idea where he learned this skill, but it was second nature to him. Scrapes and bruises were inevitable, but he never complained or fretted. Tweaked elbows and wrists were just part of the process. Ice packs became a new investment.

James's skateboard was his therapist, and pounding out kick flips in the garage was, as he put it, his "mental health time." I worried about the din disturbing our neighbours as entire Saturday afternoons could be spent at this activity. Thankfully, no one complained. Quirky videos shot by friends provide an archive of his tenacity for perfection. He would not give up, and if a trick was perfected, it had to be repeated countless times to freeze on film. Each twist of an ankle, bend of a knee, flip of a toe brought a different result, and it was quite remarkable to follow his progress over the years.

Skateboarding grew to be an overwhelming passion, and when time allowed, nothing could drag James off his board. Broken ones received a place of honour with a tale attached, and one summer he started to paint abstract designs on the shards with the intention of creating a sculpture one day. His birthday or Christmas gift was inevitably a new skateboard purchased at one of the famous shops in the Haight Ashbury. Trucks, wheels, bolts, and nuts were saved in countless jars and boxes around the house. A toolbox, stencils, and spray paint (which I had to purchase since teens were not allowed as a way to stem the tide of graffiti in the city) were added to the workbench in the garage. His annual subscription to *Thrasher* magazine brought the greatest joy, and he lived and breathed skateboarding for many years. Just recently, I discovered a photo of him sleeping under a tree with a favourite skateboard across his chest. Skateboard and boy had become inseparable.

There are many favourite haunts for skating in and around San Francisco. Pier 7 along the Embarcadero waterfront remains a mecca of sorts. The city has "knobbed" the edges of concrete ledges to prevent further scraping, but rogue boarders have figured out ways to remove the metal bolts and continue to grind away happily. Wallenburg High School on Masonic had another reputation as a prime spread of pavement with small hills and tiers of steps to negotiate. Our local neighbourhood of Polk and Lombard streets had countless gentle hills, curbs, and steps for jumping, and the Aquatic Park and Muni Pier at the end of the street near Ghirardelli Square provided endless hours of joy.

Skateboarding at Pier 7 in San Francisco

Our weekends over the years always included some hours that I would spend watching James practice his stunts. Once the bags were packed (his with gear including the music-laden iPod, mine with books and writing pads, along with the requisite gallons of water and Gatorade) we'd head out on another quest for a good venue. I relive those hours outside together constantly and feel blessed that he was willing to share afternoons with me. I was the only mother at these various locales, and the other boarders must have thought it odd to see me in tow, but we always had great fun, and I think the other guys secretly enjoyed having a loyal spectator as well. James became well known in the neighbourhood circuits, and his pride was evident.

Healdsburg, a small town north of San Francisco, in the Sonoma Valley, had the most exquisite skate park. As a way to keep their local youth active and corralled, the town had wisely created a clean, well-maintained, and patrolled spot for skaters. The myth that skateboarders are all potheads was soon squashed as I observed that to perform well, one had to be fully engaged and present. It requires great athleticism and focus to succeed in this sport. Crashing onto concrete at forceful speed is far from fun, and the skaters I observed were athletic, mindfully cautious, and sober. When James began skating, Tony Hawk was just starting to make a name for himself as a pro skater, hence skateboarding had not become as mainstream as it is now.

The last time we spent a day in Healdsburg, James forgot to pack his elbow pads and kneepads (one of the rules of the park), but he continued to skate nonetheless. Secretly, I know he intentionally left them in the garage as protective pads were seen as too immature now that he was sixteen. Of course, that was the day the police turned up; we were convinced that slapping fines on skateboarders must be the best revenue source for this small town. All the young men were hauled onto a bench, and police started taking names and presenting citations. James did not appear outwardly agitated and the officer congratulated him for being a gentleman, but all the while, he was seething under his skin. We were ordered to vacate the park, and James announced he did not want to skate there again.

When the "arrest notice" arrived in the mail (which could be dismissed through a few hours of community service and a $50 fine), we joked that he had become a felon at such an early age and how would this affect his future career chances.

Skateboarding was a perfect way to get to and from school, and the board was kept in the Dean of Students' office during school hours. How James could lug a book-laden backpack and still manage to skate at great speeds up and down the local hills left me awestruck.

*   *   *

The prior year, in October 2007 our calendar started filling up with requisite Introduction to SAT classes, early college-planning meetings, and parent-information evenings. By February 2008 we were now in full swing with James meeting on a regular basis with the school college counsellor and scheduling SAT classes as well as the eventual exam. A more in-depth school curriculum was being taught, so Saturday mornings were carefully structured to provide time for study that would still allow free time for skateboarding and baseball.

There was a new focus to James at the start of this junior year as he began to see the many future possibilities that were awaiting him upon graduation. He had started to articulate his desires and dreams, determined to embrace all available options. Taking the SAT practice classes on Saturday mornings in February was becoming harder for him, and he struggled to get out of bed in time to make it across town. Somehow we managed to do it, most often with just seconds to spare.

As Easter approached in March, James planned his first solo trip for a few days' visit in Colorado with an old childhood friend Michael and his parents. He was excited to have the chance to be responsible and travel on his own and took charge of the details, a sign of his blossoming maturity. The trip was marvellous, and he carried many wonderful memories into the following months. During that same Easter holiday, James returned midweek to participate in the Knight's annual three-day spring baseball tournament in Santa Rosa, a small town forty miles north of San Francisco. The tournament was always a good laugh, and even if the team did not play well, they had the opportunity to get into all sorts of high jinks while staying at an inexpensive motel, sleeping three or four sweaty fellows in a room, eating junk food, and being, I am sure, rather raucous. One year, James slept in the bathtub. While he returned tired from this trip to Santa Rosa, he was upbeat, and even though the team lost every game, the stories of their exploits would become the stuff of legend (or so the boys thought).

*   *   *

April arrived, and James began to complain about tightness in his upper thigh. The coaches and I put it down to a tweaked muscle. James was so aggressive on his skateboard that he *must* have pulled something. Or perhaps a misplaced step on the baseball diamond had caused the soreness? We were all convinced he had just stretched something. Massage and ice would be the cure.

Quietly, James became concerned about his strength, and his coaches encouraged him to ice and keep the leg elevated after all practices and games, which he did faithfully. The coaches would massage the area to try and warm it up before playing. During the games, we began to notice James pacing around the dugout. Sitting for long periods became uncomfortable for him, but he resisted any fussing and insisted it would go away "just give it time."

When rubbing the upper thigh, we noticed a pronounced knot, and we *all* assumed it was indeed a tight muscle that just needed more manipulation.

Heat packs were added to the regime of ice and stretching. In the coming weeks, it did not seem to improve and no amount of manipulation took away the deeper pain James was starting to feel. The longer days with late practices and games made dinner and homework time more pressured, and we had to abandon our ritual of eating in the dining room for that of sharing meals on a tray in James's room while he stretched out on the floor. Those precious, simple meals would soon become a treasured time.

James's overwhelming fatigue increased, and I became concerned with his increased difficulty in getting up for school. More often than not, our hasty departures had him arriving at the front door of SHHS down to the wire. Tardy notices started to arrive, and some days he needed to stay late at school to attend disciplinary tutorial in the library, a great frustration to him as he had always prided himself on his punctuality. He was also forced to miss baseball practice on these afternoons, which also made him sad.

The games became more tiring for James than in past years, and a few times I watched him pacing in the outfield appearing desolate, which was most unlike him. What seemed a sudden development, a troubling new weight rested on his shoulders: he was easily distracted. His running became laboured, and the coaches would substitute other players to run the bases once James managed to land on first.

James's leg continued to worsen, and he began to limp. I was concerned that something else was going on, but he refused to let me worry and dismissed all my efforts to make him go to the doctor. He was determined to work through the discomfort and assured us all that it was just a muscle-related strain due to his active season.

On a Saturday in late April, James dug out of the closet a wooden cane that I had used when I broke an ankle years before. He announced he needed it to help support his leg, especially when carrying his heavy backpack at school. Now I was becoming very worried, but he insisted that I not fuss. He was independent and had it all under control. Soon it would pass, and all would be right again. Parents of a teen will understand the power of their child's determination in becoming less dependent upon their opinion. His gait changed and his energy was diminished, yet James remained upbeat and focused, ready to work, studied, and still played hard each day as best he could. The cane became his constant companion and even when attending baseball games, James now used it to support himself during innings. Deep down in my gut, I *knew* something was wrong, but he was adamant all was fine and to stop worrying. Fussing mothers are the arch nemesis of adolescent boys.

This now is my albatross of regret. I should have acted immediately and trusted my instincts.

The school year was winding down. On May 14 the school held their annual sports award dinner at six thirty, and I had to hustle to pick up an entrée after work, collect James from home, and do the never-ending parking shuffle to find a spot close to school. James asked to be dropped at the front door while I looked for parking because his leg was once again very sore. We attended the dinner, listened to the speeches, and James was excited and very surprised to receive the Most Improved Player award from the baseball coaches. He was not expecting anything, and it really was a bit of a shock, especially since his skills had been sapped throughout the season. It was a pleasant night, but I recall feeling overwhelmed and longed just to go home and be still. I was becoming aware of a sense of foreboding, and crowds were starting to rattle me.

The following week classes were simplified as the students prepared for their final exams. On May 17, James and I attended the school play at his elementary school, Notre Dame des Victoires. The graduating class did a musical each year. James's class had produced *Cinderella*, and there was a tradition of past graduates attending the current play to show support. The youngsters on the stage seemed so young and naïve, and I had to catch myself to remember that this had been James just a few years ago.

In the late afternoon of Thursday, May 22, James headed out with cane and skateboard to work on some kick flips in the garage. Within twenty minutes he stood in the kitchen, ashen, and sorrowfully announced, "Mama, I can't skate. My leg hurts." He had little strength and confessed the discomfort had become unbearable. Immediately, I dug out the Rolodex and called an orthopaedic doctor James had seen years before, leaving a message to make an appointment. I also left a message with his GP to get a referral in place. Miraculously, both offices called back the next day with referral approved and an appointment scheduled for the following week.

In the meantime, James was due to spend Memorial Day weekend in Sacramento with his father and stepfamily. As I drove him across the Bay Bridge to catch the late-afternoon Amtrak train, there was a profound sadness about him. It was a tough farewell, and he started to cry, which was very unusual. He lugged his guitar case and skateboard, using the cane for support, and it all looked and felt like too much. As we did with each parting, I walked him on the train and then stood on the platform watching him through the window, blowing a kiss and a wave until we could not see one another any longer. Our traditional farewell parting was this: *I* (touching an eye), *love* (touching the heart), *you* (pointing to the other person). The response was the same mime with the addition of two fingers held up at the end: too!

In reflection, I marvel that I had the foresight to do this, but that weekend, I booked myself a mini-getaway at the Claremont Hotel in Berkeley, less than five minutes from the train station. There was a desperate need to be in water, and the sun and heat of the East Bay always rejuvenated my spirit. Little did I realize that in the perfect silence, heat, and solitude of those few days, I was girding my loins.

School ended shortly after James's return from Sacramento, and the final days were spent completing exams, cleaning out lockers, returning books, saying goodbye to teachers, and sharing in the seniors' graduation festivities. James was looking forward to becoming a senior himself and his final year of school after the summer holidays.

*   *   *

On Thursday, May 29, at 2:45 p.m. James had an appointment to see the orthopaedic doctor who was highly respected in the city. I had total confidence we'd get to the bottom of this leg problem quickly.

Arriving early, we quietly waited, patiently flipping through magazines, and once called into the examination room, James was taken down the hall for an x-ray. Not long afterward, the doctor entered the exam room and told us that we needed to see a bone specialist, Dr. Richard O'Donnell at the University of California San Francisco (UCSF). I was given the contact information from the office receptionist when leaving and was instructed to call UCSF as soon as possible. Nothing more was explained, and while we left the office feeling relieved that someone was going to investigate further, I thought it odd nothing else was said; we were still up in the air.

James started his school vacation the next day, and that night a group of his buddies came by for a celebratory barbeque. There was great excitement to have the junior school year behind them, and their enthusiasm for becoming seniors was infectious. I bought a bunch of their favourite foods and sodas. They were such a great group of young men—appreciative, polite, and terrifically funny. The celebrations went on until very late, and James collapsed into bed full of cheer. Summer was going to be great.

Now that vacation time was here, James would be able to get rested up and his fatigue would pass. These simple days of summer would be the perfect panacea to the discomfort and spells of sadness he had felt of late. We would turn a corner and all would be right with the world.

After no response to a call made on Friday, May30, I called Doctor O'Donnell's office again on Monday morning, June 2. James had gone out with his friends, and the house was quiet.

"UCSF orthopaedic oncology," the receptionist answered.

"Oh, I am sorry, I need to make an appointment with Dr. O'Donnell," I replied.

"Yes, this is orthopaedic oncology."

"Sorry," I said again. "I need Dr. O'Donnell."

"Yes, this is orthopaedic oncology," she replied once more.

This exchange went on a few more times when the receptionist firmly said, in total exasperation, "Madam! This *is* Dr. O'Donnell's office. He is an orthopaedic oncologist! Now, how can I help you? Madam? Madam? Madam?"

I was silent and collapsed into the kitchen chair, unable to open my mouth. The pregnant pause sucked all the oxygen from the space, and I started to cry. She must have heard my broken voice and, in a gentler tone, said, "Sorry, madam, but Dr. O'Donnell is an orthopaedic oncologist. How can I help you?"

My voice was barely a whisper. "My son . . . James . . . has to see him. His orthopaedist, wants James, my son, to see him." I could not believe I was saying these words.

"I'm sorry," she replied, "but Dr. O'Donnell is not accepting new patients. You'll have to go to Stanford."

Stanford? What? Why Stanford? What was going on?

There was nothing more to say. The receivers were hung up, and I sat motionless for an indeterminate amount of time. Tears flowed down my cheeks, and an empty whiteness had both covered and consumed me. I was floating and being buried in the ground in the same moment.

*   *   *

How long I sat there I do not recall, but I was suddenly aware that this was *not at all* what had been expected and placed a call to James's father, relaying the conversation I had just completed and to let him know I was now going to follow up with the orthopaedic office, to see what the next steps would be. Since James's health care was connected to his father's, I had to be sure that all the proper channels were informed regarding referrals, etc. Such was the state of the American health care system.

Thank God James was out. If he had been privy to this scene, it would have been incredibly difficult. I made the decision at that moment that James needed to remain oblivious and I'd share the facts only as they were confirmed. Crossing bridges before the river was formed had never served me well. Besides, his vacation had just started. His birthday was coming up. He needed to be able to enjoy these special days, and I was determined to see that through.

As I rifled about in my handbag looking for a tissue, I pulled out a small cocktail napkin from the Claremont Hotel. Starting to cry all over again, I made another conscious decision to hold on to the strength and goodness of those recent days. Thank God I had taken time to "fill my well." It was amazing how quickly I was forced to shift into a focused survival mode.

Once composed, I placed a call to the orthopaedic office, and as soon as I gave my name, the receptionist put me straight through to the doctor. This never happened under normal circumstances, and I wonder if they had been waiting for my call.

After hearing the statement that Dr. O'Donnell was unavailable, the doctor told me not to worry. He would personally take it upon himself to make *sure* James got in to see O'Donnell. He expressed deep regret at the news but hesitated to say anything further about the leg since he did not know what the problem was. In hindsight, I suppose he did not want to plant a seed or concern us unnecessarily, but the whole situation was unbelievable. He was gracious, but it must have been terribly difficult for him as he had obviously spotted something on the x-ray (but that was the extent of his ability to inform).

Although Stanford is a remarkable teaching and research hospital, he did not want us to be burdened with the huge drive back and forth. It can take over two hours from San Francisco in busy traffic. Grateful for his understanding, I told him that I would drive to the moon if needed to make sure James was going to be okay. It was left that his office would be in touch as soon as the orthopaedist had spoken with O'Donnell.

Somehow, I pulled myself together and headed over to work at the Village Well. There were some conference calls scheduled for the day and a music time at two outreach shelters that I had worked to establish relationships with. Shock had kicked in, and my adrenaline was working overtime, interestingly blocking the morning's news from my mind. Unbeknownst to me then, I was learning the survival skills that would be honed in the coming months.

Later that afternoon, the call came from the orthopaedist's office. O'Donnell would see James that week, and I needed to be in touch as soon as possible to set up an appointment.

As with my prior emotional call, the same receptionist answered the phone at O'Donnell's UCSF office, and yes, we could have an appointment on Thursday, June 5, at ten thirty. Since the doctor would be in surgeries all day, we'd have to meet him at the clinic on Parnassus Avenue.

James and I met up in the early evening after his full day with his buddies. I told him nothing of my troubling phone calls, and we carried on as normal. He spent a little time reviewing for the upcoming SAT exam and fell asleep fully clothed on top of his bed. As I tucked him in, I was overcome with a sense of doom and cried unashamedly. He looked so peaceful and happy, healthy, with his rosy cheeks and his beautiful clear skin. I quietly turned off his lights, climbed down the stairs to the main floor, and retreated to the bathtub, where I let hot water pound my face and back. Tears flowed as easily as the shower water, and I collapsed against the wall, overcome with the fatigue that accompanies horrible shock.

Crawling into my cool sheets, I prayed to every being in the universe to protect and save my sweet son from further pain and uncertainty. *Please don't let him be this sick.* The prayers were as much for me as for him. We had crossed a threshold, about to enter a corridor never explored and certainly not welcomed.

I was terrified, nauseated, and completely disconnected. How could a life be turned upside down with such ease? How could *this* be happening to James? How could *oncology* now be a word in our vocabulary? *Why* started its steady drumbeat that would become the background noise to all proceedings moving forward.

Chapter 2

Orange Juice

Good marks the spot where a page in your life
Turns so suddenly.
                                    —*James, part of his poem "The Thought," 2004*

I have zero recollection of how the coming days unfolded. Somehow I must have shared the news with a few people as I needed help at work to cover the hours I would be away. An old friend Emma, who had become a volunteer at the Well, said she'd step in and work during the Thursday playgroups to facilitate the appointment at UCSF and prevent me fretting about timing. The Village Well Board was told James might be ill. My mother and family must have been informed, but everything became a vacuum of white space and time. My journal from those days is full of intense worry and total confusion as to how this could be happening. We were stepping into the twilight zone, and I felt that any power I might have had over the outcome had been swept away.

The two days leading up to our appointment with Dr. O'Donnell felt endless. I could not sleep and already had become a mess. You enter a deep fog when news like this is presented. Oddly, having lived in San Francisco for many years prepared me for this metaphysical fog, and I knew there was no shifting of the elements to make things change. You just had to be patient and wait for the possible sun to burn away the gloom.

James did not know the severity of the news as I had not told him that O'Donnell was an oncologist. As far as James was concerned, O'Donnell was just a bone specialist that we'd be seeing in a few days. He began in earnest to enjoy his summer vacation, sleeping in often past noon, and the cycle of friends stopped by each day to play music and games.

Over the years, the Polk Street "nest" had happily become the meeting place for his buddies; I suppose because it was central and had plentiful public transportation nearby, making it easy for everyone from across the city to meet up. Our home was also close to all the places they liked to frequent, and I made sure to keep the fridge stocked with food for all the friends. I didn't want them out wandering the streets when all they really needed was a safe place to gather and chatter. It was a blessing that they liked to stop by as I adored seeing them as well.

There was a wonderful room at the top of the flat that James had transformed into his bedroom a few years earlier. It was not large but had windows on three sides that overlooked the bay, Alcatraz, and lower Russian Hill. He had managed to squeeze his drum kit, four guitars, a bookcase, and recording equipment into the space as well as his much-loved double bed. It was a hodgepodge of paraphernalia related to passionate hobbies, and the boys hibernated up there for hours on end. It was even more special in that it had a door that opened out to a flat roof. The view was amazing, all the way down to Aquatic Park and Ghirardelli Square. On sunny days and evenings there was no more perfect place to sit, and we both considered it the finest outdoor spot in the city.

The teenagers loved being out there too, and while I worried about them getting too close and falling off the edge, they were never dangerous and truly respected the space. Guitars and silly voices mimicking characters from cartoons or television shows filtered down through the skylights. Sometimes I listened, but mostly I left them get on with it. They were doing exactly what they needed to and just having them close by was a pleasure.

During those days of waiting, the roof was full each evening and many celebratory barbeques were orchestrated. James had a tiny hibachi grill, simple and funky, and it was capable of cooking two, possibly three things at a time. Its compact size allowed James to toss it into his backpack and head down to the waterfront for an impromptu dinner with his chums. They loved it. Each of the boys would bring something to share, and if needed, I would fill in the empty blanks. They were self-reliant, and James was the master chef who corralled and organized, assigning tasks and getting it done. He was remarkable at leading the charge.

Using the cane, James negotiated the stairs with relative ease, and I was happy to have him close to home. His spirits were high and his laugh robust. All the boys would be taking the SAT exam on the upcoming Saturday, so there was talk of what to anticipate. Were they ready? How did the practice sessions go? Was there a good movie worth seeing?

A couple of the boys asked me if I was okay the night of the barbeque, before seeing O'Donnell. I lied and said I was just tired . . . you know, too much going on at work . . . I needed a little more sleep. They hugged me and said it would all be okay. I cried hopelessly in the shower that night.

*   *   *

James's father came to the city the morning of June 5, and the three of us drove to the hospital in one car. Adding to the surreal element of the day was that we had not done many things as a family over the past years, and this reunion was not the sort of outing I had anticipated. We stayed upbeat and polite. James was very happy for us to be a unit once again, and I noticed him smiling in the backseat. Even the pain in his leg was trumped by this simple moment as a family.

We arrived at the monolithic buildings along Parnassus and found our way to the underground parking garage, snaking a path into the bowels of the earth. How could *so* many cars be already parked here at this hour of the morning? Many levels were already full.

After a series of elevators, we arrived at the medical-research building affiliated to UCSF. Its dark-tinted plate-glass windows make it appear like a black futuristic pod from a science fiction novel. An unshaven prisoner in his orange state-issued sweat suit, with hands shackled, was being escorted by armed guards into the building ahead of us. James and I exchanged a look of "What the!" There was an uneasiness to this entire scene. The foyer was full of people coming and going. Wheelchairs whizzed past. Every ethnicity was represented in the hallways, and the sense of urgency was palpable. We had entered a place of serious illness. Head colds and bruises were not welcome here. Each wall was dotted with multiple hand sanitizers and notices in bold:

Do not enter this area if you are sick.

Following protocol, we checked in at the main reception desk in the front hall, where a huge stack of papers was handed over for us to complete; we were then shown the way to the Pediatric Blood Disease Centre. The centre was on the first floor, at the end of a long hallway with a north western view of the city. I wanted to walk through the swinging doors and continue walking straight out the plate-glass windows. None of this was right or how life was supposed to be. Maybe by walking out the window I could also exit this horrid movie set I found myself on. But no one yelled, "Cut!" This was it.

We sat in silence studying the décor. A bright multicoloured fish theme appeared everywhere—on the walls, hanging from the ceiling, on posters, and on window decals. A large aquarium sat against one wall. It provided a distraction of sorts, but the space was almost too busy. One large wall was covered in photos of children who had obviously been patients. Lots of hairless heads in scarves stared out at me. Some children looked so incredibly sick. There were memorial programs tucked in amongst the photos. Shit, what world had we entered?

James's father and I divided the stack of papers to start the odious task of reducing our son's life to bullet points on carbon-backed sheets. His medical history needed to be documented, and I felt hopelessly overwhelmed, unable to recall the dates of anything. His last medical? Immunizations? Sight and hearing tests? How tall was he? How much did he weigh?

How could I know? This was a Thursday in June. James was supposed to be starting his summer vacation. I was supposed to be at work. James's father was supposed to be in Sacramento. How did our lives suddenly intersect with this new appointment and mountains of paperwork at UCSF?

Dr. O'Donnell had fit us into his schedule around a day of surgeries prior to leaving for his vacation in Boston that evening. The nurses at the clinic were very jolly (how could they be?) and professional, and they assured us that the doctor would be with us as soon as he finished in the operating room. So we waited. James had a book and his iPod (thank you, Steve Jobs) and was able to retreat into his world of music. His father and I chatted, small talk really. Neither of us could absorb what was unfolding, and so we tried to pick out landmarks below the large windows. Running trails through Golden Gate Park, the Panhandle, University of San Francisco, Geary Avenue, the ocean; all these old familiar sites became the focus of our banter.

Ten thirty came and went with no sign of Dr. O'Donnell. I visited the loo countless times. James was thirsty and went to find a water bottle. Minutes ticked on for what felt like hours, but finally a man came bustling into the clinic in his scrubs, hat on, still wearing his protective goggles. He checked in at the desk, grabbed a file, and called out James's name. We flew out of our seats and followed him into a tiny consultation room with hardly space for chairs. James and I sat down. His father stood.

Dr. O'Donnell explained he was terribly busy and would be leaving at six, but after the orthopaedist had sent him James's x-rays, he was committed to seeing us before heading out of town. He flipped the switch on the desktop computer, punched in his details, and up popped a screen with an x-ray of James's thigh and leg.

It was obvious, even to my untrained eye. O'Donnell took out his pencil and outlined on the screen the dark mass on James's thigh and also the pockets in each pelvis. The words I had dreaded flowed so easily from his lips without emotion: "This is cancer."

Sirens went off in my head. Everything started to spin. It was brutal and clinical, but now I know it was the only way to tell us. He had to be clear and concise. His work was not to be warm and fuzzy. No matter how brilliant he was, this was still a crappy piece of the job he had undertaken, and stating the truth was the only way to go.

O'Donnell proceeded to say he could not tell what kind of cancer but it looked suspiciously like Ewing's sarcoma, which is often discovered in teens, and the upper leg is usually the spot where it presents. The thigh and pelvis are common holding stations for this type of cancer.

He stood up and walked over to James (who had said nothing) and positioned his hands over the spot on the thigh where there resided, we had assumed for many months, a harmless muscle knot. With controlled and forceful manipulation, he wrapped his hands around the area, applied pressure, and a bulging mass appeared under the skin. "Fuck" was the collective gasp.

I was crying, and James turned and told me very abruptly to stop. He was terrified. I was terrified. He needed the adults in the room to be strong right now, and I learned at that moment a valuable lesson that I would carry going forward: I needed to pick carefully the times for expressing my emotions. If James needed me focused and strong, that is what I *had* to deliver, no matter how much it hurt me.

Further x-rays and blood work were ordered to get a better picture and make sure the cancer had not spread. The doctor instructed us to get lunch and have a chest x-ray on the fourth floor. The nurses in the clinic would do the blood draws beforehand. O'Donnell had an amputation to attend to (frankly more information than I needed at that moment) and would plan to meet us back in the clinic around 2:30 p.m. With that, he turned off the computer and hurried off to the next surgery, leaving the three of us numb in this tiny room. No escaping this one. It sucked.

A very kind and gentle nurse (was she specially selected for this task?) appeared at the door of this now-claustrophobic room and took James to the exam area, where they drew vials of blood. A hospital bracelet was hooked around his wrist, and then somehow we floated across the street to the food court and got something to eat. I recall it was a strange Chinese concoction from Panda Express, grossly dry and sticky at the same time.

James was upbeat (how could he be?) and made jokes about the menu. It was as if he was unmoved by this entire episode, but I know now that it was shock. What he saw on the screen was totally unrelated to him. His disconnect was obvious. Of course, it had to be. The chest x-ray did not take long, and we returned to the clinic to begin round number 2 of waiting.

*   *   *

Cancer. I could not even begin to get my head around the word. It was all a surreal dream, and somehow I was being manipulated to sit down, stand up, step this way, open this magazine, look at this paper, sign here. I too had entered a world of total disconnect, but surprisingly, it did not frighten me. From somewhere, I'm not sure where exactly, I trusted *someone* to catch me if I floated too far away.

O'Donnell was more punctual this time around, and once again he led us into the small room. He switched on the computer but spent much longer studying the screen without speaking. We sat in silence watching him move the mouse while staring at the computer. Click. Click. Click. Click. He put his hand on his chin and rubbed his neck.

Silence continued. Finally, he looked up and spoke with a grave tone. "I am sorry, James. The cancer is in your lungs. You need to stay in the hospital for more tests. I'll get them set up for you now. Be prepared to stay here tonight."

O'Donnell stood up and put a firm hand on James's leg and then his shoulder. James reached up to shake his hand and said, "Thank you." How did my dear son have the wherewithal to be bloody polite at this time? I was so humbled and proud of him in that simple gesture. I gave James a hug, but he was ramrod stiff and showed no emotion. This was all too much to absorb.

The wheels started to churn at the front desk of the clinic as James had suddenly become a priority. Phone calls were made, computers clicked, and serious, focused faces made sure James was moved to the top of the clinic's evening agenda. The waiting game continued, but a distinct heaviness had overcome us. James put on his headphones and retreated completely. Shock had made me light-headed and feeling faint, so the nurses got me a big bottle of water, some fruit juice, and a packet of plain biscuits. I had to put my head between my knees to keep from falling over. James refused any hospitality by the nurses. He had no intention of getting too familiar or cozy.

It must have been about thirty minutes later when a nurse came forward and explained what the next steps would be. James needed more in-depth x-rays of his legs and pelvis. Once that was complete, he'd be given a room for the night as more tests would be scheduled for the late evening and the next morning. The beginnings of what would become our huge paper trail were presented to us, including directions written on a piece of blue paper to help us find the x-ray facilities. We would now be across the street in the UCSF hospital itself.

Little did I realize that day how familiar these buildings would become over the coming months. For now, it felt like being thrown in the deep end of a very large pool with a constant wave machine, and treading water was the best one could hope for.

The labyrinth under the hospital was a rabbit warren. Alphanumeric signs dotted corners, and sterile walls, illuminated by fluorescent lights, seemed to blend one into another. We got lost within minutes, but thankfully, a technician came along to lead us to the correct doorway. A gurney with fresh sheets was parked outside the room, and James opted to lie down on it to rest. A huge panel under plexiglass describing Ewing's sarcoma hung on the wall opposite.

Photos, sketches, and text explaining the disease and treatments were welcome. It listed the ratio of success stories to diagnosis, and it all sounded positive. Each of us studied the details multiple times, and I felt encouraged while James appeared upbeat. Seeing success that outweighed failure was much-needed data right now.

The x-ray took much longer this time around as multiple angle shots were needed. When James was halfway through this session, another nurse found his father and me and told us to go to the seventh floor when finished. James would be admitted for the night.

Feeling that we had tumbled into the rabbit hole and an adventure in Wonderland, we were surprisingly not frustrated by our efforts to find the elevator to the seventh floor and the nurse's station. The human spirit is remarkable. In the midst of the darkest hours of a day that was never supposed to happen, we managed somehow to find a little humour with simple chatter. How that happened, I don't know, but I was grateful to have even a bit of levity.

The seventh and eighth floors of UCSF are dedicated to pediatric medicine. The walls are boldly painted with murals of wild animals and neon forests. Distraction remains the name of the game. We arrived to find young children with multiple tubes coming out of their bodies attached to catheters and IV drips scooting about the hallways in their slippers. Some younger toddlers, who appeared very weak, were wheeled in bright-red padded Radio Flyer wagons. Most of the children had no hair.

The first crash into the wall of sorrow. *Please, God, don't let James lose his glorious mane!* Somehow seeing these children made all the details of the day frighteningly potent. I wanted to scream and run from the place, but James needed us to be his controlled, thoughtful, focused parents, and we did our best to oblige.

"What is your name? Date of birth?" Each time a nurse or doctor came to talk with James, that was the opening line. He soon grew weary of responding, but unfortunately, these were the new rules and he had to play by them. Not quite sure how we were added to the meal list so quickly, but dinner on a tray was delivered for each of us, and we were grateful to have been given a private room. The bed squeaked and crunched from the plastic under sheets. The pillow felt like a rock. Everything was antiseptic and clinical, shrouded in that ubiquitous hospital smell. James turned to me and with pleading eyes, begged me to make sure that he *never* had to be here more than absolutely necessary. From those first ten minutes on the ward, going forward, James hated being in the hospital.

It was now 6:00 p.m., and in just a few hours, our lives had been turned inside out and upside down. The evening shift of doctors was starting their rounds, and not long after his dinner, James was faced with a room full of strangers, name badges pinned on white coats. They explained that he needed to have a series of scans and tests to try and figure out the type of cancer and its location in his body. Some tests would be run that evening; the rest would take place in the morning. He would stay the night, and one of us should go home and collect his things. The oversized chair pulled out, so a parent was welcome.

It felt as though I was on an airport-conveyor-belt sidewalk that goes on into infinity. Once on, you can't get off. With great apprehension, I realized *it* was going to decide the destination. We definitely had no input regarding this new journey, and the task now was to pay attention and try not to react too dramatically. Even in these short hours, I noticed catching only a few words that the doctors shared; surprisingly I had no questions. Somehow, almost immediately you switch off, absorbing just a few key words. Cancer. Diagnosis. Unsure. Blood draws. MRI. PET scans. It was as if my mind could only accept a limited amount of information, and today that limit had been maxed out. If someone asked me upon leaving the room what had transpired, I might have given them three or four sentences. Maybe.

The doctors left the room, and the bottom fell out for James. Totally overwhelmed, he started to cry and begged for an explanation; hating everything about this place, he just wanted to go home. He was inconsolable. The first of many moments feeling totally useless descended upon me. All I could do was let him wail in my arms.

*   *   *

James's father offered to stay the night at the hospital, and I agreed to go back home to pack a bag, including some soft pillows with a change of clothes for both of them. Even though only sixteen, James was close in size to his father, so swapping clothes was easy.

More labs were scheduled for 9:00 p.m., and a much-needed MRI was going to be booked. I had no idea that hospitals worked constantly into the night, but we were soon going to learn that this was a special facility that did not function around regular business hours.

It broke my heart to kiss James and leave the room, but I promised to return as soon as possible with his things and headed down to the parking garage. Once at the car I collapsed in a heap and screamed, pounding the passenger seat. Hours of pent-up tears flowed and soaked my blouse. Breathing hurt, and I too now was inconsolable.

Since I had been in the complex for well over ten hours, the tab for parking cost an arm and a leg, and I did not have enough cash. Through tears I tried to explain to the cashier what had happened, and he kindly let me exit the garage without charging the full amount. I wonder how many distraught families he deals with on a regular basis? How many nights does he have to bend the rules?

It is scary to think how I made it safely back to Polk Street, and now I wonder if perhaps there was some divine intervention. Streetlights, intersections, traffic, pedestrians, they all passed without me paying any attention. I pulled into the driveway, locked the car, and began the slow ascent up thirty-one stairs to the flat. James needed to be here. This was *all wrong*.

Packing a duffel bag became the easiest task of the day, and it was soon full of all the things he might need: clean underwear, toothbrush, socks, iPod charger, a few soft pillows from his bed, and not knowing what possessed me, I dug out a piece of his childhood "blankie." That always brought him comfort when young—maybe it would help tonight? I was grabbing at straws. I even hauled the inflatable Aerobed from the hall closet along with some soft sheets and headed back down the stairs to begin the trip across town back to the hospital. Since it was late, there was parking available on the street, and not having to negotiate the garage was a small gift. I was thrilled to see my boy again. It had only been fifty minutes.

A male nurse arrived at the door with a stretcher for James to head down to the radiology floor for an MRI. His father went with him, and since it was getting late, I was instructed by the nurses to go home and sleep. I needed to be back there in the morning, and as with the rest of the day, I acquiesced to their instructions and went back home. The entry in my diary that night: "Worst fucking day of my life."

It was late, but I called Emma to tell her the news, and she was heartbroken, telling me to forget about work tomorrow, she would cover and get some help. I needed to be 100 percent focused on James and the tests. Sleep was impossible, so I just closed my eyes and rested. The day played over and over in my head. I saw the faces of the doctors and nurses more clearly and sensed their worry but marvelled at how they switched into gear, almost robotically. James had cancer. It wasn't possible! How did this happen? What did I do wrong?

Guilt and sorrow frothed around me in bed.

*   *   *

By the time I reached UCSF and James's room the next morning, his father had already gone. He had to get back to Sacramento, and James was alone. It was 6:00 a.m. We hugged, and I did my best not to cry. James had slept poorly and ached to be gone from there. He was grateful for his pillows and cozy pyjamas, adamantly refusing to put on a hospital gown.

Breakfast arrived. There were a series of tests scheduled with a CAT and PET scan at the top of the list. The MRI had been done the night before. All these new terms! I had no idea what they meant and how they related to my son.

*   *   *

As college applications were scheduled for early September, many of James's classmates had planned trips to visit various colleges and universities to get a sense of what was available. I had discovered that this is a sort of rite of passage for American teens and James also had a few cities he wanted to explore. An East Coast adventure was on the calendar, and we were scheduled to depart on June 14 for Boston and then on to New York. Flights and accommodations were in place. It was going to be a special way to celebrate his upcoming seventeenth birthday. During that day in the hospital, we spent time, in-between tests, plotting our East Coast travel: what colleges to visit, how to get about, any sights to add to the list. It was lighthearted and actually fun. Cancer slipped to the bottom rung of the ladder. James now had other priorities to attend to.

More blood was drawn, and I was amazed at how comfortable James was with the procedure. I had been terrified by injections from childhood and felt squeamish watching the needles slip under his skin. The blood was bright red and looked so healthy. He could *not* have cancer. This was all a *big* mistake. Denial had become, in less than twenty-four hours, my new companion.

James did not talk about cancer. This was all just a royal pain in the ass, and once he got home, all would be okay again. We had both become quiet rebels over the past few hours, deciding that we had control over this situation, which felt good and empowering.

The day wore on, and I headed back and forth to the cafeteria to fetch fruit juices and simple snacks for James. I drank multiple cups of sweetened tea in Styrofoam cups to keep my energy up. We played cards to pass the time. It was actually a very calm day, considering the dramatic shift we had experienced. A senior nurse came in to let us know that at four thirty we'd meet with the doctors to discuss the test results.

"Great," said James. "Then we can get the hell out of here!"

At four thirty we were escorted to a small consultation room on the ward where we were introduced to Dr. Steve DuBois; his resident, Dr. Ashley Ward; and a social worker, Mark. James and I sat down with them. It was all very cordial. Dr. DuBois was on call that day, substituting for the doctor that would otherwise have seen James. We had no preconceived notion as to who would see us. We sat down at the square table in the centre of the room.

Dr. DuBois began by looking directly at James. The test results had come back and had been carefully analyzed by a number of doctors and specialists at the hospital.

"I am sorry, James, but I have very sad news for you. Your body is full of cancer. It is in your lungs, liver, bone, lymph nodes, and around your heart."

He continued, "We don't know what kind of cancer it is, but since it is in so many places, we have eliminated Ewing's sarcoma. We will need to do a biopsy of the site on the leg, and hopefully that will give us the information to reach a decision. Once the type of cancer is established, aggressive treatment will begin. I am sorry, James. This is incredibly bad news, I know."

Heavy tears flowed down my face, and I began shaking. Just as in a nightmare, I was screaming, but no sound came out. It was, up until that point in my life, the worst pain I had ever experienced. Mark held me and provided endless tissues. The box was the only thing on the table, except for the doctor's files. James sat, white faced, staring at the doctor. I reached out and held his hand. It was clammy and ice cold.

Dr. DuBois then turned to me and said that I must *not* blame myself for this. It was not because I breastfed or did not breastfeed James. It was not the food he ate or the laundry soap that we used. It was not the clothing he wore or anything related to any of his care. This was all just "incredibly bad luck" due to random genes that behave wildly.

The doctor must have known from past experience that parents immediately start to blame themselves for their child's illness and that this news was beyond anything they could fathom. Trying to make sense of it would become easier with any abstract explanation or blame that they could put upon themselves. That I had been absolved at that moment by the doctor was a huge gift. My profound guilt might have otherwise driven me over the cliff.

But for my crying, silence prevailed. James was pensive, and after a few minutes, he asked, "So what do we do about this?"

The doctor told him to go home, enjoy the summer, do what he wanted, play the games he enjoyed, and eat what he wanted. Basically, goof off. James was stunned, and his response was, "But why shouldn't I look at colleges and go to school in the fall?"

Months after that fateful meeting, the doctor shared with me how James's question had affected him. He was basically telling James to go home, have fun, and prepare to die while James's response was "I plan to live." He would remember that going forward, especially when dealing with teens facing such dire news. The doctors and social worker all supported James in his decision and said that *absolutely* he should continue to plan his travel and complete his university applications. Never again would they suggest anything but moving forward.

James had dragged us all back to the land of the living. He had not been given a death sentence. He was just going to need to fine-tune his life sentence. I witnessed that day a side of my son I had not known. His deep wisdom and infinite vision were only now going to be revealed.

There was another final test that needed to be performed, and soon yet another male nurse arrived at the door to take James on a gurney back down to the hospital basement. Once he left the room, I curled up with head on the table and wailed as I had never cried before. The team rallied around me and stayed for a long time. There were no words spoken. Like columns in an ancient temple they stood quietly, stoically protecting me from the heavens that were crashing in around me.

Eventually Mark helped me to my feet, and as I shuffled, he escorted me to an empty patient room across the hall, where I was set down on the bed. He stayed next to me holding my hand. Within a few minutes a nurse arrived to sit, and Mark asked if he could do anything for me right now. If not, he needed to step out and do some paperwork to get James into the system and help plan the schedule for the following days. He gave me a hug and left.

The nurse stayed close, confirming that this was the worst news and to not be worried about my tears. She encouraged me to collapse, and while I cried, she gently stroked my hand. I marvel now at the incredible gift these nurses, doctors, and social workers share with us. Their work is so very difficult, and *every* day they deal with these horrific diagnoses and broken, frail families. Acute pain, sorrow, and uncertainty are the common threads that tie us all together, and yet these compassionate professionals are able to make each of us feel special and uniquely cared for.

My breathing was becoming easier, and the nurse asked me what I would like to drink. "I don't know" was all I could mumble. She stood up and left me for a few minutes, returning with a big jug of orange juice and a glass on a small tray, the sight of which reduced me to fresh tears all over again.

James's prolonged birth seventeen years ago had been very difficult. There were many complications culminating with him being caught in the birth canal. Throughout the ordeal I asked to die. It had just become too much. I even gave permission for this to happen just so long as James could be born healthy. The nurses kept me with them and literally placed their faces just inches from mine, willing me to stay there, in my body, and help them with his birth. Apparently, for a period of one-half hour, I lay perfectly still, and only my vital signs showed the medical team I was still alive. The birth process escalated, finally resulting in an emergency forceps delivery requiring over seventy stitches. I did not walk with full strength or vigour for over five months afterwards.

After the eventual safe delivery of James, I lay in the operating room parched and drained. The attending nurse brought me the biggest jug of fresh orange juice, which I consumed in one fell swoop. It was absorbed into every fibre of my being, and it became a part of our shared story of survival and new beginnings. To be presented, on this day of all days, a jug of orange juice once again was just too much to bear.

James was delivered back to the room after his scan, blood work, whatever—by this point, they all blended into one, and we sat quietly, hugging one another. The same nurse came back to the room with signed papers so that James could be discharged. There would be a call from the clinic to set up a biopsy of the leg. What was the best way to reach me? My mobile number was entered into the system.

Led by some invisible force, we managed to make our way to the elevator, found the car, and presented a parking voucher that the social worker had given me. The attendant from the night before was at the exit gate. He saw the voucher and solemnly waved us through.

Interestingly, James was ravenous, and we stopped at his favourite funky restaurant on McAllister for a grilled chicken sandwich, and once it was devoured, he was desperate to get home. Pulling into the driveway I suddenly remembered that James was scheduled to take the SAT exam in the morning. Somehow I had to let the school know that he would not be there, so I dropped him at the front door and hastily backed out onto Polk and shot up over the hills to Octavia, praying someone would be in the school office.

Frantically I buzzed, squinting through the glass doors. Damn, it was Friday afternoon, and school was on vacation. Who would be there at this hour?

As I climbed back into the driver's seat, I heard a voice shout "Jean!" and there stood Tony, one of James's teachers and a school administrator. I rushed over and gave him a huge hug. Miraculously, he was just about to leave the building but stopped by the office to check phone messages. He could see me at the front door.

"Oh, Tony . . . I have *terrible* news." I was crying. "James has cancer, and we don't know what is going on. It's just awful, awful!"

Stunned, Tony asked me to repeat it—twice. Disbelief overcame us, and we hugged, both of us crying. Had I really spoken those words? Had he heard them correctly?

Once composed, the concern became the SAT exam. I had no idea whom to call or how to let people know about James's absence in the morning. Could he take it another time? Would Tony help me? He assured me this was the *least* of our worries and he'd take charge of the cancellation and any other calls. What did I need? Could he do something for James? Should he let the faculty know?

Oh, God. Now there was this sea of issues to start swimming through. I gave Tony permission to do whatever he thought best, drove home, and collapsed onto my bed.

James was in his room chatting to a friend on his phone. That evening, we both retreated into a world of silence. A profound shock like this numbs, and as others who have gone through a similar situation know only too well, there are no words that can articulate such acute anguish. Trying to grasp this truth took everything in our personal reserve. Within a few short days, life, as we knew it, had been irrevocably changed.

Chapter 3

CaringBridge

Sharing the story is as important as living it. Many people miss the essence of their biography.

—*Jean Alice Rowcliffe*

A place where days don't make events, but events make the day
—*James's poem "Untitled" 2004*

"Once you feel pain, the disease is already established." Those words, spoken by the doctors, began to haunt me. If I had acted sooner, might James have been spared this horrific diagnosis? How could we have missed it? Those weeks of James limping should have been investigated. Why didn't I force my will upon him and *make* him see the doctor? The floodgates of guilt had crashed open. This, a parent's worst horror, had just been delivered on a silver platter.

On top of the shock and inability to grasp the full meaning of what we were facing, we had to carry on with our everyday lives. There were trips to be taken, colleges investigated, plans made, meetings to be held, birthdays celebrated. The minutiae of any given day was important, and how would these details fit into our new reality? How would we make sense of it and continue living our normal lives after crashing into this wall?

Phone calls were made to the immediate family, and the response was universal: disbelief and sadness. James had started to make his calls and send e-mails. Realizing I did not have the strength to call everyone who needed to be told, I crafted an e-mail. Technology was about to become a beloved tool.

Within hours of sending this update to everyone on the list, my e-mail and mobile phone were flooded with messages. Overwhelmed by the plethora of names, I was now overcome with worry; how to respond? I wanted to crawl into a hole. James somehow managed to make individual calls to those friends he wanted to inform. He had a greater strength than I.

The first of many incredibly serendipitous moments was about to unfold. One of the calls on my mobile was from another of James's English teachers at school. Henry had a suggestion that I might want to discuss, could I call him please? What guided me, I don't know, but his was the one number I dialled. Henry proceeded to tell me about CaringBridge, a nonprofit organization that provides free websites for families facing a medical crisis. CaringBridge would host the forum, and friends could check any updated blogs that James or I would write. There was also a spot on the website for folks to leave messages. A member of Henry's family had recently used CaringBridge, and it had been invaluable. Thanks to a tech-savvy friend Christiane, who stepped in to help, she and Henry miraculously had James's website up and running within a day.

CaringBridge became the link between James, his story, and the rest of the world. It allowed details to be relayed and folks updated without my going through the story countless times, something I soon discovered is one of the most exhausting elements of being a caretaker. The early evening, when you are most depleted, is when the phone starts ringing off the hook. All the interest comes from a place of love, and that was so deeply appreciated, but the need to be silent and regroup at day's end was also crucial.

I used the term *tsunami* in my journal entries to describe much of what the coming months felt like. Sometimes the wave crashed into us. At other times it carried us. Feeling sucked out by its forceful pull became another powerful emotion, but the underlying truth was that life was totally out of control and we were now being guided by a force much greater than anything we could have ever imagined.

Holding on to the string of a kite is another metaphor. Some parents describe it as the roller coaster. Whatever the imagery, it is the knowledge that you are in a place of reacting instead of being proactive.

A journal update on CaringBridge became an almost daily ritual, and it was astonishing to see the number of people who followed James's story. Friends told friends, and we did not know many of those reading the story. I was not made aware of the scope of this worldwide following until much later. With CaringBridge in place, it left my limited free time in the coming days to start revamping the schedule. Hotel reservations and flights were cancelled. A swoosh on the grease board and all the months of organization were wiped clean. In just a few hours, James was starting from scratch and we could not get sucked into a deep hole of regret; we just had to carry on.

It was amazing how energized James became in those early days. He had a new task, a new problem to solve. His skin was clear and his eyes bright. I often wonder if other children who are given this diagnosis react in the same way. It is as if he had reset the Start button. Many parents speak of their children's renewed interest in living well, and this is certainly manifested itself in James. Fortuitously, Michael, James's friend from Colorado, was booked to come to San Francisco during the first weeks of school vacation, so Polk Street became a meeting place for all the buddies. James then had an opportunity to share his story and concerns with his close friends in an intimate setting, perfectly orchestrated, without effort.

Many of the boys were sad, and some needed to sit quietly with me away from James to cry and share a hug. They were frightened, but I assured them that everything would all be sorted out as James "still had too much mischief to get into!"

*   *   *

Tests began on Monday June 9, and as alien as they sounded that day, they soon became part of our normal conversation. The day began with us heading back to UCSF for a bone scan, EKG, blood work, and biopsy on the leg tumour. The room was cool and dark as the procedure included an ultrasound to guide the technician to the spot where the long biopsy needle would draw out fluid for analysis.

Sitting next to the ultrasound machine produced a terrible knot in my gut as the last time I had seen one was during the birth of James. The swishing sound and clicking images of the shadowy mass in his thigh made me very sad, and I was grateful for the darkness so that I could cry. James was frightened and kept his eyes glued to the ultrasound screen. Thank God the area on his leg was frozen so he could not feel the needle puncture the skin.

What seemed like an eternity was really only about an hour, and once all the tests were complete, we headed back home. James was able to spend the rest of the day out with his friends even though his leg was tender. I had to make more calls for further appointments and tests and then get over to my workplace to check in and figure out how that piece of the puzzle was going to unfold.

A meeting with the doctors was set for the next day along with an MRI of James's liver. Suddenly this new life at UCSF had glommed onto ours. It seemed we had to factor it into each day. The doctors warned that any treatment would probably include chemotherapy and radiation and as a result, James's mouth would become sensitive. I decided it was foolish to keep his braces on, and he was thrilled to visit the orthodontist to have them removed. Interestingly, his teeth had already straightened quite a bit, which pleased James and gave him the boost of a beautiful smile for the coming months.

As I go through my diary to collect these threads, I am shocked at how often we were at the doctor's office or clinic in the weeks that followed. It had all become such a blur. We were on automatic pilot, and I was not paying attention. Scans and blood work were constantly being performed as the doctors tried diligently to figure out what kind of cancer this was. It did not fit the template, and they were struggling. There was an urgency to their conversations, and they needed to see James almost daily.

In that first week we were introduced to the remarkable support system in place at the hospital. A special team of incredible social workers stepped forward to make these coming months as easy as possible for us. A parking pass was provided for the hospital garage; a temporary handicapped badge for the car also made parking on the street easier. A phone card, so that we could make long distance calls free of charge, was a huge gift.

The team was also there to listen, offer advice, and suggest treatments to keep the caregiver strong. They understood only too well how quickly I might burn out. Massage was made available, and access to the hospital pool became yet another option. They each had such a deep understanding of how fragile James and I felt, and a social worker was usually at each doctor's meeting to lend a shoulder and translate what we had heard. Much of the early diagnosis flew over our heads as both James and I struggled with why we were even there in the first place. Absorbing all the details of treatments was impossible.

Soon after his diagnosis became public knowledge, Mary, the mother of one of James's good chums, offered to come to our doctor's meetings to take notes. She had her PhD in nursing, whose specialty was brain tumours. Mary was amazing and helped by asking knowledgeable questions when we became overwhelmed. She made notes and then transcribed them into lay terms, which were e-mailed to me the next day.

Unfortunately, the results from the first biopsy were inconclusive, so another one had to be performed, this time under general anaesthetic. A larger piece of the tumour would be removed for analysis. The doctors also wanted a sample of bone marrow. Surgery was scheduled for June 16.

James turned seventeen years old on Friday, June 13. That day began with another session at the hospital for more blood work. If the blood came back as healthy, then the biopsy would move forward on Monday. One soon learns how this plethora of interconnecting treatments unfolds. The doctors and specialists are constantly monitoring the blood to see if there are any dramatic changes that might make surgery or tests risky.

Fortunately we were in and out quickly that day, and James was free to celebrate with his friends with their favourite activity, a barbeque at Crissy Field, along the waterfront near the Golden Gate Bridge. It was all spontaneous and, in typical James fashion, somehow came together. Thanks to the help of the his friends' wonderful mothers, the boys arrived with the charcoal, lighter fluid, utensils, chopping boards, condiments, drinks, cups, and plates. We all laughed when we realized that somehow James had forgotten to delegate food, so it was a quick dash over to the Marina Safeway to pick up the meat and buns. They proceeded to have a wonderful afternoon by the water in the summer fog. The parents left the boys in peace, and I sat quietly in the distance, there if James needed to leave or rest, but he stayed for hours and there are some glorious, treasured photos of his beaming smile surrounded by close friends.

James' 17th birthday at Crissy Field

James and his friends on 17th birthday

I wrote on CaringBridge how quickly James became proficient at packing fun in around his clinic and hospital visits. It was as if he knew there was no time like the present. He snatched at every moment with relish and humour. Already his will to continue living playfully was impacting the lives of others. His big spirit shone through. Reflecting on those early days, I marvel, even now, at how much he taught me about embracing every moment.

The next day, Saturday, was to have been our departure date for the trip to New York and Boston, but it started instead with yet another MRI. UCSF never closed, or so it seemed. This time the wait was long. James was weary and fractious. His frustration was obvious, and there was nothing that could make things better. The realization that there was little I could do when confronted by hospital routines was rapidly becoming a painful truth. To add more misery to the process, the technicians had difficulty injecting the dye for the test. James insisted it was because "they took fourteen bloody vials yesterday"!

Another new discovery that day was that veins can collapse, and back-to-back tests might have this effect. The morning was incredibly difficult and tested everyone's patience. Staying calm and unemotional while masking my frustration and bubbling anger was going to be a daunting but essential task to prevent things escalating during these hospital visits.

An old friend Susan had offered to drive us that day. A powerful memory I have of that long morning was of me collapsing in tears in her car once James was with the technicians. Her efforts to try and comfort me with a hug or rubbing my arm just hurt too much, and I had to ask her not to touch me. Never had I felt so bruised and raw. My sorrow had manifested in acute physical pain. This was the first of many such incidents that would provide insight for the future. *Touch is sometimes just too much.* Unfortunately, no one had warned me to expect this reaction, thus adding a new guilt over not being receptive to my ever-growing list of out-of-control emotions.

Once finished at the hospital, we spent the afternoon quietly at home watching silly *Seinfeld* episodes that Susan had brought, and it was marvellous to hear James howl with laughter after all his morning frustrations. Later in the day, we wandered up Polk Street to his favourite clothing store, Molte Cose. He decided he needed some hats, looking especially for a straw fedora. He picked out a tweed cap (which became his favourite over the coming months), and he left with the thought that he still needed a smoking jacket and pipe to complete the look.

That evening I wrote on CaringBridge of his friends starting to call the nest Camp James. Happily, they were around again that evening. In honour of his birthday, James attended a Giant's baseball game the next day with his father at Pac Bell Park. This strange juxtaposition of normal life sandwiched in between unfolding days of disease and hospital visits had become surreal.

Monday arrived, and we made our way back to UCSF for the biopsy procedure at 1:00 p.m. We had entered the big league now. This was serious surgery. The preparation area was clinical, full of white lights, oxygen tubes, and beeping machines. Up until now, we had dodged the "hospital" feeling by using the pediatric clinic and ground-floor labs.

Suddenly we were confronted by the reality of *very* sick people having major procedures performed by quiet, focused medical teams. If James was afraid, I was terrified. He changed into the hospital gown, his belongings bagged and put under the gurney, and we sat quietly holding hands. Conversation was tough, almost non-existent.

The nurses were remarkably calm, and they gave James enough information to keep him involved but not overwhelmed. An IV drip was inserted into the thin skin on top of his hand and also into his arm and a drug injected to make him calm and drowsy. I gave him a kiss, and as he was whisked away down the long corridor and through the No Entry doors, I felt a horror for the first time that James might be dying.

How long I waited, I can't recall. Eventually James was wheeled into a recovery room, and I was allowed to see him. Dr. O'Donnell had performed the biopsy, and it had been a success. He felt they had enough tissue now to figure out what sort of cancer this was. Until they identified the cancer, any treatment plan was an unknown.

My god, how tragic James looked in that room. Due to his age he had been admitted to the pediatric unit, but his almost-six-foot frame was so out of place surrounded by murals of jungle palms, monkeys, and giraffes. The only patient in this room, he was being closely monitored. He came in and out of consciousness and was swearing due to the pain. A nurse told him to watch his language (as if he could make that decision considering how drugged he was), and I reminded her he was the only one in the room. She was firm, stating that as it was a pediatric unit, James had to "watch his mouth."

It was like a scene from a Wes Anderson film. This lumbering man in a ridiculous setting, suffering acute pain, and the only concern of the nurse was his choice of words. I remained quiet and bit my tongue. He needed to be cared for, and I needed these nurses too much to rock any boats. I reminded him not to swear, but since he was delirious, it did no good.

Sitting next to James, holding his hand while beeping machines monitored his heart, breathing, and the IV drugs, I was overcome by and had to accept the realization that he was *very* sick. He might not survive this disease, and I was holding the hand of my broken son. I put my head down on the bed and cried from a deep place, never experienced before. This was serious, and James was suffering. In that recovery room I grappled with the truth that I had to prepare myself for any outcome: What if it is the worst? It was not that I succumbed to it, but I did need to try and consider this possibility. It is impossible to describe how bleak that moment felt.

James was in terrible shape and needed morphine to make the pain bearable. The incision on his leg was much bigger than I had anticipated, and the nurse and doctors kept retreating to the hallway, out of earshot, to discuss the next steps. Every groan from James tore through me. It was decided that he needed to stay in the hospital overnight. Even though this had originally been booked as an outpatient surgery, I was incredibly grateful for this decision as I knew I was not prepared or knowledgeable enough to provide the nursing care for someone so miserable. Calls were made to find a bed and an available room. The doses of morphine were being increased; James was groggy and incoherent. This was a taste of purgatory, and all I wanted was to scoop up my darling boy, wrap him in blankets, and run away to the farthest corner of the world.

The night was troubled with James, thankfully closely monitored. Eventually in the early morning the pain appeared to be better controlled. The room overlooked the wooded hills behind the hospital, and I spent most of the night staring into its shadows when not watching James and the blinking lights of the morphine drip. I had started to pray to every known entity to watch over him, including all the white-light mantras I could think of. My line was out to the universe trolling for a solution. I needed some indication that all would be fine. Friends had started to talk about miracles, and e-mails poured in with remarkable stories of battling the odds. People *did* survive cancer, and James was young and strong. He had everything going for him, and he was a fighter.

Positive energy—that was the ticket to solving this dilemma. Surely, it could all be managed through careful, thoughtful choices. I refused to think I was delusional; anything and everything would be on the table to save him from this horrid pain and suffering.

The doctor's rounds in the morning included a large group of residents, and there seemed to be great interest in James's case. He was still groggy and uncomfortable but acted like a caged lion who wanted to break free. He was direct with the doctors about an exit strategy. How soon? What was needed to speed up the process?

Dr. DuBois came to see us after the rounds had been completed and was thankful for the biopsy as it had provided enough tissue to send it off to various specialists for their review. He should have word in the coming days and would schedule a meeting with us the following Friday to discuss the findings and plot our treatment plan going forward.

Crutches needed to be ordered and delivered to the hospital room before our trip back home, and the wait for this final piece was interminable. James growled incessantly with zero patience. His leg hurt, and he wanted to be gone from "that hellish place." I needed to keep dipping into the pool of patience to keep things relatively calm.

Pat kindly volunteered to provide transportation to and from the hospital and was waiting outside the front door as James fled the building as fast as he could on crutches. Knowing his leg would be sensitive to jolts, she picked a route home that would dodge the myriad of potholes that plagued the city. She was so right! Even with her careful planning and execution, we still hit a series of bumps, and James jumped out of his seat with a few choice words. No one was telling him not to swear now.

David, a neighbour and the dear father of one of James's friends, met us at our gate to help us negotiate the many stairs that confronted us. He provided the strong arms and back to support James on the very slow ascent. The orchestration of these many helping hands was one of the greatest gifts during the coming months. Emma and Pat became the keepers of the matrix, and I owe them the deepest thanks for the rest of my days. I could not have survived without their organization and selfless giving.

As the days and weeks began to unfold, I continued to update CaringBridge as a way to keep everyone up to speed. In rereading it for the writing of this book, I am shocked at how bloody positive many of the entries were. I know I had to stay upbeat for James, but they really were far from true. I did not record the excruciating tests, the drugs that failed to ease the pain, ongoing blood work that left deep bruises, all mixed in with my the pervasive horror and sense of doom. It was a simplified and partial telling of his story that everyone read, and my inability to be totally honest troubles me now.

Perhaps this is why it became so important for me to write this book. I wanted to tell, as truthfully and completely as possible, James's story and how it impacted the lives of those around him. I found myself recording in my journals that I was living a lie. On the surface, the public face was one of optimism and courage while beneath that veneer I was full of rage and uncertainty with an ever-growing fear that I was not going to be able to save James. How would I ever be able to go on? As I have discovered, there are *many* who share a similar story, and perhaps through the authentic telling of our collective stories we can help others while also preserving the legacy of those we love.

Chapter 4

Chess

Life is a game of chess. Don't rush to checkmate too quickly, for then it is over.

—Jean Alice Rowcliffe, written in a journal at age 13

The more you seek, the less you find.

—Zen saying

During the afternoon of June 18, while recuperating from the hospital visit, we decided to pull out the chessboard. James was still in a lot of discomfort, and the pain meds did not seem to work for long. Ice packs rotated on and off the biopsy site for the rest of the day, leaving the skin white and frozen, but James did not mind. He wanted it numb.

Distraction was crucial now, and interestingly, chess became the panacea we both craved. James's friends called and made plans to stop by, but in a staggered fashion so as not to overwhelm. I marvel at how thoughtful these young men were. They figured out very quickly what worked and what didn't without guidance from James or me. My respect and love for these boys was only going to increase over the coming months. James adored their upbeat company and humour, and watching them interact made me feel all things, even a cure that would produce a completely healthy son, were possible.

The doors of the Village Well stayed open thanks to many remarkable volunteers, and I managed to pop in and out during the days in between clinic visits. The news of James had spread like wildfire, and I was shocked at the number of families who already knew our circumstances. Many mothers had started to bake for the morning tea. Some willingly lead the circle times and help oversee the playgroups. The shadow of personal worry over this new nonprofit and how it would continue weighed me down, but I had to put that concern on the back burner. My journal entries show inklings of fear that I could easily go mad from being so completely overwhelmed. How would I keep all the balls in the air? I dared not share this with others for fear of looking feeble or incapable.

A gifted carpenter, my father had placed on his workbench an amazing large box filled with many small drawers. All carefully organized, he would keep little bits and pieces in each one. A few matching screws in one drawer. Bolts and rubber rings in another. Batteries and plugs in yet another. It fascinated and brought me comfort as a child, knowing you could go anytime to that one drawer and get exactly what you needed.

My life was now that oversized box. I found small drawers to house the worry over work and finances. James's cancer, unknown treatments, pain control, future plans were each assigned their special drawers. By carefully popping each concern into a tidy space, I could cope. When needed, the one drawer could be opened, explored, and then closed again, waiting for the next drawer that needed attention. The mind and spirit has a marvellous way of seeking balance, and this metaphor worked for me.

Interestingly, during these weeks, the famous wild parrots of Telegraph Hill started to fly over the house. What possessed them to make us part of their flight path remains a mystery. They would swoop down, off of upper Chestnut Street, pass over our home, and do an abrupt swing over the apartment building across Polk, flying then back up to Chestnut Street. Their distinct squawking cheered James, and we found them fascinating. This daily ritual became like clockwork.

The weather turned humid, and the ice packs melted quickly, forcing me to use bags of frozen peas, corn, berries, mango—whatever I could lay my hands on. We joked about the goopy mess that would ensue if any of the bags broke. Interestingly, one bag of berries did leak and left a slight pink tinge on a comforter which remains to this day.

James had spent the days since the surgery sleeping in my bed to avoid climbing the stairs to his room. I curled up on the chaise at the end of my bed to be able to help him during the night. While he elevated his leg on Sunday afternoon, I sat quietly on the chaise doing some bookwork. I looked over at him propped up on a mountain of pillows, and suddenly there was a radiance about him that was shocking. I asked him what was happening, and he described feeling overwhelming love and contentment that he could not contain. He said there was nothing that could make him feel any better than *being* in that moment; he saw a warm light and felt incredible peace.

His eyes were glowing, and he seemed bathed, literally, in white light. It was remarkable.

I told him he had experienced what is called *satori* and that many people search for this sense of enlightenment throughout their entire lives and never find it. Somehow James, in the midst of all this troubled, painful uncertainty, had stumbled upon it. He spoke about the experience for weeks afterwards, of how good he felt and the overwhelming love he had for all things. I was desperate for this euphoric feeling to last.

∗   ∗   ∗

Thankfully, humidity does not last long in San Francisco, and the air shifted; fog rolled in, and a cool breeze wafted through the windows before our meeting at UCSF to find out what the biopsy had unearthed. I was convinced that once we knew what we were battling, it would become easier.

I wrote on CaringBridge at the end of the day that it was considered good news that James had a "rare form of cancer." Only fifty people were diagnosed with it each year. Why I thought that good news, I will never know. I suppose it was because the biopsy, bone marrow sampling, and blood work had at least helped the doctors successfully give the disease a name:

> MICROPHTHALMIA TRANSSCRIPTION factor associated tumours (miT) which includes clear cell sarcomas (CCS), alveolar soft part sarcoma (ASPS) and translocation—associated renal cell carcinoma (RCC).

The translation was impossible, but we were made aware that there would now be a lot of researchers and doctors keen to befriend James. The truth that we had to grasp now was that chemotherapy and radiation had not yet proved successful in treating this strain of cancer.

A new experimental drug trial was presented as an option. It was in its early stages, and only six people were taking it. James would be the seventh. It targeted this type of cancer specifically.

We then entered the realm of what this treatment might look like: what other treatments might be possible and what were the potential side effects. After weighing all the information, James was very clear:

He did not want a shunt or a permanent IV line in his body, if at all possible.

He preferred oral medication.

He did not want to lose his hair nor have invasive procedures.
He wanted to continue to go to school and look at colleges.
Boom. That was it.

The trial drug was a pill, to be taken twice a day. James would not have to stay in hospital for treatments. He would not lose his hair. He could continue to attend school, and yes, a trip to Boston to look at colleges was possible. Scans and blood work would be required before, during, and after the trial to track the progress of his tumours. Since UCSF is a research hospital, Dr. DuBois had access to the drug, and James could begin taking it in the coming days. In hindsight, I suppose what made it a good day was having a name and some sort of plan in place to start moving forward. It did lift my spirits.

Another bit of rare serendipity was that Dr. DuBois, who was on call the day that he met James for the first time and told him the terrible news that cancer was throughout his body, was simply subbing for another doctor who would have normally been assigned to James. It now transpired that Dr. DuBois was one of two doctors in America studying this type of rare cancer, which we now referred to as alveolar soft-part sarcoma, and so, of course, he would continue to be James's oncologist.

Months later, the doctor confessed to me quietly that he had been waiting for this cancer to be delivered to him for his research studies, but he was terribly saddened that it had to be James. We were told that this research would be invaluable for other patients down the road, and James, feeling he needed as much good luck karma as possible, agreed to partake in a series of special blood draws over the course of some days once he had begun the trial.

*   *   *

Do not act as if you had ten thousand years to throw away. Death stands at your elbow. Be good for something, while you live and it is in your power.

—*Marcus Aurelius*

We suddenly felt an urgency and desire to do everything we could to enjoy life. There was a newfound enthusiasm and humour to our days. James was lighthearted and adored having crowds of friends around. He went out every day and evening. He ate what he wanted, grabbed any spontaneous suggestions for fun that came along, played games, bought new red shoes and a Fender guitar. The Guitar Centre on Van Ness became an even greater source of endless hours of exploration. James lived each day as completely as possible, collapsing into bed at night, totally exhausted. I can, with all honesty say, that it was a magical, shared time.

James at the Guitar Center on Van Ness Ave.

The next week began with more blood work and a PET scan followed by fasting, and then the drug trial would begin. The PCRC unit on the sixth floor became our new daily destination. The drug trial ARQ 197 began in July and had to be carefully monitored. Pills were taken at the same time each day; the timing of blood draws had to be exact; any reactions and changes were carefully recorded. James had been assigned a number for the trial as the drug company wanted no extraneous information that could influence their results. He really was a guinea pig, a human test tube, for a possible future cure. James felt he had been given a gift, and that meant everything. He was willing to endure the strict discipline of the drug trial in exchange for more time of continued health.

We lugged a big canvas bag back and forth to the hospital each day packed with his laptop computer, chargers, and the trusty chessboard. I think we were the best equipped of any family on the ward. While some of the days at UCSF were over fourteen hours long, we managed to fill them with big doses of joy. James had figured out how to stream Lewis Black monologues on his MacBook, which would have us in tears from laughing so hard. Some of the nurses commented on our ability to stay upbeat. It wasn't an act. We were, during those moments, genuinely having a good time in spite of this disease.

James was determined not to let it take him down. He was convinced that *he* had power over *it*, and these were going to be good days. I did not doubt him (nor would he let me), and so we carried on. The windows of "What if?" and "Why not?" were wide open.

Reflecting, as I write this, on his genuine ability to stay upbeat and positive leaves me now in total awe. He really was amazing and his example humbling.

James became tired during the early days of the trial, possibly due to the early risings to get the UCSF each morning. He came home and rested but then headed out with the pack of friends for the evening. A new visualization entered our lives as we decided to switch off the neon Diner sign inside his body. The drug was going to stop the cancer cells expanding and growing. There would be no food for them to consume.

James worked hard at pretending that the cells were starving and crinkling up. He developed daily bouts of hiccups during this first round of treatments, but otherwise he felt fine. Simple pleasures like chicken soup and peonies cheered us, and we both were surprised and pleased at how good the days felt.

James's first espresso at La Boulange on Polk Street

One morning we walked to La Boulange bakery on Polk and Green Street and sat outside while he drank his first, and only, espresso. Though not a coffee drinker, he wanted to try one and felt very European surveying the passing traffic from his wicker chair.

When he was not out wandering with his buddies, we managed to play a few games of chess each evening, and James proved to be a tough adversary. He did not want to lose, and both of us played aggressively. Nine times out of ten, he won, and I now realize that these games gave him a sense of control that he was lacking. James felt empowered when manipulating the board. I knew he wanted to play hard, so I did not intentionally let him win. They were memorable games that tested us both. A few of his friends played as well, and they would settle into competitive matches that lasted for hours.

New doctors and more social workers were introduced to the mix. It was wonderful that James shared a good rapport with them as it would have been hell to not have the ability to share candidly with your oncologist, especially as a teenager. James felt comfortable enough with Dr. Dubois to call him Dr. Stevie. Their bourgeoning relationship became another blessing in the midst of this awful story we had wandered into.

Interestingly, James had started to refer to his cancer as an "inconvenience," and he was unequivocal that he was going to lick this thing and move forward with life. His determination made it impossible for anyone else to think otherwise, and we all rolled along in his bubble of confident cheer. He started to see a physical therapist at UCSF to get his leg strong again with the intention of getting back on his skateboard, which sat waiting patiently at the front door. Going to work was tough for me on many days as being around the young babies and their families left me sad. They were supportive of my plight and all wanted to be empathetic, and the community was incredibly dear and kind to both of us, but this strange juxtaposition of two colliding worlds continued to hang over me. I cried for long lonely minutes quietly in the shower at night, which remained my only place of refuge.

The early days of the drug trial appeared a success, and the follow-up PET scan showed no new development in the tumours. It seemed they were being held at bay. James was happy, and I felt huge relief but could not shake a sense of doom. The doctors did not see *new* tumours, but that meant the old ones were still sitting there. Doing what? I did not trust them.

The entries in CaringBridge started to hold more questions of why and how do we live well with this uncertainty hanging over us every day. I had started to look at each twenty-four-hour-period differently and did not have time for pettiness or unnecessary stress.

> We all have the ability to make each day count—standing together at the edge of the precipice not knowing what the next day will hold. All the issues that we think of as so important quickly evaporate when you awaken each morning and the most important thing you have to do is make sure you hear your child breathing. (CaringBridge, July 6, 2008)

Within a few days, the "possible" nausea and fatigue that we had been warned about set in. Even a simple walk to the corner left James depleted, and he craved peace and quiet. Fortunately, these days did not last too long, and he patiently regained his vigour. A favourite daily outing now was to drive out to Crissy Field in the late afternoon for our game of chess at the table where he had celebrated his birthday barbeque. Some days he'd watch the joggers and cyclists with a melancholy that horribly exacerbated my feelings of helplessness.

As a way to distract him, we would tack on a drive through the Presidio to the Haight Ashbury to look for the ultimate plaid flannel shirt at Goodwill or instruments at their community music store. He had decided to create a recording studio in his bedroom, so the quest for microphones, speakers, amplifiers, and mixing equipment became the new undertaking. One afternoon James purchased a glockenspiel, and his evening musical creations were becoming quite amazing.

The doctors stayed on top of the pain medications for James and at each appointment took extra time to review his tolerance carefully. During one such meeting Dr. Dubois asked me if there was a gun in the house, leaving me shocked at the question. "Absolutely not!" was my instant retort. "Did James have access to a gun in other people's homes"? How could I know? I was terribly stunned by the suggestion but realize now that, of course, the doctors were concerned that if James became despondent, a gun might provide escape. The statistics of suicide from self-inflicted wounds is staggering in the United States.

The question made me bristle and was so alien to anything I had ever contemplated. This bloody cancer, without any thought of how it would affect us, had invaded our world so completely and with such ease that it left me incredulous. The thought of watching out for gun violence was really the last straw.

So far James was doing fine with the pain management and beyond occasional twinges did not appear to be suffering. Straight out of the shoot, James was taking oxycodone oxycontin and, within a few months, a low dose of methadone. The combination seemed to work as one drug supported the other and relieved the different types of pain. I was so naïve, I had not realized just how potent these drugs were, and the fact that my son needed them to function had not sunk in. Even as I'd wait at the pharmacy for these controlled substances to be prepared, I was in a world of disconnect. James looked and acted fine, so all must be well but the only way he could function was because of powerful drugs that were keeping much of his body numb.

My entries on CaringBridge continued being upbeat as James was able to read them and also check in on the greetings that friends had posted. I did not dare go into the full story of how weary he felt some days or my uncertainty of whether or not this drug trial was working.

By mid-July, after a break of a few weeks, the second round of the trial began with more of the daily timed tests at the PCRC unit. James was becoming more tired and had started to lose weight. He kept focused every day on being creative and having fun, but his energy was starting to lag. I would never share my uneasiness and sorrow with him, but my personal journal was full of it.

Chapter 5

Peter Gabriel

"I didn't think my heart could love this much."
—James, sharing his devotion for his pet, December 2008

James and "Micha"

James had always wanted a pet. Sadly, his ongoing allergies had prevented anything beyond a cricket (found during one of our glorious Yosemite vacations); a frog; a fractious cockatiel named Micha, who sadly grew to hate us for being deserted all day; and Ocean and Coltrane, two odd tiny fish who lived in a small clear plastic box.

While none of the pets had a great shelf life, Ocean surprised us all by living for over four years. He remained in the same spot in the kitchen for fear that any shift in his habitat might be dangerous, and he became the stuff of legends. When Ocean eventually died, he was taken out to the Pacific to be carried out to sea. James thought it only right. Coltrane, who had died years before, was laid to rest under a tree in the "secret garden" near our home at Fort Mason.

After his diagnosis, James resurrected the idea of getting a pet, and in our spirit of "What the hell?" it was decided that we might as well get one. If James had cancer in his lungs, surely a bit of wheezing from a furry animal could not be any worse. Our thought process was all over the place.

James had always wanted a rabbit, which interestingly had also been my childhood pet. We did our research and discovered a number of possibilities in the area. Sadly, that spring, there had been some horrible wildfires in northern California, and many rabbits had been scooped up in an effort to save them from the flames. They had ended up in a number of local shelters, and there was a desperate need for welcoming homes. After work on July 14, we made a trek over to the South of Market animal shelter to take a look. James expressed concern that we'd find the right one, asking, "How will we know?"

I assured him that somehow the right one would be there for us, and if not, we'd look elsewhere.

"But how will we *know* if it is the right one?" James asked again.

"We need to trust," was all I could offer. Deep in my gut I had great hope that success would be certain as James needed a boost.

My only prerequisite was that the rabbit be house-trained as I had no intention of picking up droppings in my few spare moments. We had to complete a long questionnaire upon arrival at the shelter, and James worried we might not fit the bill. Dear love, he would sometimes fret over the silliest of things, and I reassured him that the shelter wanted to find homes for these stray animals, so they would not be as exacting as the paperwork suggested. We were taken into the area where the rabbits were housed, and immediately our hearts melted. There were many to choose from, and I reminded James to look for those that were house-trained. Each animal's cage bore a profile tag.

As predicted, there was one perfect white rabbit who jumped up and put his paws through the cage when James stopped to read the tag. He was smitten. House-trained. Perfect. His name was Gabe. Without hesitating, we asked the shelter staff if we could take him home.

All was in order, except the rabbit needed to be neutered and the shelter asked us to wait a day before collecting him, giving them time to perform the procedure. James was devastated. It was the first time I had seen him so heartbroken since his diagnosis, and I was suddenly aware that afternoon that even with his positive energy and outlook, James was extremely fragile. Since we had to get all the supplies in place, I convinced James to let Gabe stay at the shelter overnight, and we'd get the cage, food, and other trappings at the local pet store on our way home; that way, we'd be all set for tomorrow.

My brother Bill arrived on July 16 for a few days, and en route from the airport, we stopped at the shelter to pick up Gabe and bring him home. What a wacky night! We really had not thought carefully through what having a pet in the house would mean, and I had forgotten how crazy a rabbit can be. Gabe hopped everywhere, disappearing under chairs, bed, and tables. He spent some time on James's bed *and* under it.

I tried to hide how frantic I felt as James was having a blast. He laughed so hard he cried; and interestingly, once Gabe had exhausted himself, he sat happily for ages in James's lap, letting James stroke his long white ears and furry back. They immediately bonded, and if James called him, Gabe would come bolting across the slippery wooden floors towards him. We teased that he was really a cocker spaniel in disguise. While we were warned that rabbits were skittish about being handled, Gabe was totally at ease curled up for hours in one's arms.

Sadly, my worries were realized; within a day, James developed a terrible wheeze. The dander made his eyes water, and while at UCSF for his next round of drug-trial blood work, I discussed with the social workers how to find a replacement home for Gabe. James was desperate not to lose him, but I could not allow the allergies to overwhelm his already taxed system. James wore a face mask and washed his hands after holding the rabbit; Gabe's arrival in our home was rapidly becoming an issue.

A few e-mails and notices were posted, and I waited to see who might step forward. Some local families expressed interest, but surprisingly, within a day of preparing Gabe to move, James stopped wheezing. His eyes cleared, and he felt as though nothing had happened. He could hold his rabbit without suffering; it was decided to let him stay put. Perhaps the mythical charm of the white hare had worked. The transformation was nothing short of miraculous.

James christened the rabbit Peter Gabriel, after Beatrix Potter's Peter, but of course, the connection to musician Peter Gabriel was lost on no one, and surprising us even more, the rabbit responded to *both* names. It was quite remarkable to see him hop towards you in response to either "Peter" or "Gabriel."

James's friends grew to love him as well, and it was touching to watch them coo and fawn over this ball of white fluff. Marc, a dear friend for many years, had raised rabbits growing up in New Hampshire, and he teased me mercilessly that PG was going to be in our lives "for a long, *long* time." Rabbits easily live as much as fourteen years. How would we take care of it? He'd grow to be huge, taking over the flat, or at least he'd need his own room! James loved the notion. I started to cringe. We *really* had not thought this through properly.

Somehow though, all worries evaporated once Gabe nestled into your arms and nuzzled your elbow. He was not going anywhere, and for the first time since James's diagnosis, I felt hopeful. James had renewed energy and started to look at clothes for the upcoming school year. He studied online stores for great deals on skateboarding shoes and nifty backpacks. We went to Urban Outfitters and trendy city thrift stores.

The next round of trial drugs did not seem to leave him as tired and nauseated. His blood work looked good, and scans revealed no new tumours. Everything was in check.

Peter Gabriel was the light of the day, and even though he had taken to chewing on furniture and the sea-grass rugs, we overlooked all his shortcomings in exchange for the joy. I started to take Peter to work for the young children to play with, and they were also delighted. Friends, when leaving cookies for James and me on the front stoop, also left bundles of fresh carrots to make sure PG had a treat too. This cunning rabbit even figured out the drawer in the fridge where the carrots lived and would get up on his hind legs, begging for one when we opened the door.

Music was taking over the flat, and James's buddies were over every day to record. There was now a complete drum kit as well as the keyboard, four guitars, and a new banjo that Doris, an old friend (his "fairy godmother"), had sent from LA crammed into the small room. James's recording equipment sat on an old wooden library table. There was hardly space to turn around, but he loved it that way, and I washed my hands of any attempts to organize.

James working on his music recordings

It was perfect in his eyes, and that was all that mattered. The boys experimented with a variety of instruments and sounds. A hanging saucepan clanged next to the bass drum. James played his acoustic guitar using his great-grandfather's violin bow, generating a sound like a medieval psaltery. The creative process was dynamic, and somehow, each week he managed to fit in a visit or two to the funky music stores in North Beach or the Haight to poke about. He could spend hours lost in thought with the instruments and LP collections. His energy was once again infectious; I was swept up in this enthusiasm and creativity. Days were simple and happy. James had his appetite, and but for all the dates on the calendar for upcoming scans and labs, I would never have believed his body was full of cancer. This was a golden time in our days together.

*   *   *

Actor Heath Ledger died in January 2008 from an overdose of oxycodone/ diazepam (some of the drugs that James was taking each day), and his last film *The Dark Knight* opened mid-July. The movie's release and chatter about Ledger's death triggered James's concern about possible addiction issues due to all the drugs that he was taking. Trying to ease his worry, I reminded James that he *needed* these narcotics for the relief from legitimate pain, and his body absorbed these medicines differently than those who were recreational users. It was experimental drug use that messed up the head and body.

James's meds were essential for targeting very specific pain. He would not become an addict. His doctors reinforced this at each of our meetings, especially when the doses had to be increased.

I drove James down Van Ness Avenue to the AMC theatre to meet his friends for the evening viewing of *The Dark Knight*, but at the conclusion, he called to come home. He used to have the energy to be up for a few hours of fun after a movie, grabbing a bite, taking the bus, or even walking home. I carried my mobile fully charged at all times now to be able to collect him whenever he needed to retreat. When I pulled up curbside, James stood alone outside the theatre, propped on his cane. He had enjoyed the film but looked white and so terribly tired. It was becoming more and more difficult to suppress my concerns at these times and not fuss, but I had to stay strong and to present to James a life unchanged.

Peter had become a constant companion, and once in the door and up the stairs, James would lift him from his pen to cuddle or let him freely hop around the flat. After much trial and error, we had settled upon a pen that was set up in the kitchen. Using accordion wire frames, meant for containing dogs, there was room for Peter to hop and stretch, eat and curl up in a "nest" box lined with towels. Hay bedding, chew toys, rabbit food, and additional bunny treats were added to the weekly shopping list. I was amazed at how quickly Peter Gabriel had settled into life with us and how James felt such a deep attachment. This magical white rabbit truly was meant to be a part of our lives and had become in a short space of time an incredible friend and gift for both of us.

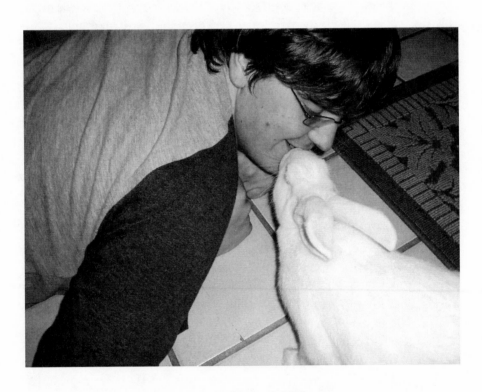

James and Peter Gabriel

Chapter 6

Wishes

Everything is possible.

—*James, July 2008*

In early August, James and I managed to follow through on our postponed trip to Boston to look at colleges, and James was excited to submit his various applications once school started. We loved Boston, and the ability to wander and explore it on foot, for the first time, was a treat. James needed his cane but managed to walk to the sights and tour the colleges on his list. Sam, a fellow Stuart Hall classmate, was in town at the same time, and the two boys started to plot what college life would be like, free from the structure of home and secondary school.

While continuing to take his chemo drugs each day, James still had energy and none of the predicted nausea, so the trip was easy, straightforward, and a huge success. We carried our chessboard with us in our large canvas bag each day and spent time on the Common playing games while resting in between college visits.

Traveling chess board

We managed to visit Harvard, Emerson, and Boston College, and James experimented with his retro "Diana" camera that allowed him to take a variety of artsy photographs. He enjoyed especially manipulating exposures and commented on how he wished he could do the same with his cancer. Another childhood friend Teddy, who loved to compose music with James, was also in Bean Town at the same time, and we enjoyed a lively family dinner with his folks at the famous Union Oyster House. The banter of the young people was infectious.

James's appetite was good but not voracious, and while starting to lose weight, he still looked fit and healthy. Due to the East Coast time change, we were able to stay up to watch the late-night talk shows hosted by Jay Leno and Conan O'Brien. I had not watched them for years and adored hearing James's hearty laugh. These days of exploring uncharted territory unfolded with ease, and seeing him well and optimistic for the future filled me with hope.

It was only when visiting Northeastern University that I was reminded that James was ill. He felt that he had to dismiss this college as an option because the campus was too expansive, and he'd not be able to walk between the buildings.

We returned to San Francisco on August 13 tired but full of enthusiasm for Boston. James looked forward to sharing his findings with the doctors the next day. Within twenty-four hours of our return, James fasted once again in preparation for a full day at UCSF; a PET scan, an MRI, an x-ray, and blood work had all been scheduled. My journal entry that evening started with "James weary."

All too quickly the goodness of our recent trip evaporated. The reality of cancer came crashing back into both our lives. We had managed to dodge it while in Boston, but living with cancer was very much the reality in San Francisco. The coming days revolved around attending physical therapy for leg-strengthening exercises, tracking blood work, and beginning the third round of the trial chemo drug. All fingers were crossed that it was going to work, but I knew the outcome was never a sure bet.

After the scans, it was decided that radiation was needed to try to slow the growth of the tumour in James's thigh, which had started to apply more pressure to the leg. Hence, we were introduced to yet another suite of lab rooms deep in the bowels of UCSF. The preparation for radiation is a meticulous process, requiring painstakingly tattooing the target area on the skin. James was horribly uncomfortable lying in a dark room on an icy-cold slab table, and while he remained gracious and followed the doctor's instructions, I could tell he was miserable during the process.

The head of radiology, Dr. William Wara, was a delightful grandfatherly figure who worked closely with us explaining how radiation worked and its possible side effects. Fatigue and nausea might well be on the horizon, and he offered suggestions of how to counteract them. So far James had been lucky not to suffer with either, and I dreaded what these symptoms might do to him. The dark rooms, flashing red lights, biohazard signs, and an ever-growing uncertainty made me terribly sad.

In the waiting room, I cried quietly, and the technicians and nurses faithfully checked in on me. Many days, I felt a dark swirling fog descend upon me, and I prayed that we just get through the procedure, arrive home safely, and retreat from the world into the calm quiet of the nest. Our home had become an even greater safe haven for both of us since the diagnosis, and we longed to close the door and pull up the drawbridge at the end of each day.

James continued to remain remarkably upbeat and just wanted to get on with life. He found the tests an inconvenience and doctors' visits a bore, but he was adamant that he not stay in hospital, so the trade-off was the daily to-and-fro for the numerous tests and treatments in exchange for living at home, spending time with his friends, and attending school with the goal of university upon graduation.

"Quality of life" had become the key phrase in all discussions with the doctors, and in my naïveté, I thought we were all just talking about how to ensure James got through these tests with some degree of comfort. James, too, thought of it as an excuse to live well. It would take me months to fully grasp what the quality of life message really means.

*   *   *

Months earlier, on the day of James's biopsy, Anne, a UCSF social worker, met with me for tea in the cafeteria. She was wonderfully calm and non-judgmental, a trait I would soon come to appreciate greatly once the ensuing months started to unravel. She explained that due to his age, James qualified for Make-a-Wish, and if he'd like to put thought to that, she would get the wheels in motion with the Bay Area chapter. She expressed a sense of urgency for the granting of any wish, implying that it needed to be done before James turned eighteen. In truth, as I was to learn later, it was the dramatic terminal nature of James's cancer that hastened the offer and wish fulfilment. Simply put, the team at UCSF did not know if James would live until that birthday.

When James learned that he qualified for Make-A-Wish, he began to ponder what that might be. Meeting Radiohead was one of the top wishes; sitting in on a writing session for *The Daily Show* in New York City or meeting Lewis Black, our favourite satirist, were also high on the list as were parachuting from a plane or spending a week in the Caribbean with his close friends. The fantasy provided a welcome reprieve from the uncertainty that had started to permeate James's days.

I was heartbroken throughout this wish exercise. James deserved a lifetime of special wishes, not just *one*. A gnawing sense of doom sat heavily with me. This was somehow all wrong. James did not need a "wish." He was going to beat this disease and live to a ripe old age with grandchildren to fawn over. This feeling that I had wandered on to the wrong movie set was pervasive. I continued to pray for someone to yell "Cut!" but still, no one was stepping up to grant my wish.

After a day or two of kicking around ideas and making the list of pros and cons, James decided he'd like to meet then—presidential candidate Barack Obama on Election Night in Chicago. We had entered the final months of the campaign, and James and his peers were swept up in the excitement of all that Obama represented—a youthful, candidate who wanted to shift the tide of America. He was positive, hopeful, invigorating, and charismatic. James was enthusiastically following the campaign and longed for the opportunity to vote; next year, when eighteen, he'd be proud to cast his ballot.

In the early days of the campaign, Obama had visited San Francisco to address the crowds at the Bill Graham Auditorium. James had just started using his cane, but he was determined to attend. After a hasty dinner we drove down to the civic centre and miraculously managed to find parking nearby, making the hobble to the long queue bearable. We were stunned at the turnout. Over five thousand had gathered, and the lines were enormous. Thanks to their mobile phones, James met up with some of his classmates, and they managed to cluster together to watch the proceedings. We did not have a seat and had to stand on the main floor of the auditorium for hours. James curled up next to a wall to sit down, and I held a place near the stage for him to join me when the time was right.

I had never been to a political rally before and was amazed at the organization and crowd control. The seats above us slowly filled as everyone had to pass through security checkpoints, and after a two-hour delay, while hammered by blues and R & B soul tunes over the sound system, the event got under way. It was magical. Beyond the politics or issues, watching Obama command the auditorium and speak of better days that were attainable was uplifting and inspirational. While the politics of Washington would in time beat a drum to try and drown his message, I will always remember that night as one filled with exuberance and hopes for positive change.

James was incredibly energized at the end of the night, and his upbeat friends all shared a new and passionate interest in the American political system. If nothing else, Obama encouraged young people to lose the shackles of indifference and participate. Become involved. Find your voice. All valuable lessons for young people to be reminded of, and for James, over the coming months, it gave him a deep sense of hope and belief in a bright future, even as this ugly cancer slowly ravaged his body.

The larger community of friends and the support team at UCSF were incredibly kind and started working on their own special treats for James as well. The greatest was acquiring tickets, thanks to the generosity of local radio station KFOG for the inaugural Outside Lands concert at Golden Gate Park, from August 22 to 24. The headliners for opening night were James's favourite band, Radiohead. He was thrilled.

It was all arranged that I would tag along to be onsite for opening night should James want to leave early, but I was to remain in the background as best

I could. The disabled-access seating was on a raised platform near the main stage, but to my shock, there were no seats available. It was just a flat open platform that anyone seemed to be able to climb on to. Using his cane, James wandered around the Polo Field with his good friends, Keaton and Anthony, to the various smaller stages where other bands performed (the array of artists was quite amazing for this first-time event) while I tried to find a chair for him to sit on. I knew he'd get tired as the evening wore on and the cold damp night air, so common by the ocean, was probably going to make him uncomfortable. I rattled the cages of every event staffer I could find to try acquire a chair for him, to no avail. The mother bear was growling, and I was desperate to take care of my cub, come hell or high water.

Just as I was losing my temper, I heard someone call my name, and there in this sea of humanity was an old friend Edith, attending with her two children and husband. They had purchased tickets in the upper level, and when I explained my dilemma, she immediately went to a row of folding chairs, picked one up, and handed it to me across the dividing fence. Once again, the universe conspired to give us what we needed, and I was so grateful. We soon became separated by the crowds, but I clung to that chair with my life and James was indeed grateful to have a place to rest as the night wore on. The concert was amazing, and James was ecstatic to hear Radiohead live. He treasured the memories and framed the poster to hang on his wall. For months following that weekend, he relived every moment, adding to the swell of music emanating from his room.

*　　*　　*

During the early months of drug trial, the days were punctuated by visits to the doctors and labs with on-going MRIs and PET scans. UCSF was a destination every week, and it was discovered, very sadly, on August 19 that the first drug trial had not been successful in halting the growth of tumours. In fact, two new lesions had formed in James's liver and sit bone; it was crucial to come up with another plan quickly. Radiation would hopefully slow the growth and ease the pressure in his thigh, but we had to remain open to possible radiation in other parts of his body. Every stop was being pulled out.

There might be another drug that we could explore that would target the tumours' food supply that was being delivered through his blood. Surgery was not an option as the cancer had spread too much in his body.

We were all amazed at the thoughtful questions James asked the doctors. He was totally engaged in the decision-making process and remained calm and alert while weighing options. He was teaching all of us how to walk this path. While James was busy living life to the full and cramming as much music and socializing into every day, the doctors were scrambling to find a solution. I felt a quiet desperation, and I think the doctors did as well. It was not expressed but was very real, and in reading my journals, I am reminded of how frightened I was becoming. The doctors tried to keep me focused and calm, but we were all on the same page. This was a runaway train, and we did not know when it would crash into the station.

*   *   *

Graduation photo 2009

The senior school year began the week of August 28 with one day set aside for the graduation photos. The young men of Stuart Hall have a series of pictures taken for this final year, some in their casual clothes and others wearing a tuxedo shirt and jacket. The end result is a lovely collection of poses for parents to purchase. One picture is chosen for the yearbook. Another is picked for a large framed class picture that hangs in the foyer of the school. James did the photo shoot and then immediately headed back to UCSF for the first round of radiation treatment, which would last seven consecutive days. His photos were beautiful, and all who have seen them are amazed at how well and beautifully calm he looks. His skin is clear, his hair thick and radiant, and there is a lightness and peace in his eyes. These pictures have become some of the most treasured from his short life, and I keep one of him, wearing his tuxedo, close by every day. Within days of completing this first round of radiation, the predicted extreme fatigue and nausea set in.

I made an appointment with Gordon, Head of school, and Rachel, the Dean of students, to put together a game plan that would make it possible for James to participate as fully as possible in the school year. He was determined to attend Stuart Hall every day, apply to colleges, graduate, and get on with living his life. James continued to call this cancer his "great inconvenience" and was positive he would beat it. His strength and tenacity was rapidly becoming a source of incredible inspiration for everyone, from the doctors to the school community, his extended family, friends, and even beyond.

Thousands were by now closely following the CaringBridge blog, and the greetings page rapidly filled up with expressions of hope and devotion from around the world. The outpouring was amazing to me, but James found it embarrassing. He always hated a fuss. I would read the greetings to him in small batches as he was starting to find it all too overwhelming.

*　　*　　*

The evening of October 15 was a giddy one when the team from the Bay Area chapter of Make-a-Wish met with us at home. The opportunity to be creative and whimsical and indulge in wishes was a perfect anecdote to the glaring reality that was staring us in the face. James told the team of a few of his ideas but settled on the notion of meeting Obama and sharing in Election Night in Chicago. The Bay Area chapter had never had a wish of this magnitude. Most children opt for a trip to Disney World or meeting a rock star, but James's wish had tapped into their creative juices and very quickly energized the entire organization. James chose not to share his wish with others until it was in place, and we agreed to respect this. I know that the Make-a-Wish team were not at all sure they would be able to fulfill such a wish, and they were happy to keep it a secret too. Failure is not something they wanted to advertise.

James and his classmates followed the debates and campaign assiduously and spent a lot of time with the political science teacher during lunch breaks discussing the possible outcome. Everyone in our circle was rooting for Obama, and once Sarah Palin entered the ring, they were all convinced that Barack had the election in the bag. Election Day 2008 was November 4; Barack Obama and Joe Biden would be in Chicago's Grant Park to follow the results with their team of supporters. It would hopefully be a night for celebrations. James, for one, was convinced they would win.

Chapter 7

Details and Distractions

It is in every one of us to be wise.

—*Anonymous*

The senior school year was now under way with the college application process moving full steam ahead. James had decided to apply to several East Coast and Midwestern colleges and universities as he wanted to live away from home for these next four years. To even out the mix, he also applied to a couple of local universities but felt that San Francisco would be the perfect place to return to upon graduation. He was determined that I continue to live on Polk Street as he had great plans for life there one day, and it needed to stay in the family to give him that option.

James carefully crafted the requisite college essay, which he shared only with his college advisor. I did not see it nor, as far as I know, did any of his teachers. James was very clear that this was *his* work and no one was to influence him. His strength and tenacity, traits I had always known he had, were now being honed and shared generously with his community of peers. They were deeply moved and inspired by his commitment. He went to school every day, and if radiation or doctors' appointments were part of the mix, so be it. His attitude was clearly "I will not squander this year."

The head of school met with me to discuss his classes and workload, and we all agreed to take James's lead on what he was up to on any given day. There would be no master plan to adhere to. Over the coming months we would become astute readers of James's energy and abilities. The faculty confessed their amazement with all that he contributed to their classes. He was mature, asking incredibly thoughtful questions and willingly sharing his insights. Living with disease had broadened his perspective on many things, and his spiritual side was blossoming. Many of the faculty shared with me that they were becoming better teachers having James in their classrooms.

Peter Gabriel continued to bring great joy to our days, and James had forged a deep attachment to this magical crazy pet. The two of them could communicate in their own special way, and I was amazed at how tame Peter was in James's arms. He would burrow into the crack of James's elbow and sit, unperturbed, for hours. When James played his guitar or a video game, Peter sat quietly close by. Reflecting on those moments, I am reminded what magical beings they both were and thank God their paths intersected so completely. Each day was rapidly becoming a gift as I grappled with the fragility of time.

Radiation was targeted to James's bones, and he had started to carry a doughnut cushion to school so that he could sit with greater ease on the hard classroom chairs. James's teachers were hugely supportive, allowing him total freedom to stand, walk about the classroom, or even lie on the floor, whatever was needed to ease his discomfort.

Patter, his art teacher, placed a large beanbag chair in the studio so that James could relax or even take a nap in his final class of the day.

* * *

Two new drug trials were placed on the table to explore: Sunitibin was in Phase One but would target the blood supply to the tumours. Again, it was an oral drug, which was preferred, but doses and side effects, still under study, were iffy. A list of likely, less likely, and rare-but-serious side effects had to be considered. James would take the pill for twenty-eight days and rest for fourteen. Trabectedin was designed to treat unusual sarcomas. It would be administered for twenty-four hours a day every three weeks via a semi-permanent central IV line. Hospital stays would be necessary. Side effects would be the traditional ones of nausea, headaches, fatigue, and probable hair loss. Red and white blood cells would be tracked constantly. With both of these drug trials, as with the first one, James would be sharing his story to further research and develop cures while hopefully healing himself.

Dr. Dubois's and James's special relationship had deepened over the months, and it was wonderful to observe their honest friendship. James was totally confident and at ease with Dr. Stevie and never doubted that he had his best interests at heart. To help James decide what drug trial to undertake, a conference call was placed to Dr. John Goldberg in Miami, the only other doctor in the country who was researching alveolar soft-part sarcoma. It was hoped that Goldberg might bring new eyes and perspective to the case and help advise as to which drug might be more effective. He would act as a consultant going forward, and James felt empowered having these two experts watching his back.

Dreading an IV line and time in the hospital James opted for the Sunitinib. He could continue with an oral drug, attend school, and live at home. The twenty-eight-day cycle would begin as soon as the drug was obtained.

The UCSF research programs are world renowned, and the hospital is regularly lauded as one of the top ten in America. Consequently, the exceptional and respected doctors within its network have access to drug trials that might not be available elsewhere. In the early days of James's diagnosis, while we were struggling to come to terms with the horrid shock and reality, many folks took it upon themselves to look for alternative treatments, medical facilities specialists, and doctors. They all meant well and their suggestions came from a place of love, but one of the greatest gifts was a message I received from a dear friend in the United Kingdom. She shared an old friendship with a Nobel prize winner for immunology, and after reviewing James's notes, he was very clear that we "must not doctor shop." He was totally confident that we had the very best possible care, and his message gave me permission to let go of any guilt that I might be holding based on fear of not doing enough.

I have learned through this experience that each family and individual deals differently with a diagnosis of this magnitude. Some want to explore every possible *why* and research all treatments and contingencies. Unable to fully grasp or dissect, and probably triggered in part by my state of shock, I entered a state of "Ignorance is bliss" and made the conscious decision not to dig too deeply. *Perhaps if I did not become too engaged with the reality, it would go away?* Who knows what motivated me, but I continued to see my precious son as robust and healthy. He was strong, complete, and beautiful, full of vigour and oozing with life. His love and attachment to relationships was powerful, and sharing in his joy was how I intended to walk this path at his side.

At no time during his illness did I see the complete set of x-rays for James, and I asked that the doctors not give me a prognosis. His father requested that, and I left the room during their discussions. I was not going to live by someone else's timeline. This was James's story, and since he had every intention of living well and moving forward, it was my job to help facilitate that as best I could. Getting caught up in all the details of the disease would take me off-task.

That said, I *was* still willing to hear what the doctors told me. I did not block out important facts and participated fully in necessary decisions, but I was very aware that this time together *now* was incredibly precious, and we were not going to waste a moment. I resisted allowing the disease to become the most important part of the story. James did not ask me to do this. For right or wrong, it was my personal decision. Interestingly, it empowered me and perhaps provided the necessary strength to keep going as the days unfolded.

Some well-wishers, I am sure, were disappointed that I did not become more aggressively engaged in alternative treatments or philosophies, but the reality of running on fumes and staying strong for James was exhausting. Perfecting my stolen moments to grieve (so as not to trouble him) and juggling the day-to-day agenda while scrambling to find time to be still and process what this illness meant was all-consuming. I was James's advocate for living well, and I pray that my decision served him best.

Thankfully, James was blissfully unaware of all the behind-the-scenes machinations and questioning. He was doing exactly what he needed, and his friends, school, music, and creativity brought him peace. He was living life to the full, and like the detective from the sixties' television program *Dragnet*, James wanted "Just the facts, ma'am." He asked that we give it to him straight, present the options, make a decision, figure the out the drugs or next step, and get the hell out of the clinic. That is how he wanted it, and we all tried to oblige.

For years I had felt at odds with San Francisco and craved a simpler and less-expensive place to live. After the horrible diagnosis of cancer and being fully embraced by UCSF, I was never going to doubt that we were indeed in exactly the right place at the right time. The research opportunities and medical care could not have been more exemplary.

San Francisco, for all its difficulties, was the perfect setting for this chapter. James *adored* the city, and I let go of my frustrations and for the first time in years allowed the city to display its magic. There was a blessing in my renewed willingness to give it a second chance.

James and guitar 2006

Appointments were made at the clinic on Parnassus for the further scans and tests that were required before starting Sunitinib. In the midst of all this, James experienced increased lower back pain, and new drugs, some with higher doses, had to be introduced to help manage his discomfort.

There were a few days when, for the first time, he entered the realm of extreme agony, which was unbearable to witness and left us all feeling totally helpless. The daily doses of oxycontin and oxycodone were increased with lorazepam and a higher dose of methadone added to the mix. James's doctors asked us to track when the doses of meds were increased (James was given control of when to administer) as this would indicate when they would need to tweak or explore the next level of opiates. I soon discovered that the fine-tuning of pain meds was just as important as trying to slow the growth of the lesions. In hindsight, the doctors understood fully what was going to be needed as they tracked the cancer's spread, but they allowed James to remain fully engaged in the moment and did not attempt to orchestrate. James was thus empowered, and he had a sense of control in this unravelling scenario. Intelligent, compassionate support was as much a gift from the doctors, nurses, and social workers as finding a cure.

Alternative pain management was suggested with acupuncture high on the list. The Osher Center on Sutter Street is at the forefront of integrative medicine, and since it is part of the UCSF network, James's scans, x,-rays and

MRI results were easily transferred for review by the Osher practitioners. I had always been fascinated by acupuncture and was more than willing to share the experience with him.

On September 18 we attended the college information night at school, and at 8:00 a.m. the following morning, we were at the Osher Center to explore acupuncture treatments. It all felt surreal. "Continuing education" was certainly the essence of our days now. Before the first treatment, James had an intensive consultation with Beverly, the head of the program. She discussed the treatments James had already pursued, what drugs he was using, the areas of most discomfort, and what the goal of acupuncture would be. We both had an hour's session and were shocked at how great we felt at the end of the treatment.

It really was amazing. James's colour was great, his cheeks rosy and his eyes clear. We both felt incredibly mellow and warm, and I could feel surges of energy running through my body. My liver was blocked, and the stress of the past months had clogged the flow of blood and fluids. I was instructed to eat more hot foods as my system was cold and "like a swamp." Beverly targeted areas of James's body where the lesions existed in an effort to lessen their pain. We both became incredibly aware that day of the power of energy in the body and mind and promised to be more mindful of our thoughts. After months of struggle, these would be the only "treatments" that we'd both actually look forward to.

That evening James, his good chum and classmate Keaton, and I drove up to Lake Tahoe for the weekend. A friend and Village Well board member had graciously offered their parents' mountain home for a little break, and it proved to be a magical getaway. The rental mini-van was loaded up with guitars, favourite foods, and games. Being seven thousand feet up in the mountains did us all a world of good, and the pristine waters of the lake and spectacular views filled some hitherto unacknowledged empty spaces. It was the first time since James's diagnosis that I could sit silently in nature and try to make peace with the universe for allowing this to happen to my son.

While the boys played guitars and chatted on the deserted beach, I was able to wail at the end of an isolated pier. Stress fatigue had become the norm, and deep sleep was a welcome respite. James swam in the pool and soaked up comfort from the heat of the sauna. It was a perfect time in so many ways, except that the new pain had manifested in James's lower back.

During the drive up the mountain and many times throughout the weekend, James was unsettled. Sitting and even lying down was difficult. He was uncomfortable for long stretches, and to ease the pressure, we used heating pads and layers of pillows. Driving back to the city, we had to stop multiple times for him to get out of the car to walk and stretch. I reported this to the doctors first thing on Monday, and another visit to the clinic was set for Tuesday.

Within twenty-four hours a PET scan and MRI were scheduled at a new additional UCSF campus on Berry Street, near the PacBell baseball stadium. These scans, performed as an outpatient, would let the doctors know if James could begin the Sunitinib and would maybe explain the extreme back discomfort. We headed to the clinic on the morning of September 24 for what had now become routine scans.

Everything went terribly wrong.

James could not lie flat on the table for the MRI, and while the technicians worked to prop him up or find a better position, James was beside himself with agony. Tears flowed as he cried out in pain. It was the worst I had seen him. The technicians were baffled, and they thought he might be exaggerating, but I assured them that this was not like James. He didn't whine or complain. There had to be something wrong. After multiple attempts the scans were halted, and I made an emergency call to Dr. Dubois.

Plans for the scans were aborted, and I was told to get over to the hospital as quickly as possible. Miraculously, a bed was available for James. The scan and MRI would have to be performed while under sedation. On autopilot, I sped across town and checked James in on the seventh floor. He changed into a hospital gown before being wheeled down to the hospital basement. Mark, the technician who had performed the past scans, was waiting next to the MRI machine in his uniform Hawaiian shirt. James was relieved to know that he would be performing the tests.

During all the uncertainty of these months, we both found great comfort seeing the same faces for blood draws, tests, and scans; all these technicians had become our extended family. We would end up seeing more of them in the coming months than anyone else.

We now had the routine down pat. James was injected with the radioactive dyes and sugar waters through an IV line in his hand. He had to sit quietly for about forty minutes to let the fluids enter his system. In simple terms, cancer apparently likes sugar, and by injecting the glucose, the cancer cells would be activated. The injected dyes would target these active cells in the tumours, making it easy to get a clear picture of what had grown, where the cells were accumulating, and what might be problematic.

This time, an anesthesiologist had also been sent for. A lot of frantic scurrying and phone calls between offices generated a heavy tension in the room. Fortunately, Dr. Stevie was on staff that day, and he calmly explained to James what was needed to get the scan results. James immediately exhaled. This doctor had an amazing effect on us all. How the procedure came together so quickly, I will never know, but James was soon groggy and able to lie flat for the tests to be performed. The technicians allowed me to stay in the room until he was peacefully asleep, and then I wandered the corridors. It would take at least two to three hours before I would see him again.

En route to the small waiting room that had become all too familiar in what sadly seemed such a short time, a young man in a neatly pressed dark suit with a shockingly white shirt and black tie came around the corner pushing a shrouded gurney, and passed in front of me. Of course, I suddenly realized that this lower level of the hospital also held the morgue. The sight of that shrouded corpse played over countless times in my head for months to come. Even now, years later, I see it vividly, so clinical and final, routine and yet awesome.

I then had a moment of extreme clarity and vowed not to let James die in the hospital. He would *not* be wheeled out of this cold, generic basement by strangers in dark suits. Until that awful afternoon, I had not acknowledged that James might die. Somehow, I had to get my head around that possibility, but it was such an overwhelming notion that I quickly shelved it. Like Scarlett O'Hara, I would think about it another day.

No longer would I be able to say that I was a proactive parent. This day changed everything. From now on, I would just be rebounding from whatever occurred at any given moment. I lost all sense of power, and my fear of failing became acute. We were all being thrust into the unknown. Sticking to plans and being in charge would no longer be a reliable gauge of how days would unfold. It was terrifying, having zero sense of what I was to do beyond this moment. Perhaps, in hindsight, it was a subtle gift as we were being nudged gently to accept the Buddhist thought of living in the moment, detached from outcome. Any attempts at being superwoman would fall flat. Through this new, unexplored territory of vulnerability, both James and I would find our courage.

We stayed in the hospital that night so that James's pain could be managed. Morphine was generously administered, so he was groggy for most of the night. The nurses and doctors were, as I wrote on CaringBridge that evening, "incredibly gentle and kind." We would be discharged the next day, and hopefully the scan results would give us the all-clear to begin the next round of chemotherapy.

The results were not encouraging. The lesions had spread, and the sit bone was full of fractures. The cancer had eaten through the bone, exacerbating the great pain in James's lower back and bottom. Higher doses of methadone, along with additional long-lasting drugs, would be introduced to the arsenal and carefully tracked by the pain specialists at the hospital. There would be no solution to fixing the bone fractures; managing the discomfort was the task now.

We left UCSF in the early afternoon, and James asked to stop at school on our way home. It speaks volumes to the importance of this community that he would choose to stop at school, of all possible places, after such a traumatic twenty-four hours.

Within an hour of getting home, eight young men descended on the house for a visit. Emma and I performed a quick run to Safeway and brought in lots of food and drinks, which the boys inhaled. It was a glorious reprieve from the past days to hear their laughter and silliness again, and a number of them decided to sleep over. The recent presidential debate was a hot topic interspersed with *The Simpsons* and a nonsense zombie game on the PlayStation. Peter Gabriel was in the middle of the zaniness, and I my spirit was instantly lightened, surrounded by all this life and exuberance. These young men erased, for the moment, all my anguish.

*   *   *

James attended school faithfully every day and was producing some of his best work. His writing had a new depth, and he asked questions that were powerfully thought provoking. He greatly influenced not only the teachers but also his peers in those months. He was busy working on his college applications and, while tired, was determined to graduate and move on to the next chapter.

The increased dose of methadone worked a charm at helping ease the pain, but it took a number of days for him to get over the grogginess it produced. For at least three days after the dose was increased, James would be a zombie, tired and distracted with lots of fumbling about. It was frightening the first time to watch him act like a drunkard, but once his body adjusted to the opiate, it somehow all balanced out. We accepted that there would be these days to negotiate whenever the dose was tweaked. The pain relief it provided was amazing, and it gave him a new lease on life once it kicked in. Methadone is a powerful drug, yet he did not run the risk of addiction as his body used it efficiently. It still amazes me how the brain is capable of sorting out how to improvise and adapt.

After an EKG on September 29 James was given the all-clear, and the next chemo drug trial, Sunitinib, began. There were no reactions for the first week, and all seemed to be going well. The pain meds made it possible for James to attend school each day, and the chemo treatment did not have any side effects, so we both had a few days of uninterrupted routine.

On Sunday, October 5, James complained of numbness in his left groin. The doctors did not want to mess about with that, and immediately an MRI was planned for the following morning, and we were told to suspend Sunitinib. The roller coaster was switching into high gear. We made a visit to the Parnassus clinic prior to the MRI, and within twenty-four hours, more radiation was booked with Dr. Wara.

This time the tattoo would target a new lesion in James's back that was applying pressure to the nerves, causing the numbness. This type of cancer did not respond to lengthy treatments, so short strong bursts of radiation would be the routine going forward. These detested lesions were appearing, expanding and cutting off circulation, doing whatever they wanted, and we seemed to have zero control over them.

The level of helplessness escalated, and while continuing to keep buoyed and upbeat in front of James, I was crumbling within. So long as he did not feel pain, then everything was fine in his eyes. He did not want to know the extent of the disease. Just let him live well and graduate. His eyes were constantly on the prize.

In the midst of all this, James continued to compose music, and his friends left their instruments at the house so that they'd be ready for the call. *Thrasher* magazine arrived each month, and the first article James would devour was the music review. Over the years he had acquired an enviable command of the alternative music scene and was extremely knowledgeable about bands and singers worth following. His evenings and early mornings were spent downloading music to his computer, and he started to think more about following his passion by becoming a music critic one day. Thoughtful comparison and a keen intuition were two of his many traits.

Physical therapy continued in a valiant effort to make James's leg strong enough to skateboard again. All the technicians and support team supported him 100 percent in his desire to move forward. It really was remarkable how engaged we had become in his future aspirations. James would go to school and then head over to UCSF for the radiation treatment in the afternoon. The routine was becoming second nature, and other mothers offered to help with the hospital run if I could not be free from work in time to get him there.

I tried not to miss the appointments as he was so sad if someone else took him, and I hated arriving home to find him despondent. More juggling was in order to prevent feeling guilty, and I'd move heaven and earth for future appointments to be there for him.

The predicted fatigue was now manifesting itself, and James would sleep in the car going across town and then again in the waiting room until his treatment. Physical therapy and radiation would be organized consecutively to make efficient use of time. While the pain meds and radiation played havoc with his waking hours, James still amazed us all with his determination to be at school each day. His drive and focus were hugely inspiring and many of his friends confessed to me that they had no right to grumble over their small worries when James remained upbeat, positive, humourous, and honest about what life had to offer.

Peter Gabriel was given free run of the home each evening as a reward for staying penned in during our long days at school, work, and hospital. He was becoming incredibly bold and cunning, and one night in early October he went missing. We were beside ourselves, tearful with worry and hunted everywhere, to no avail.

While pulling our hair out, we heard a rustling under the kitchen sink. Upon opening the door we found Peter perched on a box of dishwasher soap feasting on branches of stargazer and Casablanca lilies that had been tossed out in the rubbish bin. His face and paws were covered with yellow stains, and he looked very sheepish. Somehow he had opened *and* closed the door, remaining hidden for some time. James and I howled and were both stunned at this rabbit's cleverness. We worried that evening how the plants might affect PG's stomach and went to bed that night more focused on our rabbit's well-being than our own.

*   *   *

The October Columbus Day weekend falls at the finale of Fleet Week in San Francisco. It is a week when a collection of ships sail into the bay, most of them from the US navy and Fisherman's Wharf, and the local streets fill with sailors. The week is capped off with a three-day air show that highlights the supersonic Blue Angels. James was terrified of them as a youngster, and there are many who dislike their death-defying antics over the city. They are, after all, planes of war, and I have always said that if I lived in a war zone, I would not be thrilled to hear them screeching towards me.

Polk Street, which runs parallel to Van Ness (the main north-south street in the city), was the flight path for the planes, and their entrance and grand finale occurred over our home. Sometimes they would fly so low that we could look through the jet windows. Scary now in hindsight.

My mother and sister came to visit that weekend (as it coincided with Canadian Thanksgiving), and it was the first time they had seen James since his diagnosis. It was a poignant reunion, and I especially enjoyed being close to family again. James continued with his socializing and packed a lot of fun with his friends into the three-day school vacation.

On the Sunday, I hosted an afternoon tea at home to reconnect with many of the families and friends whom we had not seen for ages. My mother especially enjoyed seeing faces from past visits. Sadly, James became terribly overwhelmed during the day with all the extra people in the house, and he took me aside to reprimand me for not telling him.

What I thought would be fun for him turned into a difficult and extremely emotional afternoon. This would be the last time many of them would see James, and as hard as it was for him, I am still grateful to have invited them. We never know when our last visits with anyone will occur, a truth learned during this awful ordeal. The screaming jets, while appealing to the guests who had assembled, only amplified how rattled James was.

James and Justin on the roof October 2008

That evening he went to a movie at a local cinema on Chestnut Street with his friends, and when I picked him up at 11:00 p.m. he looked defeated, crouching on the ground next to the cinema. I vowed that night never to put *anyone* in his path that he did not want. From that day forth, I too retreated from the world of socializing.

*   *   *

The current round of radiation made James very nauseated and extremely tired. He experienced increased pain due to swelling of the lesions brought on by the radiation, so the doctors decided to increase the doses of the pain medication and added prednisone to the mix, just to get him through this rough patch. He was stubborn and courageous and continued to go to school each day while the caregivers played a game of cat and mouse.

He thrived being with his peers, and nothing was going to keep him from attending school each day. James's energy kept me going. It kept all of us going.

Chapter 8

Obama

I will never give up hoping. It is all that I have.

—James November 2008

My hopes are not always realized but I always hope.

—Ovid

Make-a-Wish had pulled out all the stops to try to bring James's wish to fruition. Meeting Barack Obama on election night had proved to be a challenge, but this single wish had energized the nationwide organization. The school quarter was drawing to its October close, and James was fully focused on completing any outstanding projects.

His teachers were in awe of his calm resolve. The college list was complete, and he worked diligently on completing the final applications. Sadly, James's pain threshold kept diminishing, and it was decided that an additional treatment would be added to the routine.

Zometra is an IV therapy that targets bone pain. Anyone who has suffered with bone cancer understands how acute this discomfort can be; it cuts deep into one's core and is extremely difficult to treat. An EKG was followed up by the first Zometra treatment, and if the side effects were kept in check, it might just provide more uninterrupted time for the quality of life we so desperately wanted for him.

The evenings at home were simple and quiet with Peter Gabriel, our goofy "lapdog" rabbit happily following us around the flat. James confessed that this silly white bunny was the best thing to come into his life and he "was overwhelmed with love for him." Secretly, I tried to conjure up every bit of magic surrounding that four-legged creature in hopes that some miracle might bring James back from this horrible place.

Magic did indeed come our way as James's Make-a-Wish unfolded. On October 30 I received a call from Patricia Wilson, the Executive Director of the Bay Area MAW Foundation, stating that they had achieved success and James would be able to attend election night in Chicago on November 4. With the help of Speaker of the House Nancy Pelosi and countless others in the Democratic Party, James would be flown to Chicago, given accommodation with the press and campaign staff at the Hyatt and VIP seating in the honorary tent at Grant Park with the opportunity to stand near the stage for the final election results.

I was able to share all this with James when he came home from school, and needless to say, he was completely overwhelmed. We sat for ages discussing the plan, but even though he was deeply touched by the offer, he was uncertain since they could not guarantee that he'd *meet* Obama. James was very aware that we would be one of millions at Grant Park, and he did not want to spend his "one wish" on being part of a massive crowd. It broke my heart as I knew only too well that James had grappled with the fact that he qualified for this wish because of his terminal illness and he did not want to squander it. More than ever, he deserved a lifetime of wishes.

We kicked around the idea all evening long, and MAW gave us until noon the next day to give them his final word. They were so understanding and patient and knew only too well the turmoil many young people have concerning these wishes. Apparently it is quite common for them to wait for the green light to proceed, which made me feel better.

Until the wish child gets into the car on the way to the airport, he or she has the opportunity to back out of the plan, which only illustrates how remarkable this organization is to keep all options open until the last moment.

James went to bed, still uncertain, and I told him to sleep on it and let the morning shed new light on his dilemma. When he awoke, he was leaning towards the plan but still was not completely sure. He knew that MAW needed an answer by noon, and I drove him to school with the suggestion that he talk to some of his teachers about his quandary. They were his mentors, and I was convinced they could help him reach a comfortable decision.

There was a large costume Halloween party at the Village Well for our families, and I was so distracted during the day that I did not put any energy into the wish until my mobile phone rang at eleven thirty. It was James. He had decided to move forward with the Chicago plan after talking with his teachers, who all said it would be the chance of a lifetime and James would be witnessing history, important history for America if Obama were elected president.

Immediately I called Patricia, and loud squeals erupted from the support staff in her office. She would move forward quickly, and we should wait for the next message as to how this would all unfold. When I collected James from school, he was energized and there was great excitement from his friends, who all agreed he had made the right decision. A number of the boys were going to get together to go out for the Halloween night prowl, and James's plan was to rest for an hour or two and then be ready to join them. His energy was positive and upbeat.

The recent increase in pain meds had eased much of his discomfort, and once again the future looked bright. Ongoing pain was terribly debilitating but when it was in check, the increase in James's energy was miraculous.

We were home by 4:00 p.m., with the kettle boiling when the phone rang. It was Patricia, telling me to sit down. They had just received a call from the Obama team saying that Barack would like to meet James the next day in Henderson, Nevada. Obama had heard of the wish, and knowing that the election night would be an unknown, he wanted to meet James beforehand. It was a shock for all of us. A car would be sent to collect us in ninety minutes for a flight to Nevada. We'd stay overnight at a local hotel and attend the rally the next day. Obama would meet with us after the rally, and then we'd fly home Saturday night. The bonus was that James *still* had his trip to Chicago for Election Night to look forward to. It was an astonishing opportunity, which left us both speechless.

Suitcases were yanked out of the cupboard and a few clothes tossed in. Computers and chargers, phones, toothbrushes, and clean underwear made up the bulk of the items. I have never packed so quickly. We were both on an adrenaline high. James made a few hasty calls to friends saying he'd not be joining them for the Halloween festivities (which interestingly made him sad), and by five thirty we were at the front door, ready for this amazing adventure to unfold. The limo arrived promptly and drove us to SFO to catch the short flight to Nevada. Every step was a breeze and not until we were settled into the evening desert heat of the Green Valley Resort in Henderson did the reality sink in.

James was so excited, and we were both deeply moved by this senator candidate who was willing to take time, three days before the election, to meet him personally. "What a difference a day makes," James said numerous times during the evening. He was stunned that his decision to move forward with the Make-a-Wish plan in the morning had triggered this remarkable domino effect.

We slept soundly but needed to be awake early for a simple breakfast before another car collected us at six forty-five from the hotel. We were driven to Coronado High School, where the Obama staff greeted us and took us under their wings. With press passes pinned to our shirts, we had acquired free roaming privileges, but we opted to file onto the stands behind the podium as a way to take in the spectacle. The crowd kept multiplying in front of our eyes. James recalled the night when we had to wait four hours for all the attendees to file into the Bill Graham Auditorium in San Francisco.

This Nevada crowd was electric, whooping and hollering and chanting, "Yes, we can!" and their spontaneous joyful roar was infectious. The dry Nevada heat soon descended, and even though it was the beginning of November, by 10:00 a.m. it felt like a summer's afternoon. Signs and flags were handed out to the crowd by the campaign staff to ensure a sea of "Change" would be visible once the cameras started rolling. Controlling the masses and orchestrating the look seemed effortless, but I later thought there would be many staff with ulcers after this intense campaign.

Loud police helicopters overhead signalled the arrival of Barack Obama, and within minutes, Senator Harry Reid was warming up the crowd and introducing "the next president of the United States."

With his slow and easy stride Barack Obama walked down the raised platform to the podium. Much to James's embarrassment, I was crying. Even though as a Canadian I could not vote, I was still deeply moved by the thought that here was the first African American presidential candidate who represented such sweeping change. I had grown up in the days of Martin Luther King, and at this moment, it felt that his "dream" truly was close to being realized.

The promise of a new future through these shifting tides was powerful and had given James faith that a healthy, pain-free adulthood was indeed possible. Obama's well-rehearsed stump speech was familiar yet still sounded fresh and vibrant. He managed to energize the crowd to "Vote, vote, vote!" on November 4 and make their voices heard.

After the event, a number of videos appeared on YouTube, and as fate would have it, James is clearly seen behind the podium in some of them. A wonderful keepsake of this magical day, it is still available on Youtube: Henderson, Nevada, November 1, 2008—3 days out. James can be seen at Obama's left elbow/shoulder while looking at the screen.

Following his speech Senator Obama worked the rope lines while James and I were whisked away by the campaign staff to a portable classroom on the school ground. The senator's personal assistant, Reggie, was the only person in the room at that time. He was busily setting out a number of books, shirts, and other pieces of memorabilia that folks in the crowd had asked to be autographed. Apparently at each stop, the campaign staff would gather up these items and have them signed by the candidate so that they could be returned at the end of the event. It was well orchestrated, and I was impressed at how efficient and thoughtful this team was with their genuine interest to accommodate all.

James and I sat quietly on two folding chairs, feeling quite nervous. There was a rock star quality to Obama, and James was especially anxious. After the meeting we would wonder why we felt so jittery, but our excitement was palpable.

A few minutes later the door opened, and we heard the now well-known mellow voice ask, "Now then, where is James?" Leaving his security detail outside, Barack Obama strode in without escort, fanfare, or press. The only staff present was his photographer, who fortunately took some wonderful pictures of the meeting, which he e-mailed to me immediately afterwards.

Obama grabbed a chair and walked over to sit with us. Handshakes and a hug were exchanged, and then James and Barack sat face-to-face, man to man for what was to become a long and very personal conversation. James felt as though he were the only person in the room. They talked about school, colleges, and choices for the future. Obama liked James's idea of colleges in Chicago and encouraged him to "dream big dreams—everything is possible."

I was instantly captivated by Obama's charm, manners, and confidence. Here was a presidential candidate, three days before the most important day of his life, all mellow, tranquil, and more than happy to chat with James for as long as they wanted. I wondered how many other politicians would be so accommodating and willing to share this time, without including a press entourage in tow to later advertise the moment. His genuine humility deeply touched me.

James had a few things to be signed, and out came the assortment of Sharpie pens in every colour of the rainbow. I was shocked, and Obama teased that they had to be organized and "ready for anything." Connor, a schoolmate, had taken some photos of Obama at the Bill Graham event many months before and had Photoshopped the Stars and Stripes along with the word HOPE into the pictures. Obama autographed two of these photos, one with the word HOPE, the other with the message "Dream big dreams."

James treasured these pictures immensely, and they were framed and hung on the wall as soon as we got back home. We asked the senator when he'd next see his daughters, and he beamed, saying it would be later that afternoon in

Colorado. He was visiting three more stops before the day ended. James was inspired by his stamina, and Obama returned the compliment.

I have met many people in my life, some with great stature and prestige, but there was something about this meeting that will surpass all others. Here was a man who, even in my youth, would *never* have been a possible candidate for president, standing strong and confident yet also deeply gentle and humble, on the cusp of great transformation in America. That he took precious time to share with James and treat him as an equal was a powerful gesture and would become the inspiration and highlight of James's final months.

James and candidate Barack Obama

Obama was genuinely excited that we'd be in Chicago for election night and wanted us to be sure to visit the University of Chicago as well as Loyola when in town as he thought they'd be great college options. When James told him of his love of history and politics, a visit to the White House was suggested as well as the Inauguration in January as, Obama put it, "if all goes to plan!"

We were escorted from the room elated, and James was exhilarated that he had been privy to this experience. I still hope that Barack Obama knows what a remarkable gift he gave to James. His team walked us back to the car, and we were driven to the hotel for some lunch and time by the pool to absorb what had transpired. We welcomed having the time to digest the excitement of the morning before our flight left that evening. We stretched out on king-size beds in huge cabanas by the pool to watch the surreal scene around us. *Lost wages* was our code word for Las Vegas, and the crowd at this resort did not disappoint; numerous bleached blondes in spandex leggings and tight tank tops floated about the pool patio on the arms of aging sunburned men. Mauve desert mountains on the horizon, dry heat, and this cabana scene added to the unreality of the past twenty-four hours.

VOTE! was the message we relayed on CaringBridge that night.

I e-mailed the photos of James with Obama to the folks at MAW, and unbeknownst to me, they, in turn, sent them along to the *San Francisco Chronicle* newspaper. They appeared in the Sunday edition with a lovely article about James's meeting and wish. Suddenly, there was press interest in his story that was about to go viral.

We arrived home that evening and had twenty-four hours to repack, sort out a home for Peter Gabriel for the next few days, and prepare for the next flight to Chicago. Thankfully the pain meds had everything in check, so James was comfortable and full of energy. The team from MAW arrived on Sunday afternoon with balloons, a bag of goodies, tickets, et al., for the flight the next morning. They had even laminated an Obama *Hope* poster by artist Shepard Fairey, which James immediately hung in his room. We both had our Make-a-Wish pins to wear, which the team assured would open doors for us.

I cannot say enough wonderful things about the UCSF social workers and the MAW Foundation. Together they worked tirelessly to create magic, all the while making it appear so effortless. I know there were countless people in the wings pulling it all together. The "Wish" team were giddy with the prospect of us being in Chicago and were stunned by Obama's willingness to join in the fun at the eleventh hour. James's request had taken on a life of its own, and everyone felt good about it. Enthusiasm was growing throughout the broader community; and the number of CaringBridge followers, many of whom we had never met, had grown greatly. Somehow, we had all been swept up in the tide of wishes, and what would one choose if given this opportunity? It captured everyone's imagination. I still find myself asking, "What would my one wish be?"

On Monday, November 3, yet another limo picked us up from home (James was starting to like this mode of transportation) for the flight to Chicago. The Make-a-Wish pins *did* work magic, and we were greeted and ushered through the various airport lines with incredible ease. Even though needing the cane, James refused to use a wheelchair, and he walked the long distances to the gates in both San Francisco and Chicago.

Upon our arrival in the Windy City we received news of the death of Obama's grandmother, which made us both very sad. Obama had spoken of his love for her when we met on Saturday and how important she had been in his life. It felt such a cruel twist of fate that she would die on the eve of one of the most important days of his life. It must have made the election day very bittersweet for him. Not long after this, I would wonder that perhaps the only way she could share the day with her beloved Barack was to be there in spirit.

We settled into our room on the twentieth floor of the Hyatt with the lights of the *Chicago Tribune* building glowing below. It was one of those glorious balmy Indian summer nights, and since this was our first visit to Chicago, we headed out for a stroll of the neighbourhood and a bite of dinner. Interestingly, the streets were very quiet, but we realized the next morning that already many roads had been closed and traffic diverted to help control the millions of spectators expected to pour into the city for election night. As we chatted to folks in the hotel lobby and restaurant, we perceived a cautious optimism and the sense of being on tender hooks.

Whatever the outcome, it was still an incredibly historic day for the country to have its first African American candidate for president. James and I both clung to the thought that maybe miracles *were* possible after all. "James is humbled, excited, and ready to sleep" was my final entry on CaringBridge that night.

Election Day, November 4, 2008

The press had found James, and I was getting calls from MAW to see if he would be willing to do interviews with CBS and ABC. CBS wanted him to fly to New York after the election. I had to monitor these offers and run them by James as he had to base all his decisions on his energy level, but for now we were focused only on November 4. After fifteen hours of sleep, James awoke energized and ready for some breakfast in the lobby.

The buzz was electric; the polls were open and the day was racing to its conclusion. We had been instructed to check in with the campaign staff before 3:00 p.m., so we made that our first stop before heading out for a walk. A huge press room with banks of television screens, tables crowded with computers, and acres of cords snaking everywhere was assembled in a lower-floor ballroom of the Hyatt. We checked in, and our passes, neon-green wristbands for Grant Park, and information packet were ready.

The autumn morning was glorious, and we shared a wonderfully leisurely walk through the city to Grant Park. The pepperberry trees were dense and the fall colours outstanding. One of James's good friends Andrew had loaned him his digital camera to use on this trip, and I was able to capture some wonderful pictures of James and the scenery. We had put on our to-do list that day to buy a camera of our own, but Andrew's filled in the blanks until we found a shop that was open. Interestingly, many stores were closing early to allow folks to attend the rally or just stay home and avoid the crowds. I had not grasped just how huge this event was going to be.

Chicago, Election Day November 2008

We sat resting at a park table overlooking Lake Michigan and pulled out the cards to play a few hands of rummy. We both agreed this was the best day in ages. James looked radiant and so well, but now as I revisit these photos, I see the dark circles under his eyes and his thinning face. The drone of massive television screens set up around the park reminded James of a horse race, and we supposed, in many respects, that this day really was one. Stopping at the famous reflective bean sculpture to capture more great shots and other sights along the way filled the hours, and we even managed to find a digital camera literally five minutes before the store closed en route back to the hotel for a rest.

While I was busy updating CaringBridge later that afternoon, James received a call on his mobile from a number he did not recognize. Hesitantly answering the call, he immediately sat upright on his bed, becoming *über*-polite. He mouthed, "Nancy Pelosi," while pointing to the mouthpiece. Speaker Pelosi hails from San Francisco and had worked with MAW to help bring this dream to life. As fate would have it, her children had attended the Sacred Heart School on Broadway, and James's secondary school was one of their network schools as well. She and James chatted for quite a while, and she was so excited that he was going to be at Grant Park that night and wanted to know if everything was going well, and did he need anything?

The good, generous souls who had embraced this wish and worked to make it happen were obviously plentiful, and we were both tearful after the call, trying to grasp how amazing the whole experience was. James was unsure how to thank them all, and I reassured him that their thanks came in knowing it was going to be a great night and that bringing him joy would be a gift to them. James took time to call some of his friends back in San Francisco. Many had voted for the first time that day. He was secretly envious but vowed that next year he'd join them. They were all floored by this adventure, and it was great to see James once again giggly with excitement. Following a quick dinner and lots of water to hydrate, James decided he wanted to get to the park as things were unfolding quickly on CNN.

Once outside the west wing (how apropos!) of the hotel, we joined a sea of humanity gathering to board one of a long line of trolleys that would take us to Grant Park. We recognized many familiar faces from the press as they joined us on board, and I recall feeling like the out-of-town cousins at a big family wedding; everybody seemed to know one another. The campaign staff looked haggard and nervous even while slapping backs and exchanging robust kisses. Some folks, probably the big donors, were layered up in their casual outdoor Ralph Lauren jackets and boots.

James became lightheaded from the expensive perfume wafting through the air. The assembled must have wondered who James and I were, but I suppose the Make-a-Wish pins told our story adequately.

The ride to the park went quickly as all the roads were now shut to traffic and huge barricades kept pedestrians away as well. A police escort accompanied each trolley to the north side of the park, where we were deposited to join a long security queue. All electronics and phones had to be left on, bags opened, pins taken off. I thought it odd that phones could be left on; we did not have to remove our shoes. The lines moved surprisingly quickly, and we soon found ourselves on prefab wooden sidewalks that led to various VIP tents. Our green wristbands gave us entrance to the National Financial Committee tent, which was electric with excitement by the time we reached it. Chairs and tables laden with plentiful food and drinks were set out, but we were totally focused on the jumbo televisions positioned in each of the four corners of the tent.

When the news broke that Obama had won Ohio, the screams were deafening and I called a few friends back home to let them hear the excitement live. James sat down to rest for a few minutes, and I told him to wait there while I got the lay of the land outside the tent.

Within a few feet of our tent were other tented enclosures each designated for "Biden Guests," "Obama Guests," "Political Guests" as well as a mammoth tent covering the elevated bleachers for the press. Cords dangled, small satellites poised skyward, loud speakers and television screens echoed results from various states. CNN's Candy Crowley, perched on the edge of an elevated platform with her shoes off, looked very serious. All the press appeared exhausted.

I have been a big proponent of paying attention and allowing kismet to play its role in life. One of the biggest kismet moments was about to unfold. I turned around, and out of the millions of people assembled, there stood the young man who had been our campaign escort in Nevada just a few days earlier. Sadly, I cannot recall his name, but he was incredibly charming and kind. We were both shocked to see one another again, and after exchanging a few pleasantries, I asked if there might be any way that James could *sit* in the outside area of the park since standing would be difficult as the hours wore on.

He told me to go back to the tent and wait for him there; he'd meet us in a few minutes. I half-expected that would be the last time I would see him, but true to his word, within five minutes, he popped his head through the tent's door, told James to grab his chair, and follow him.

He escorted us to the fenced-off VIP area on the left side of the stage, where only eight people stood. This thoughtful Obama staffer whispered something in the ear of the Secret Service agent in charge who opened the chain-link fence gate and directed us in on condition that we couldn't exit again until the end of the night. It was an amazing location; James was ten feet from the stage. The view was perfect, and there were no crowds as yet pushing into us. James was able to sit on his chair and read his Charles Bukowski novel uninterrupted. On an enormous screen above our heads, CNN blasted out all the results from the various states. We had no idea how long all this would take, and James's novel helped to steady his nerves.

Four others standing in the area had won an essay contest, "What the Election Means to Me" while the other four in this area were Obama family friends. It was incredibly intimate and blissfully uncrowded. The other side of the fence was packed with countless supporters and celebrities such as Oprah Winfrey, Spike Lee, and the Reverend Jesse Jackson. After the election there would be many photos taken of those gathered in the VIP area, and I am sure they wondered how we managed to be in such a comfy situation.

Jumbotron at Grant Park calls the election for Obama

The tension was building, and suddenly, a thunderous roar erupted; CNN had called the election for Barack Obama. I will never forget the sound of that night. Everyone was crying and screaming. James and I hugged and also cried. Almost immediately, what had been an empty space filled up with Obama and Biden family and friends. It became just as packed as the outer spaces were. Fortunately, James had saved his place up by the fence, and surrounded by Joe Biden's brother, sister, and son, he had a perfect view of the proceedings. There was a lot of pushing and jostling, and we had to hold our own, but with extraordinary resolve, James stood firm and strong.

To be so close to the stage when the Obama family came out was truly amazing. Their joy looked genuine and sincere. The speeches were moving, but I must confess it would be only in film clips, after the fact, that James and I would hear what was spoken; we were swept up in the emotional tide that surrounded us. James started shouting, "Yes, we did!" and soon a chorus rose around us until everyone was repeating it. We waved our flags and smiled. Again, in press photos and film clips after the event, there would prove to be some wonderful pictures of a beaming James, especially poignant shots for all those who loved him. Back in San Francisco, MAW were beside themselves with joy, and they called to check in, but it was impossible to hear one another.

Grant Park Election Night 2008

I had a deep sense that this was a particularly special moment in time as the bigger picture suddenly crashed in around me. Would James be here for the next election? Would he be able to vote as he so desired? What would Obama's four-year term look like? Did he know how much this meant to James? I saw this young president who suddenly had the responsibility of the world placed upon his shoulders. "See the power in hope." James and I had to cling to that message; it was a positive directive that so many were desperate to believe in.

This really was a defining moment in history, not only for America but also the world, and being on the cusp of great change gave James a renewed sense of belief in miracles and the future. He kept repeating, "Everything is possible." The powerful subtext was "This cancer can be beaten," and he was determined to make that his outcome.

My tears flowed from joy but also from sadness. Only in the coming years would I understand how naïve we all were. The drums of bitter noise and discord would escalate, and Obama would be thrown many curveballs. He and James would be tested beyond all measure, but for this one electric and positive night, all was right with the world.

When all the speeches were over and the Obamas had left the stage, we embarked on the task of exiting Grant Park. This is when the only glitch of the night occurred. We boarded our trolley, travelled a hundred yards, and then came to a grinding halt.

There we sat for almost two hours while police helicopters circled overhead with their search lights focused on the ground below. We were given no explanation, and we started to fade. The man next to me looked so familiar, and I am sure he wondered who this woman was who kept staring at him. I guess I was not very subtle. The next day I would see him do the first interview with president-elect Obama: it was Steve Krofft of CBS's *60 Minutes*.

Finally a passing transit policeman informed us that the Secret Service were escorting Obama and Biden out of the area and everything had to be halted and secured until they were well away from the park. James now became aware of what their lives would be like with constant protocol, security, and schedules. He decided it would not be easy giving up the freedom of anonymity.

In the wee small hours of the morning we finally arrived back at the Hyatt, which was crawling with people. A loud and elated sea of humanity filled the sidewalk. The lobby bars were packed, and parties were about to erupt. I could only imagine all the sore heads the following morning. James showered, took his evening meds, and curled into his bed to watch some of the late shows on television. He kept saying, "He did it, Mom!" as if only constant repetition would reinforce the truth. We both fell asleep to the sound of the television reporting the news.

The next morning we rushed out to get some newspapers to keep as mementoes, but every newsagent was already sold out. I hoofed it over to the *Tribune* office to hunt one down, to no avail. Apparently the daily papers were scarce in all cities that following day. Kind friends in San Francisco saved the *Chronicle*, so we did have that to keep.

After a much-needed hearty breakfast we headed over to Loyola University on Lake Michigan for James to explore. I stayed a few paces behind, giving him his freedom and ability to blend in with the students. There was such excitement on the campus that day, and James was light and breezy. He sat for a long time on the water's edge reading his book, and I wandered into the small university chapel. It was incredibly quiet, and being alone in solitude moved me to tears. I was overcome with a sense of peace and joy that I did not think possible. Since James's diagnosis I had not found a moment of *deep* peace, yet this tiny chapel in Chicago provided that for me, and even though it is difficult to ever think of going to Chicago again, I would not mind visiting that chapel by the water one more time.

MAW called with some possible TV interviews if James felt up to it, and I ran the idea by him. He was a bit unsure about all the fuss and not confident that he wanted to do them, so it was left that he'd make his decision once back in San Francisco. James never craved the limelight, and even though a big-spirited leader, he was still an introvert.

We walked for miles, and James's leg must have been in agony, but he was not going to give up. He stopped at Urban Outfitters and bought a grey wool pea jacket and plaid shirt that would become his favourite during the coming months. He felt preppy and smart, and I was thrilled to see him growing in stature.

I wrote that night on CaringBridge that James was "full of hope and promise." Make-a-Wish had given both of us the most amazing memories and a gift of time.

Returning home was easy, and we both marvelled at how perfect the weather had been for election night as the following morning erupted in torrential rainstorms. The past six days had given James a renewed confidence, and he could not wait to share his exploits with his friends and teachers. He felt energized and ready to tackle whatever came his way. He was also excited now by the prospect of applying to colleges in Chicago as he had discovered a new beauty in the autumn colours, something we did not have much exposure to in San Francisco.

Thank you for sharing this journey and sending your wishes of goodwill. James is touched by the number of strangers who have embraced this adventure. We are all threads woven on a great loom and the wonderful canvas keeps evolving moment by moment. (CaringBridge, November 6, 2008)

*   *   *

During the editing of this book I received a wonderful e-mail from Tony (who is now head of Stuart Hall High School). Apparently a board member from Make-a-Wish had recently shared a "James" story with him that he, in turn, wanted to share with me.

James's Obama wish ended up energizing the entire countrywide MAW organization, which is very rare. It became a rallying point for all with the collective shout to the various chapters asking for help to make the necessary connections. Apparently they received an incredible response. Piecing together all the logistics was a huge undertaking, but Obama was very excited to meet James and there was a full court press with everyone involved to make it all come to fruition.

With three or four campaign stops per day in those final hours, by the time Obama reached Henderson, Nevada, he was exhausted. However, when he met with us and heard James say, "You give me hope," Obama told his staff he felt renewed energy to power through the next few days and ultimately on to victory.

Tony added, "James, dear James giving strength to others, up to and including our current president of the United States."

We never know when and how we will touch the lives of others.

Chapter 9

Grassroots

"Did we really just do that?"
—*James and Jean, upon leaving Grassroots for the first time*

November began with great enthusiasm, and James continued to exclaim spontaneously, "Mom, he did it!" We rode the wave while watching all the daily news surrounding Obama's transition to the White House. James decided against the television interviews for the New York stations as he would need to be up for 3:00 a.m. filming, and he did not feel strong enough. I followed his lead entirely on this.

He confessed to experiencing wild dreams at night and would awaken full of vivid images. One of my regrets is not taking time to write them down before heading out to school as they might have provided some insight as to what he was feeling and processing. He was busy applying to colleges and relived the magic of his wish every day, feeling so close to and engaged with politics and history. We both wholeheartedly accepted the wisdom in planting a seed and letting the universe conspire to make things happen.

Peter Gabriel returned home from his days away, full of tales from his adventures with the Goldsmith family who had a pet tortoise. Rest assured there were never-ending references to the Aesop fable. James was convinced the Obamas should get a rabbit for their pet, but I reminded him that the White House furniture would be a tad more valuable than ours and they would probably not want rabbit pens set up all around the place.

School was going well, and James's energy seemed good, but the pain meds needed frequent adjusting, and I was concerned that his discomfort was becoming more of an issue. Nausea had started to trouble him on some mornings, and it was tough to watch him suffer when we had nothing new to offer him. Some days we'd have to stop while driving to school for him to open the door and vomit in the gutter. How he continued on for the rest of the day, I will never know.

At one of our weekly clinic meetings I asked Dr. DuBois if James would qualify for medical marijuana since I had heard about its ability to ease pain and help with nausea. "Absolutely!" was his response, and he immediately wrote up the referral for James to get a medical marijuana identification card. James was delighted with the prospect, and he confessed, as we drove away from UCSF, that he had already tried pot to see if it would control his nausea, and it *had* worked. Within a day, we were up at San Francisco General Hospital applying for and receiving, on the spot, our cards. I was given one as well to allow me access to a pot club if needed.

Getting our medical marijuana cards at SF General hospital

The woman who helped us was an amazing character who shared more of her life story than we were ready for, but her genuine concern for James's well-being was heartwarming. She was a recovering crack addict who had found the power of healing through her work and faith. She was inspiring, and in the coming months, James often mentioned her reinforcing, once again, that these fleeting moments are often enough to touch one another. She suggested a number of medical marijuana clubs in decent neighbourhoods, and since Grassroots was close to our home, we decided to make that our first stop.

I need to explain what a *huge* turnabout this was for me. For years I had been the zero-tolerance, antidrug queen. James knew that I would not allow marijuana, and there was no wriggle room. Marijuana had a disgusting smell, and even though I had never tried it, I could see no merit in it. So for me not only to suggest this option but *also* to escort James to get his card and then to the shop to buy the stuff was a pretty big deal for him. He was in shock, and in an odd way, I think it brought us even closer since he knew I was going against my principles to bring him comfort. Afterwards, I wondered why I was so draconian, and now I am quite happy to lend my voice for the legalization of medical marijuana as I have seen first-hand its incredible power.

The Grassroots club was on Sutter and Polk, near a local fire station. It was not a great neighbourhood but certainly better than deep in the Tenderloin, and I felt quite safe parking on the street. It was next door to the Diva Club, where female impersonators performed, and in true San Francisco fashion, we'd often bump in to "Barbara Streisand" and "Cher" having a cigarette on the street, which always gave us a laugh.

Having never entered a pot club, I had no idea what to expect but was immediately struck by how organized and professional it was. The bouncer at the door checked our photo ID cards and unlocked the gate to let us in. Tall stools were lined up along a Victorian wooden bar—such as one would see in a saloon—and scales and illuminated magnifying glasses dotted its countertop. The mirrored shelves behind held large carefully labelled apothecary jars filled with marijuana while baked goods and liquid concoctions were kept in a fridge at the end of the bar. In hindsight, we must have been quite the spectacle: a teenager with his basket-toting mother in her paisley skirt, who was keen to learn all about the process. With no need to be covert, everyone was totally up front about it all, and I think they actually enjoyed our visits.

I willingly confessed having no experience or knowledge, and the staff were most happy to educate. Sativa and Indica are the two main types of marijuana, and each one has various plants and blends under their respective headings. I was shocked at the variety and how knowledgeable each of the staff were concerning pain management. A delightful Irishman helped us, and we spent over an hour going through the various blends and how they could help James. He wanted a full rundown on the location of the lesions and what sort of drugs James was taking. In addition to providing strains that would manage pain, the staff would be able to find those that would help balance the side effects of the meds (something I was about to discover in the coming months); it felt as though we were in the hands of ancient healers.

We were shown the buds under the magnifying lights to see what Tetrahydrocannabinol (THC) looks like and how to choose plants wisely. Some cannabis is good to wake you up while others put you to sleep. Some strains help with appetite, others pain control. It was overwhelming, and I tried to write down as much information as I could to help with future visits, but it transpired that the staff would be very helpful, walking me through the process at each visit.

James's needs would also change, and the staff stayed right up to speed with us. All purchases had to be paid for with cash only, and they always threw in some extra treats for James such as lozenges, lollipops, or baking. It was not cheap, with each visit running at least $60 to $100 for a few buds, priced according to weight (hence the scales), but it was worth every penny. They suggested that we get a vaporizer to avoid smoke inhalation that could irritate the tumours in James's lungs. Fortunately, there was a smoke shop around the corner, and after we picked up our generic paper bag of pot, we headed over to Smoke Signals for the next step.

This shop was full of hookahs and every variety of pipe imaginable. I would soon learn that most of the accessories were for smoking pot. We had a knowledgeable Middle Eastern man at the counter who walked us through the process, and eventually we decided upon a more-expensive vaporizer that had a good reputation.

James picked up a pocket grinder (used to break down some of the buds) and a dark blue San Francisco ashtray. It was a methodical and thoughtful afternoon, and I left the store feeling jovial and silly for being so negative in the past. James was upbeat and excited to try out the new "toy," and we laughed heartily at how strange this must look to the world; certainly his friends would find it bizarre. "What have I done?" soon evaporated into "Get over it, Jean!"

The vaporizer took a little experimenting to get used to, and I went back to the shop the following day to get another tutorial. It ended up working like a charm, and the results were immediate. Water in the main bowl helped turn the smoke into steam, which was easier to inhale down a long clear heavy plastic tube. In addition to becoming very mellow and calm after using the vaporizer, James would gain a robust appetite.

The early days were quite experimental, and he tried the different blends to see what effect they had on his pain. I did need to get used to the smell, but over time, it did not bother me. I actually have moments now when I miss it.

Its scent represented a lifeline to my son, and I would give everything to have that tangible back. At times, when I walk down the street, I'll get a faint whiff of marijuana, and I feel James next to me, sharing a laugh.

The only rule I implemented was that James only buy his marijuana at the club and not from someone on the street. Buying from strangers was risky, and since he had a local place, where his mother would even take him, he had no need to purchase it elsewhere. The pot from the club was actually more potent as it was pure, fresh, and not mixed with anything. He agreed.

Knowing that James had permission and freedom to use, I felt it only fair to let the parents of his friends know that there would be marijuana in our home. I did not want to be secretive about any of this. Grateful to be told, all of the parents responded favourably. Interestingly, by being open and honest, the thrill of being covert was lost, and the boys never behaved badly or took advantage. James carefully organized the various marijuana blends in a collection of labelled glass jars, which he kept, along with his other pot accessories, in a designated drawer in his room. I understand now how empowering it was for him to control some aspects of living with disease. Taking charge of his personal space was one way to accomplish this.

The days unfolded with more kismet, and early November was proving to be a good month. One day a padded envelope sent by a Mr. Yorke arrived in the mail from the United Kingdom. I had no idea who he might be, so being a bit suspicious, I stayed close by while James opened it. Enclosed was a handwritten note to James from Thom Yorke, the lead singer of Radiohead. Thom had heard about James's story and did not know what to say, so he burned two CDs of his own favourite music for him.

James was speechless. Meeting Radiohead had been one of the possible wishes James was considering. The gift was so unexpected. We did not know who was responsible for making it happen, but a thank-you went up on CaringBridge that night. James set up a second shrine in the house. One was for Obama, and now Thom Yorke also had a place of honour.

Within twenty-four hours we found out who was responsible for making the Thom Yorke connection. I wrote on the blog, "What do vintage Dior, Madonna, and Radiohead have in common? A very convoluted tale that leads back to James." Doris, our LA friend, owns a wonderful vintage clothing store frequented by many of the Hollywood elite and their stylists. She was at her store when she received my e-mail informing friends of James's cancer, becoming terribly distraught at the news. The stylist for the singer Madonna, was with Doris at the time and took great interest in James from that day on, following his story on CaringBridge. Long story short, she somehow tracked down Radiohead and Thom *et voilà*, this connection had brought about the very special packet for James. Serendipity had once again come to visit. James decided to burn a CD to send back to Thom as a thank-you, which he worked on over the coming months. I would send it in August 2009.

I wrote on November 10 of being in "awe of James's resolve to do it all" and loved to hear his musings. He now wanted to spend some time in Paris after graduation, living as a Hemingway expat. He planned to "take in the sights, smells, and sounds of that city while writing his first novel."

The days were busy with school and college applications. My days at the Well were full, and we'd both happily retreat and hibernate at night. Socializing for James was becoming more about being with his closest friends and less with the larger world. My energy was slipping and I did not have time for a lot of chatter. Being still and alone was becoming more important for me than in the past, and I found myself clinging to the need to rejuvenate whenever possible.

The doctors were pleased with how stable things looked for James, and it was decided that he could resume the Sunitinib, which had been put on hold for his radiation treatments, the trip to Chicago, and Thanksgiving. If he could tolerate the drug, it would be increased in strength, and the next series of scans and MRIs were scheduled for December. It was a little reprieve, and we called it our golden time.

James was feisty and in good spirits. Work was going well, and I mustered up energy to juggle all the moving parts. My brother Paul was due to arrive for a weekend visit, and there was a party planned on November 22 for James's graduating class at the Flood Mansion on Broadway.

Paul arrived on Friday evening and was happy to escape the two feet of snow that had already fallen in his home town of Owen Sound in Northern Ontario. James was happy to see his uncle again, and everything was unfolding nicely. For months, I kept postponing my annual mammogram, and I needed to follow through with it before the year ended, all for the insurance nonsense that was so pervasive at that time in the United States. Paul and I headed out for the appointment on Saturday morning, leaving James at home to rest and get ready for the party that evening. We'd be gone for about an hour.

Within a block of the breast health centre, my mobile phone rang. It was James. He was coughing up blood.

Breaking all the rules, I made a majorly illegal U-turn in the middle of the road and raced home again. Paul called the clinic to cancel my appointment, and once home, I bounded up the stairs. We found James standing at the door of his room that opened out to the roof, with his hand over his mouth. He had coughed blood over the outside railing and wall of the building next door. There was also a small pool of fresh blood in his hands. He was terrified.

Shaking, I immediately called the on-call doctor and told him we were heading over to the ER at UCSF. Thank God for Paul as he helped clean up James, and we carefully escorted him down the stairs. During the drive across town, James was silent and coughed up a little more blood into a hankie; I was determined that the doctors see what it looked like. It was troubling as the blood was fresh and bright red. Thankfully, we did not wait long to be seen by a doctor, and a chest x-ray was performed along with blood work. As he did now for all hospital visits, James had brought his computer and sat listening to music with his headphones on, anything to be distant and distracted. He was white and very weak.

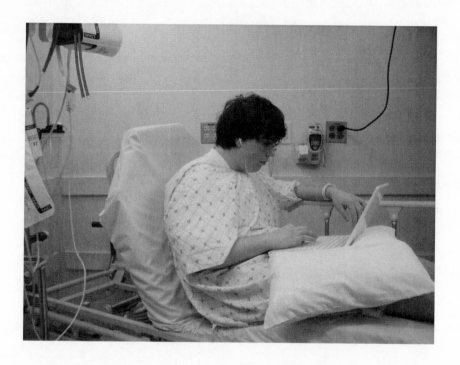

James surviving hospital visits with laptop and headphones

The shock had kicked me in the gut, and I stood in the hallway crying while Paul kept James company. This was all so terribly unfair and wrong.

The ER doctors said it was a tumour in the lung that was the problem and we'd need to see the oncologist on Monday. They monitored James throughout the afternoon, and we waited to see if there would be any more bleeding.

In the early evening it was decided that James could go home, and we stopped at Grassroots to pick up some more supplies. Paul took the car and drove around the block while I took James inside, but when we came out of the shop, there was no sign of Putters.

Unfortunately, Paul had been moved along by the police and ended up lost in the one-way system so pervasive in that part of town. We connected via our mobile phones, trying to figure out where he was and how to direct him back to us. It became a convoluted adventure, which under normal circumstances would have made us chuckle. Sadly, James was in no mood for escapades.

Once home, we collected ourselves, and James miraculously said he would go to the school party. With some marijuana in his system, he was much calmer, and if he felt up to it, Paul and I were willing to take him. It turned out to be a very large gathering with many families we had not seen in years. While it was billed as a party for the graduating class, it really was being hosted to honour James, though he was never told this in advance as he would have been mortified and embarrassed by the attention. There were friends from his early childhood and elementary school days. Had I not been in shock, the evening might have been less surreal. We had just spent the afternoon with James coughing up blood from his fragile lungs, and then here we were at a party full of giddy reunions. It was a remarkable community that supported him totally, and they would grow to be an anchor for both of us in the coming months. Many generous and incredibly kind families sweetly had started a fund to help cover the cost of a chairlift that would help carry James up the long flight of stairs at our entrance.

As the night wore on, James became overwhelmed, and after a couple of hours, he asked to return home and get into his bed. I was amazed at his ability to stay that long. He slept until mid-afternoon the next day and stayed close to home and Peter Gabriel. There was a new melancholy about James, and I worried as to what the Monday meeting would reveal. "Fuck cancer," I wrote in my journal that night.

*　　*　　*

Why did the chicken cross the road? Paul sent the following joke to me after his return to Canada, and it was a perfect tonic for the following week. I include it now as it brought a much-needed laugh to James's days, which sadly were becoming more complicated:

WHY DID THE CHICKEN CROSS THE ROAD?

SARAH PALIN: Before it got to the other side, I shot the chicken, cleaned and dressed it, and had chicken burgers for lunch.

BARACK OBAMA: The chicken crossed the road because it was time for a change! The chicken wanted change!

JOHN McCAIN: My friends, that chicken crossed the road because he recognized the need to engage in cooperation and dialogue with all the chickens on the other side of the road.

HILLARY CLINTON: When I was First Lady, I personally helped that little chicken to cross the road. This experience makes me uniquely qualified to ensure right from Day One that every chicken in this country gets the chance it deserves to cross the road. But then, this really isn't about me.

GEORGE W. BUSH: We don't really care why the chicken crossed the road. We just want to know if the chicken is on our side of the road, or not. The chicken is either against us, or for us. There is no middle ground here.

DICK CHENEY: Where's my gun?

COLIN POWELL: Now to the left of the screen, you can clearly see the satellite image of the chicken crossing the road.

BILL CLINTON: I did not cross the road with that chicken. What is your definition of chicken?

AL GORE: I invented the chicken.

JOHN KERRY: Although I voted to let the chicken cross the road, I am now against it! It was the wrong road to cross, and I was misled about the chicken's intentions. I am not for it now and will remain against it.

AL SHARPTON: Why are all the chickens white? We need some black chickens.

DR. PHIL: The problem we have here is that this chicken doesn't realize that he must first deal with the problem on this side of the road before it goes after the problem on the other side of the road. What we need to do is help him realize how stupid he's acting by not taking on his current problems before adding new problems.

OPRAH: Well, I understand that the chicken is having problems, which is why he wants to cross this road so bad. So instead of having the chicken learn from his mistakes and take falls, which is a part of life, I'm going to give this chicken a car so that he can just drive across the road and not live his life like the rest of the chickens.

ANDERSON COOPER, CNN: We have reason to believe there is a chicken, but we have not yet been allowed access to the other side of the road.

NANCY GRACE: That chicken crossed the road because he's guilty! You can see it in his eyes and the way he walks.

PAT BUCHANAN: To steal the job of a decent, hard-working American.

DR SEUSS: Did the chicken cross the road? Did he cross it with a toad? Yes, the chicken crossed the road, but why it crossed I've not been told.

ERNEST HEMINGWAY: To die in the rain, alone.

GRANDPA: In my day we didn't ask why the chicken crossed the road. Somebody told us the chicken crossed the road, and that was good enough.

ARISTOTLE: It is the nature of chickens to cross the road.

ALBERT EINSTEIN: Did the chicken really cross the road, or did the road move beneath the chicken?

COLONEL SANDERS: Did I miss one?

* * *

Monday's visit to UCSF involved an EKG and further x-rays. The Sunitinib was back on hold. Bleeding or coughing up blood was one of the "rare but serious" side effects of the drug that had been explained when first presented as an option.

On Wednesday, November 26, I updated CaringBridge with an entry, stating, "It was a tough day for James that just seemed to go downhill from the start." The CT scan of his chest had been difficult as it took six attempts for the technicians to find a vein that would work. He now hated getting jabbed, and as I was told later, the bloody disease was causing some of his veins to collapse. It finally worked, and he had a subsequent meeting with the oncologists for the follow-up. Tragically, the chemo drug had not worked at shrinking or eliminating the tumours. Coughing up blood was a dangerous side effect, so it would be suspended immediately.

Yet *another* new lesion in James's lung had caused the Saturday bleed, and so a further round of radiation would be arranged to target it. There was discussion of performing a more complex procedure, which would involve going into the lung through the airways and cauterizing part of the tumour, but radiation would hopefully do the trick without being so invasive. UCSF had access to the CyberKnife, which was state-of-the-art radiology. If the doctors thought that would be helpful, they would use it.

The day went on and on with more bad news piling up on top of the next, becoming incredibly disheartening. James was desperate to leave the hospital, and I wanted to crawl back into a hole and push the restart button. This was all unreal and could not be happening to my sweet son. Disbelief was becoming my daily mind-set. Those golden days of a few weeks past felt like a lifetime ago now.

We got home as soon as possible, and when we pulled in the drive, there were some of the buddies waiting for James. What remarkable young men they were. Knowing when to be there and when to retreat, they had a sixth sense about James and his needs, and I pray that gift of intuition serves them well in their lives.

Later that afternoon I received a call from Dr. Wara. The tumour that needed attention was too close to the heart for the intense power of the CyberKnife, so after blocking out the site on Monday, we would proceed with a ten-day session of radiation on Tuesday.

It was the four-day Thanksgiving holiday, and the time off could not have been more welcome. A new cough medicine had been prescribed to help settle the lung and hopefully give James peaceful nights. Thankfully, it worked, and he managed to get some solid sleep. My personal journal records that I was now deeply moved by how honest James was about his needs. We had always been close, but there was a deepening relationship unfolding that would be one of the greatest legacies of these coming months. I would learn to follow his lead and let go of my need to control outcome. In my own life now, I find myself drawing on his example as I try to walk a path of diminished expectations and honest authenticity.

James November 2008

We attended Thanksgiving dinner with his father's extended family in Marin. James was tired, and we did not stay long. He really had lost energy and patience for large gatherings, and I had grown weary of always needing to be "on." I updated CaringBridge with my gratitude for all those who had touched our lives and to remind that every day should be one of thanksgiving. Staring me in the face was the fragility of moments, combined with a growing sorrow that I had no idea if any of these days would come again.

Our tradition had always been to get our Christmas tree during the Thanksgiving weekend. James and I adored this time of the year, and we'd put the tree up as soon as possible and leave it up for as long as was safe, sometimes into early January. James took such delight in searching for the right tree, and we swore that by choosing them earlier, our trees were always fresher and longer lasting. The tree lot we frequented, just down the hill from us at Filbert and Van Ness, was sponsored by Delancey Street, a local charity that helped homeless men get back on their feet. We would often stroll by in the cool evenings just to smell the evergreen.

We headed down to the lot again this Thanksgiving weekend, but this time trusted friend Marc joined us. He was fit and strong, and I needed him to help me haul the tree up the stairs as James was sadly unable to. The search took less time than in the past, and James was convinced he had found the best tree in the lot. Marc tied it to his large van, and we had it up the stairs in record time. It was indeed the best tree we had ever had, perfect in its size and proportions. It fit the space in the front window with ease, and immediately the flat was filled with its glorious smell. This would be the last tree we would share together.

Multiple Christmas boxes were lugged up from the garage, and in record time, we had the rows of lights and all the old favourite decorations hanging from the branches. I was determined to make the house perfect this year, and we did everything to adorn all the corners. James even had a tiny tree upstairs in his room, something he had especially requested. There was now a small fridge at the end of his bed to keep some of the medicines refrigerated along with Gatorade, yogurt, and some marijuana-packed baking that helped to settle his stomach whenever the drugs made him nauseated. His tree was placed on top of the fridge, and the lights cast a beautiful glow at night. He was happy and content. We were determined that this Christmas would be perfect.

His friends poured in and out of the flat playing music or games on the PlayStation, one of which was a nonsense World War II game that concluded with "Zombie Nazis." The team of boys had managed to scale the difficulty ladder, and James was particularly good at the game. It was gross and violent and scared me to watch, but it served a purpose beyond having fun.

I had recently learned that a teenager, suffering with cancer, had designed a game for cancer patients where they attacked the diseased cells, killing them in the process. Through testing, it was discovered that this game increased the positive endorphins, and doctors actually saw some improvements in their patients' well-being. Having a way to focus frustrations, anger, and vulnerability while empowering the patient served a valuable purpose. The power of the mind over body was an important aspect of attacking these zombies, and I would happily encourage the raucous sessions.

Our visits to Grassroots were becoming a weekly outing, and James was experimenting with a variety of blends. Night-time and early-morning nausea were more frequent, and one particular blend of marijuana helped enormously. James would wake up early enough to allow himself time to vaporize before heading out to school; it made the day easier.

I made an appointment with the head of School to let him know that James needed all these drugs to make it possible for him to get through the days. Gordon was wonderful to give James carte blanche, and the community continued to be amazed and delighted that he made the effort to attend school.

That, for James, outweighed anything else. When tired, he continued to make use of the art room's beanbag chair or the offer of a couch to stretch out on.

There was a time when he would have resisted these offers as they represented a sign of weakness, but in those final days of 2008, he would take advantage of them more frequently. I was quietly and sorrowfully becoming fully aware of his failing strength.

We prepared for Christmas by rolling out all our favourite traditions, including viewing *How the Grinch Stole Christmas* narrated by Boris Karloff. Since I was a child, this animated special was an important part of the build-up to December 25, and I recalled watching it in black and white long before a colour television came into our home. Viewing it with James this year made me incredibly sad, and I cried unashamedly at its conclusion. James, for the first time since this terrible ordeal had begun, did not ask me to stop crying, and I confessed to being too soft. He reminded me that I would cry at the opening of a card.

James talked about the fun he'd have sharing these films and stories with his children one day. As in years past, our favourite Christmas books were piled up by the tree, and we both enjoyed sitting in the evening by the fire, flipping through their pages. We kept the fire logs going, and the scene was next to perfection.

One night James asked me to read aloud *Peef*, a story about a Christmas bear who wants to be real, but I could not complete the book through my tears; it was all too poignant and incredibly painful.

James was gentler these days and not at all judgmental, especially when I became weepy. The feisty, indestructible James who had refused to seek medical treatment for his sore leg months ago was now more tender and thoughtful. I think on some deep level he was quietly preparing us for the coming months.

The next round of radiation would target two spots on James's lungs, and the tattoo markings were in place for December 2 session to begin. Shortness of breath and increased fatigue would be two probable side effects. As forewarned, the ten days would be tough on James, and his fatigue became acute; he slept longer in the waiting room before treatments and then again in the car coming home. He'd manage somehow to get homework done at the end of the day and have some fun with Peter Gabriel, but he would crash into bed early every night. His appetite was diminishing.

The CaringBridge site was proving to be an invaluable resource. I had absolutely no energy to chat with people and dreaded having to tell the story over and over. Updating one page on the blog was so much easier. It had become the one reliable link to family and friends. Emma and Pat had, without being asked, become the gatekeepers, and I will always be indebted to them. They became the conduit for people to reach out to and also for me to seek assistance. They made sure the Well kept going on the days that I could not be there and buffered me from any issues or worries that might break my spirit.

Somehow everything kept ticking over, and I knew there were many angels waiting in the wings. I may not have been gracious at the time to acknowledge all these kindnesses but hope that these friends know how much James and I appreciated them.

*   *   *

James's back was increasingly more painful and finally he took the advice of his teacher Matt Woodard to let one of the boys carry his weighty backpack from class to class.

Almost immediately his back felt better, and he learned it was okay to ask for and receive help. His efforts to stay strong did not need to raise his pain threshold. We craved the weekends as a time to regroup and sleep. Turning off the alarm was the biggest treat.

Radiation continued every day, even on weekends, so that was factored into the schedule. Halfway through this radiation session, James's breathing became shallow and his chest tight. The main lesion in his lung was swollen due to the targeted radiation, and as it was close to the airways, it caused the struggled breaths. James took things slowly and quietly. Emma laminated a "Do not ring the doorbell" sign, which was hung on the gate when James was resting.

The medical team struggled to come up with a new plan for chemotherapy. The first option was a daily pill, and even though taken orally, it would be potent with the more common side effects of fatigue, nausea, and the dreaded hair loss. His red and white cells would be closely monitored. The next option was the traditional drip chemo that would require twenty-four hours in the hospital every twenty-one days. Dr. Goldberg in Miami was consulted, and a possible trial at Stanford might be available. The doctors could not recommend one above the other. It would be James's choice.

Christmas and the increasingly potent "quality of life" were the goals that the doctors hoped to reach. I was totally detached from the truth of what this meant and continued to cling to the optimism that James manifested and desperately needed. He was going to beat this; we were going to experience a strong future; he would have children to share Christmas stories and shortbread with. Total denial is a powerful tool.

James needed more space—from doctors, clinics, even me—and tough as it was, we all made great efforts to be sensitive to this reality. He desired to be creative more than anything and remarkably decided to get some beginner piano lessons as he wanted to explore jazz composition. The drums and all guitars were constantly in use, and when his friends came over, their jam sessions were loud and productive. He carried a Hemingway Moleskine notebook and composition book with him in his messenger bag every day, jotting down ideas for music, art, and poetry.

Some of the instruments in James's bedroom

As the school vacation was fast approaching, James found a renewed drive to complete his projects at school and be ready for that term's final exams. His doctors continued to be galvanized by his drive and determination. They had so often witnessed teens in this situation switch off, retreat to their rooms to play video games, and detach from life and the future. James was striding headfirst into the unknown and was determined to succeed. He had set an example for many to follow.

I found it hard to grasp that a mere seven months earlier, I would have dismissed this story as total fiction. Now we were deep in the throes of this unwelcome reality that was dictating to us our every move. We'd play chess aggressively in the evenings. It felt like another lifetime when our days were light, simple, and uncomplicated.

Together, we were determined to make this Christmas extra special; I was reminded of all the traditions that families share and how, through these, we are tied together. Our collective stories are more powerful than those that divide. I was constantly being reminded that sometimes simple gestures, the ones we feel may go unnoticed, are, in fact, the most powerful. James asked us all to remember Make-a-Wish in their end-of-year charity donations. His wish continued to bring such joy, and many friends and family did make donations to this incredible foundation in his honour.

Early December was cold and frosty, which we loved. James wished for snow, but that was a rare spectacle in San Francisco. At least a few mornings with some ground frost made it feel like winter. With the fireplace aglow in the evenings, the nest felt cozy and festive. Prednisone was now introduced to help with his tight chest, swallowing, and the ensuing pain. Pain management had become such an important piece of this puzzle, and the team working with James was exemplary. His daily medicines kept increasing, and how his organs managed to process all these drugs astounded me. That he was able to function each day, attend school, and continue to be creative speaks volumes of his tenacity and strength of spirit.

It was decided that the next round of chemo would begin after the Christmas break, affording him full days to enjoy the holidays. The doctors were intuitive in reading his needs, and as James weighed the treatment options, he continued to ask circumspect questions. Even though James was in charge of decision making now, they were, nevertheless, decisions that he should not have had to face.

During the final days of 2008, the school performed a festival of carols that included the entire population of the elementary and secondary schools. James was asked to be one of the announcers, so he brushed up on his French. This special assembly was not open to parents, but I went anyway and asked the faculty to let me stand with them. They welcomed me with open arms, and we watched from the upper gymnasium gallery. It was incredibly moving, and the staff were understanding and hugely supportive, providing many hankies and shoulders. It was difficult for them to watch as well.

James, shockingly, refused to use his cane to walk to and from the microphone, making his hobble even more heart breaking. It had to be incredibly painful for him to put full weight on the leg, but he was determined not to be singled out or different from the other students. Each class performed a carol in Latin, French, or English.

The senior students performed last, and their voices were mature and confident. The graduating class wore their grey pullovers with the school tie to differentiate themselves from the rest of the students. It was a proud moment for me to see my sweet James, looking handsome and strong, reach this point in his life. The thought that he was full of cancer was the most alien thing imaginable. I crept out before the students returned to their classes and sat in the car crying. Each of these special moments was becoming harder to experience. They were all so beautiful yet fleeting, and it felt like I was holding on to the string of a balloon that could fly away at any time. Finding safe places to grieve was becoming my personal priority.

*   *   *

In mid-December, Quincy Jones appeared at the Herbst Theatre in San Francisco to record a program for the "City Arts and Lecture" series on National Public Radio. I purchased tickets for James, Keaton, and me to attend, and we had great seats overlooking the stage. It was a fascinating evening, and the stories Quincy told were hugely entertaining. His outlook was upbeat and positive, and he shared the sentiment that he felt as though he was just "warming up." His stories of producing albums with Frank Sinatra were worth the price of admission alone. Once again, James was given the message of the power of mind over circumstances and of letting go and learning to trust.

The boys were energized as they left the theatre, determined to compose and create as much music as possible over the holidays. We stopped off at the Guitar Centre on our way home to look at microphones and drum machines.

James was inspired both musically and artistically. The home office was transformed into an art studio with an easel, a lovely gift from a past client, as well as paints, canvases, and brushes all at the ready. Creative juices flowed through both of us, and the coming holiday would bring great results. The "Do Not Disturb" sign was on the gate, and the phone could be unplugged; we both longed for many nights of golden slumbers.

Chapter 10

Christmas

"Dear Santa, please bring me that long-overdue dog and good health."
—*James December 24, 2008*

The school vacation started on December 19, and it could not have been more welcome. Knowing we'd have a short reprieve from chemo drugs, radiation, and clinic visits with oncologists was such a relief. Taking pain meds would be a daily occurrence, nothing changed that, but they had become almost like multivitamins, just an addition to the day that would keep James healthy. We had both detached from the big picture, and denial continued to be our blissful companion.

That said, James's energy continued to wane and he tired very easily. The recent bout of radiation had taken its toll. The plethora of medicines were diminishing James's appetite, and he needed to vaporize before most meals to have any interest in eating. Simple foods like yogurt, soft bread, pastini, and soup became more popular. The prednisone helped with his breathing but had its own side effects as well. We had learned that along with the benefits of any given drug, there would be a side effect—some insignificant, others more dramatic.

I was grateful that medical marijuana was in James's life as it did provide relief and much-needed balance. He had made the decision that he would move forward with the oral chemo drug as he did not want the invasive IV line in his body, and he dreaded the thought of hospital stays. This new drug would actually be a combination of different drugs that would hopefully inhibit the food supply to the lesions.

Since his cancer was so rare, there was very little data available as to what might work. I wrote that "we were collectively joining hands, holding our breaths, and jumping into the deep ocean waters."

Jumping into favorite water hole at Yosemite

Simple things like baking shortbread, drinking cocoa, visiting with his friends, playing the guitar, painting, and drawing filled the days before the Christmas eve. I made every effort to keep things easy and uncomplicated. Each evening the lights of the tree would be ablaze, and when I finished my late-afternoon walks, I'd make a point of crossing the street to look up at the window and enjoy the glow. A few neighbours would catch us in passing and comment on how much they enjoyed the lights as well. When it turned dark, James had taken to turning off all the lights in the flat to let the tree illuminate the space. The spectacle lightened our spirits.

Ever since he was a young child, James never wanted December 25 to arrive. He adored the build-up to Christmas more than the actual day. He did not want the presents; it was the atmosphere and anticipation that meant more to him. This truth was even more so this year, and he begged that we turn back the clocks and calendar to add more days and postpone the inevitable. We had made a commitment to keep the gift giving to a minimum. Neither of us wanted anything; just happy, pain-free days together would be the best possible present. Peter Gabriel would, of course, get some special treats, and the local pet store had a wonderful igloo-shaped fleece nest for him that would be perfect. We wanted to take a picture of him in a silly elf costume, but he would not oblige.

Nonetheless, the thought was fun. I made a stop to see our friends at Grassroots to pick up some special blends to pop into James's stocking, still amazed at my ease in embracing this new life with marijuana.

Some evenings James asked to go for a drive to look at the lights in the city; Huntington Park on Nob Hill and the large tree at Union Square were always popular. We discovered later that Make-a-Wish had sponsored the tree this year, and James and his wish were honoured in the opening ceremony. On December 24 I popped out to Blick's art store on Van Ness to pick up some final gifts for James, and just as I reached the cashier, I received a panic phone call from him.

There was a horrible shooting pain running up his leg, and he could not stand. I dropped everything and rushed back home. Dr. Ward was on call, and she told us to head over to UCSF immediately. She was concerned there might be a blood clot causing the problem. Here we were, yet again, back on the roller coaster.

The emergency room was busier than anticipated, with many sorrowful-looking patients waiting to be seen. I had a glimpse, for the first time, of the truth that perhaps the holidays were in fact the *worst* days for many who remain silent. I would learn this truth over time and now often think of that crowd in the ER that night, looking for solace and peace, when there is none to be prescribed.

Another x-ray was performed and the dreaded blood work. Nothing was found that could be problematic for the next few days, so James could go back home, but we'd need to talk to Dr. DuBois at the beginning of the week. By now James was weak from hunger, so I set about to find something for him to eat. The neighbourhood was shrouded in fog, and nothing was open. The hospital cafeteria had closed, and the only food available was dried ramen noodles or Twinkies from generic vending machines on the fourth floor.

Crying and feeling desperate, I pulled out a packet of cheese snack crackers. Here it was, Christmas Eve, the most magical night of the year, and we are back at the bloody hospital, on a miserable bloody night, my sweet son in agony from bloody cancer, and I can't even get him bloody proper food to eat! It was a very low point for me, and any reserved strength was rapidly sapped.

Miraculously, Pat called to check in, and I told her the saga. She was with her good friend Maria, making a traditional dinner of cannelloni, salad, and sugar cookies. Pat said she would bundle up some food and bring it right over to us. Her arrival was such a gift, and James literally inhaled the food while standing in the ER driveway. Even though his appetite was off, this was one of the most wonderful meals James could remember, and he was so grateful. He often recalled that meal in the parking lot during the ensuing months.

Pat and Maria became two of the best Christmas angels, and it made me realize that there is a need for warm meals on nights like this when restaurants are closed. James and I thought it would be good to deliver food to the hospital to feed folks like us next year.

By 9:00 p.m. we rolled into the garage, incredibly relieved to be home. It was not the day we had anticipated, but that seemed to be the story of our lives now. James showered and climbed into his flannel pyjamas (which had been warmed up in the dryer) to sit by the tree. He was subdued, and once again, we turned off all the lights in the flat, except the Christmas tree. He picked up his guitar and started to play some of his favourite songs. It was a sacred moment. I pulled out my camera to take a picture but, due to the low light, was unsure if it would come out. It did, and that captured moment became a much-treasured photo that I would share in the coming years. But for his strumming, we sat in silence, and I was overwhelmed by an acute sorrow, which felt like an arrow being shot through my heart.

Christmas Eve 2008

James was desperately ill and his pain constant now. I could do nothing but provide fringe comfort, and a dire hopelessness that I must not show him sat heavily on my shoulders.

As was the tradition, James wrote a note to Santa, set out shortbread cookies, milk, and carrots (for the reindeer) on the hearth, and slowly made his way upstairs to bed. He never asked to know the truth of Santa, and I never told him. This was a magic bubble that he did not want burst, and so we never discussed it. Each Christmas morning he would awaken to find the cookies and milk gone and carrots nibbled, alongside a thank-you note from Santa. It brought him real joy and I suppose a peacefulness in seeing the tradition continue.

We set out our respective stockings, and in the morning there would be presents, wrapped in special Santa paper, for both of us. This year would be no different from any other. He crawled into his beloved bed exhausted and slept soundly while I scurried about to set out the gifts in the stockings, including Peter Gabriel's. A deep sleep was so welcome that night; I had dreams of James as a robust, healthy, and bubbly toddler, my perfect Christmas present.

After opening the gifts and sharing waffles—James's Christmas morning choice—I drove him up to Marin to spend the day with his father and extended family. I returned to the city to get chores done and regroup as the dramatic change the day before proved we would now need to abandon our plans for a week free of medical appointments. Upon his return to the city, James went to see the newly released film *The Curious Life of Benjamin Button* with some friends. It must have been a powerful story for him as it explores birth, death, and the time in between. I would not see this film for a number of years and found it profoundly moving and difficult when I finally plucked up the courage.

On Monday, December 29, we needed to see Dr. Dubois to get a sense of what was going on with this new pain. James used his crutches again to keep weight off the sore leg, and we headed back up to UCSF to have more scans, an MRI, and blood tests. We needed to establish a blueprint for any upcoming treatments. Another injection of Zometra would be given on Tuesday before meeting with the doctors, who would have the test results in hand. I had learned from my first meeting with the doctors that a social worker would also be present for any meetings that might have difficult news. Every meeting had a social worker in attendance. Every meeting had a box of tissues on the desk. Why it took me so long to grasp the severity of our situation I will never know.

Albert Einstein said that there are two ways to look at the world: as if everything is a miracle or as if nothing is a miracle. We had opted for the first choice, and this belief had carried us through months of difficulty and uncertainty. We clung to the miracle that all our lives had intersected at the right time. Perhaps it was folly, but it did provide us with a shared time that was positive and loving. It would have been easy to slip into bitterness and anger, and as I would discover, there would be plenty of time for such sentiments, but somehow our gratitude and joy through living well each day had become more powerful, at least for now.

Section 2

The Last Tear

Chapter 11

Washington

We know what we are, but not what we might be.
—*William Shakespeare*

The meeting with the doctors on Tuesday was not encouraging. New lesions had appeared, this time not only in James's lower leg (source of the recent pain) but also in his head. The low-dose oral chemotherapy pill would begin the next day. James had an attack of asthma, which triggered a cold, so some more quiet days were needed to help get his strength up so as not to be too depleted going forward. As well as the chemotherapy, it was decided to begin yet another round of radiation at the same time. It was not recommended to overlap radiation with chemo, but there was little choice now.

I wrote on CaringBridge that we all marvelled at James's unflappable spirit and willingness to tackle all these obstacles by staying focused on the future and moving forward with his plans. Inside, I was crumbling.

In the midst of all that had been put on his plate, James received a message from Speaker of the House Nancy Pelosi's office, stating that she had set aside tickets for us to attend the Inauguration in Washington in January. He was once again deeply touched and appreciative, and so we decided to try to make it happen. The offer gave him yet another wonderful distraction and opportunity to act upon Obama's message to "think big," and we believed that somehow the pieces would come together. James would need to complete the radiation treatments beforehand, and hopefully he'd be less fatigued. It felt much more daunting than his trip in November. How could his health be even more precarious in such a short space of time?

*   *   *

Another episode of coughing up blood during the first week of January had us rushing to the emergency room with hearts racing, but miraculously, we were told it was not related to the other earlier lesion in the lung (but I wonder now if, in fact, it was), and after some observation, James was sent home. The combination of the chemotherapy pill and radiation would increase his fatigue and other side effects. I was quietly taken aside and warned to pay attention to *any* sudden or dramatic changes.

Instead of a tattoo to block the zones, a wire-mesh mask was created that was a perfect copy of James's head. He would slip the mask on for treatments, ensuring his head was in the same exact position each time. The beam of radiation had to be perfect. He thought of taking the mask when finished and creating a plaster cast of it. It is the one thing we did not do, and I regret it to this day.

He was missing more days of school now, and it troubled him as this next term was important since it lead to his graduation.

I put full steam into making plans for Washington and, using my air miles, managed to get first-class seats. James had never flown this way, and I thought it would be a treat as well as make him more comfortable. The Sacred Heart school community rallied to try and find accommodation through their network. There were a few offers on the table, but James was concerned that he needed privacy since morning nausea had started to become much more of an issue. I had told him about the fund that was established to provide a chairlift for the many stairs at home, and he was horrified. That people had doubted his ability to climb stairs left him mortified, and he refused to allow anything like that to be installed. The chairlift fund was abruptly modified into our Washington fund, and it was greatly appreciated as accommodation, for the Inauguration had gone through the roof! Rooms were selling for over $1,000 per night, *if* you could find one. The predictions for millions descending upon the capital felt daunting to James as he was more easily rattled and agitated. We would not have the support services of Make-a-Wish for this trip, and I needed to trust that transportation would not be an issue as we negotiated the crowds. We clung to the mojo that seemed to be working for him and once again threw our cards into the trust pile and prayed everything would go well.

Claire, an old friend from college days in the United Kingdom and mother to my goddaughter Caroline, lives in Virginia, and her family worked magic to help find solutions. Her sister Pippa had contacts in the hotel industry, and she managed to find us a room at the Capital Hilton, a few blocks from the White House. Claire found a wheelchair and also offered to pick us up from Dulles airport at midnight. All roads in and around Washington would be closed for the Inauguration, so we needed to stay in town and not depend upon any bridges for access to the city. A base camp to retreat to was essential.

James was clearly no longer strong enough to tackle huge crowds or uncertainty. The weather was an unknown until we arrived, so all contingencies had to be taken into account. Speaker Pelosi's office sent e-mails with instructions as to how and where to collect tickets once in Washington. There were many warnings of long queues and increased security.

CaringBridge was updated with lots of upbeat messages, which excited and energized all those following us, but I was terribly uncertain about the trip, if indeed James was up to it. I would never let him know my concerns but rather forged ahead and prayed that any angels that had helped thus far would keep us in their sights. I was burying all my worries, sorrow, and fatigue, unsure when I'd be able to address them. I have now the deepest empathy and respect for those who support and care for the terminally ill. The strain to keep everything ticking over as normal, while life falls apart, is unbelievably draining as well as acutely painful.

The Washington trip was booked from January 18 to 23.

Nancy Pelosi's office was marvellous at keeping us informed on all the activities in Washington during that time, and the local Make-a-Wish office once again stepped up to offer their magic in helping with some of the logistics. Executive Director Patricia even dropped off hand and foot-warmers. They became essentials for the incredible cold that we were about to confront.

Everyone was rooting for us, but James was in agony as the lesions that were being targeted with radiation were swelling, causing terrible headaches from the increased pressure. Marijuana brought great relief, and the pain medications were steadily increased. NBC news did an interview with James that was broadcast to the local stations. They chatted about his meeting with Obama and the election night in Chicago. There was great interest in his upcoming trip to Washington, and James seemed to enjoy this little foray into the world of being a celebrity.

Here is the link to the interview:
http://ww.nbcbayarea.com/news/local/SF_Students_UnlikelyRoad
to_D_C_Bay_Area.html

Even though feeling less than perfect, James dressed up and attended the school Winter Ball with his classmates the Friday before our departure. Up until the morning of January 18 I was not sure that James would make the trip; I had added on cancellation insurance so that we could bow out at any time. James was fatigued and uncomfortable; the weather forecast was for extreme cold in Washington. Multiple warm outfits, gloves, hats, and the many hand-warmers had been packed; yet even with all contingencies in place, there was still a cloud over James as he felt nauseated so much of the time. The doctors were working on coming up with some sort of new concoction to help, but for the moment, they increased the methadone, oxycodone, oxycontin, and lorazepam.

January 18, arrived and although weak, James decided to move forward with the trip and hastily packed his carry-on bag, which would include his laptop, headphones, a collection of funny DVDs, all his medicines, doctors' letters explaining his medical condition and, of course, his iPod, which was groaning with music. We did not carry any medical marijuana as it was not legal in DC. Our friend Susan drove us to the airport, and James was subdued. He was secretly dreading the flight. That he should feel so hesitant in what seemed only a few weeks since Chicago was shocking.

This trip, he did not resist the use of a wheelchair, and the airline was great at helping with all disabled access. Prior to boarding at the gate, a team of Homeland Security boarded the plane with sniffer dogs. A portable x-ray machine was set up, and all passengers had to pass through it once again before walking down the gangway. It was unusual, and we wondered what the big deal was.

Once seated and just moments before the doors closed, Leon Panetta and his wife were escorted on to the plane and sat in the front row of first class. Mr. Panetta was at that time slated to be director of the CIA. He would go on to be Secretary of Defence in the Obama cabinet. James joked that we were probably on the safest flight that day.

While James dreaded the cross-country flight, it went smoothly, and with the help of his laptop, we spent time watching our favourite Lewis Black and episodes of *It's Always Sunny in Philadelphia*. Laughing made the flight pass quickly, and we arrived on time in the late evening. Collecting baggage was another matter, and it took almost *two* hours for our bags to arrive on the carousel. It was shocking, and other travellers grumbled that this was the norm at Dulles airport. I wish we had been warned.

With the mobile phone signal down, I had no way to let Claire know what the holdup was, but she kindly waited patiently, and we dragged ourselves into her car well past two in the morning. We drove into a silent Washington with many streets blocked off; I did not expect to find this hub of power under a sleepy cloud. Needless to say, we collapsed into bed, and thankfully the hotel had left a plate of fruit and cheese in the room so James could eat a small snack.

The next day, after sleeping in until very late, we wandered out to get the lay of the land. It was bitterly cold. James hobbled on his cane and managed to walk a few blocks, but we needed to make many rest stops along the way. The excitement on the street was infectious. Vendors were everywhere hawking T-shirts, buttons, water bottles, bookmarks, homemade baubles, every imaginable commemorative souvenir all labelled with an Obama photo or logo from the campaign. One of the funniest shirts had Obama as Superman opening his shirt to reveal the iconic campaign "O."

While James rested in the afternoon, I wandered over to the Cannon Building near the Capitol to collect the tickets for the Inauguration. As predicted, there were enormous queues at each of the entrances, and I placed a quick call to the speakers' assistant Stina to make sure I was at the right spot. She very kindly sent out another assistant with our tickets, sparing me hours of waiting.

The walk to and from the Cannon Building was longer than I anticipated, but it did give me an opportunity to absorb the sights and massive crowds who were gathering. Thousands were already staking a claim on the expansive lawns in front of the capital building. Total strangers exchanged hugs and kisses. It felt like a large family gathering playing out in the nation's capital. Sidewalks were packed with parents and children all bundled up under layers of down jackets. There was such a sense of important history to this moment. Security fences blocked pathways in an effort to control the flow of humanity. This Inauguration was going to be a huge undertaking, and I carefully plotted out a path to follow the next day should transportation become an issue. Thankfully I had a wheelchair to push James, if needed.

Once back to the hotel, I booked a car for nine the next morning to drive us to the Capitol. James decided on an early dinner at a local restaurant. The cold was biting, and he was tiring easily, so we walked back to our hotel just as many were heading out to celebrate.

There were parties everywhere, it seemed, with restaurants and hotels advertising special events. After his initial apprehension, James was now happy to have the opportunity to be in Washington and told me he looked forward to sharing the tales of this with his children one day.

Washington 2009, eve of the Inauguration

Inauguration Day Tuesday, January 20

> The trilogy comes full circle. First, meeting Barack Obama, then the election night in Chicago and now the Inauguration. Not many are able to complete a cycle so completely and we feel very blessed. (CaringBridge)

The day was icy cold, and we layered up as much as possible to be ready for the car at nine. The driver was concerned that we could not get close to the Capitol building as all major artery roads had been blocked off. I asked that he try to get us as close as possible and we'd wing it from there. Only limos, taxis, and emergency vehicles were allowed on the streets, but even without personal cars, it took over an hour to drive a relatively short distance. Most of the streets had become pedestrian walkways, but fortunately the crowds moved smoothly.

The driver could get us only a few blocks close to the north side of the Capitol, and we needed to hoof it over to the south side, the location for the Cannon gate entrance and "orange ticket" holders. There was a swarm of humanity as far as the eye could see.

While James had resisted the thought of the wheelchair to begin with, he was grateful for it within a few minutes of alighting the car. He would never have been able to negotiate this walk on his cane. Security lines greeted us at the designated main gate and then another long queue to enter our specific gate area. Once on the Capitol grounds, we headed over to Section 12. There was an elevated area for wheelchairs, and even if it was not as close as we could have been, I decided to hold fast instead of trying to push James over the rough frozen ground.

Jumbotrons, set up around the entire area, made it possible for the over two million gathered to follow the proceedings. "Could it really be that number?" we kept asking one another. James had been given a small camera from CBS to film his personal experience of the Inauguration. This footage would be added to others, and their hope was to create a montage for broadcast. James was so cold that he did not film much of anything, and I returned the camera to them at the end of the day. We took photos on our new digital camera and were pleased to have some special pictures for him to share once back home.

James freezing cold at the Inauguration

The Inauguration ceremony was powerful, and to be a witness to the spectacle was incredibly moving. James was thrilled to be a part of it even though the cold was settling in and making him terribly uncomfortable. Since he could not walk to warm himself up, a couple of kind folks took it upon themselves to help shield him from the biting winds. As an example of just how cold it was, I had kept my mobile phone in my pocket, and when I took it out, the glass cracked.

We would not really be able to enjoy the entire ceremony of the Inauguration until back at the hotel, watching it on endless television reruns.

Inauguration of President Obama 2009

James became so miserable from the cold that he asked to leave before the end of events to try to beat the crowds. We headed towards the Metro but quickly abandoned that idea with the throngs that were already flooding into the system. My hitherto brave and unflappable James was now terribly nervous about the crowds. I suspect being in the wheelchair made him feel more vulnerable.

Walking was the only option left, so I headed off on my pre-planned route from the day before, pushing him towards Massachusetts Avenue and the two-hour walk back to the hotel. The workout felt great, and we shared a number of laughs trying to negotiate the humanity, curbs, vendors, and general craziness on the streets. It actually ended up being a mini tour of Washington, which James managed to enjoy, and we both agreed that we would have missed it had the Metro option worked.

Once back in the warmth of the room, James collapsed on the bed and was able to watch the parade outside the White House on the television. But for the extreme cold, it had been a good day, exhausting but also exhilarating and I was so glad James had been able to experience this marvellous opportunity.

Sleep was deep and solid that night, and we awoke the next day rested, but James felt terribly nauseated and it took a long time for him to get his legs under him before we could head out. This morning routine was sadly becoming the norm, and it troubled me greatly that he started each day vomiting before showering. We needed to nurture a new patience, but it was becoming difficult. My rage towards cancer was now becoming all-consuming, yet I had nowhere to channel it.

For the first time in my life I considered doing what I had forbidden James to do and seriously contemplated looking for some marijuana on the street for his use. He was in such agony and unable to enjoy eating; I would have risked arrest to help him. I resisted the urge, but the notion made me realize that the various state laws controlling medical marijuana were all muddled and antiquated. The last thing we needed was a Make-a-Wish mother tossed into jail, so James suffered in silence. I felt once more, totally useless and helpless.

I had arranged for the same car and driver to be available to take us on a tour of the city so that James could at least see some of the important sights. He was subdued throughout, and we sat in silence for much of the tour. A stage used at a concert on Monday night was being taken down at the Lincoln Memorial as we climbed out of the car and used the disabled access to avoid the queue. I was determined that he see the monument and views of the Mall.

Lincoln Memorial after Inauguration

A stranger took a photo of the two of us and it became one of the nicest ones of these past months. James stood tall and looked proud. The view of the Mall was littered with chain-link fences, cranes, television crews and satellite trucks, mountains of equipment, and overflowing rubbish bins. The driver took us past all the important Washington landmarks, and we snapped photos through open windows. It was shocking how little energy James had, which translated into a lack of interest; I feared the Inauguration had sapped too much of his limited reserves.

Once back at the hotel, James slept while I walked out to meet up with Claire and Caroline, both of whom I had not seen for over twelve years. It felt good to reconnect, but I was aware of how different my life was and how all-consuming this cancer had become.

We stopped at St. John's church where the prayer service was held before inaugurations. The needlepoint footstools for past presidents were lined up at the front pew. President Obama's was in the process of being made. The history was rich. Heavily scented flowers hung out of overly stuffed alter pieces. Tea later, at the Hay Adams, was a small taste of civility in the midst of all the crowds and hustle of the past days. Once again all these strange juxtapositions crashing in to one another.

When I arrived back at the hotel in the late afternoon, James felt more energized, and we bundled up again to walk over to the White House through Lafayette Park. The sun was setting, and the streets quiet due to the lack of cars. We stood near the gates to the White House and saw lights coming on in different rooms. James wondered what it must be like for the family to have moved in yesterday and how strange it must feel for them. He thought that democracy and the transfer of power worked in America with such ease.

Feeling bold, we had dinner at a nearby Brazilian restaurant, and I was amazed at how upbeat and relaxed James was. We played gin rummy while waiting for the meal, and he thoroughly enjoyed his Cuban sandwich. We laughed, made jokes, enjoyed our meal, and the night was perfect. This would be the last meal that I would recall James enjoying with such gusto.

Curled up in our beds back in the room, we watched television and got sucked into season premieres of *24* and *House*. These programs had cult followings, and even though they had been in production for years, I had not watched either of them. We got hooked, and we would follow both faithfully once back in San Francisco.

House was a favourite television program for James, and he downloaded many episodes to his computer. The lead character, a brusque eccentric doctor by the name of Greg House, was the Sherlock Holmes of medical mysteries and as such was capable of solving what appeared the most impossible of dilemmas.

Over the coming months I would realize that secretly James was longing for a Greg House to find the cure to his rare disease. I am sure that each episode's denouement provided James some encouragement that a solution might be found.

The let down from all the recent excitement and battling the cold weather had left us both exhausted. We turned out the lights before watching any of the late-night talk shows. Our return to San Francisco was scheduled for the next afternoon.

January 23
A heartbreaking start to the day.

James awoke to find chunks of hair on his pillow. The dreaded hair loss that the doctors had warned us about had begun, and he was devastated. His hair was lustrous and thick, and he was so proud of it. Often people would stroke or rub their hands through his hair when talking with him; they found it so inviting. A dreadful morning nausea overcame James, and he spent the first hours of the day positioned on the floor next to the toilet, weeping and cursing at the same time. It was awful.

I tried to console him as best I could, but it was all pretty feeble. This grief cut to his core, and all I could do was sit there and share the moment. Sadly, I would rapidly learn, there are no words for times like this. He was afraid to shower for fear of losing more hair, and he wore a plastic cap on his head. I spritzed his head with a light solution of water and baby shampoo to try and be as gentle as possible, but even with just the slightest touch, his hair continued to fall out.

Getting ourselves pulled together took forever that morning, and we both felt as though we had been smacked into a brick wall. Fortunately, James had his tweed hat to protect the top of his head (where the problem was most pronounced), and we did wander out eventually to get some food at a local café. His appetite was off, and he wanted just plain yogurt and light toast. These would become his foods of choice for most days going forward.

The flight from Dulles was delayed on the runway for over an hour, which agitated James even more, and touching down in San Francisco never felt better. His bed provided welcome relief, but sadly the coming days would unfold with pillows covered in hair, and like the biblical Samson, James's energy and spirit would diminish with every lock that slipped through our fingers.

Chapter 12

Time Is too Slow

This equation does not add up,
And yet I'm holding the answer.

—James, *Coastline* poem, 2006

James returned to school the next Monday and was ready to share his stories of Washington with his teachers and friends, but first we had an early-morning start at UCSF for blood work and x-rays before meeting with his oncologists. The tumour in his liver was causing greater discomfort, and James was more severely fatigued. No matter how we tried to slow the progression, his hair continued to fall out, and mornings were the worst as he'd awaken to find long wisps on his pillows, sheets, and comforter. Interestingly, the line of loss was a square on the top of his head, which fit the mapped area of the recent radiation. His bangs, sides, and back of his head remained intact, so when he wore his hat (part of his daily wardrobe now), he masked the great sorrow underneath.

We discussed the possibility of getting a wig, and to my surprise, James was very keen on the idea. There is a wonderful organization in San Francisco called Friend to Friend that provides wigs for cancer patients. We made an appointment with Gunther (who was a wig master for the opera and volunteered his time), and James chose a style and colour that looked similar to his own. It was ready to be picked up within a few days, but James wore it only a few times, choosing instead to wear his hats. I kept the wig for years before plucking up the courage to let it go and donate it to another patient in need.

James began a new chemo regime called Etoposide, which was scheduled to run for twenty-one days. Now there were pills to balance other pills, pain meds to control new and old pain, drugs to prevent the nausea from all of these drugs, and pills to hopefully prevent infection since his immunity was low. I tried to stay upbeat on CaringBridge, but it was hellish perpetrating this façade. James's hair was falling out, he was so terribly tired, he had little appetite, the pain was increasing, and there was *much* more talk about the "quality of life" from the team at UCSF.

Memories of Washington sustained us, and we enjoyed buying the commemorative news magazines; many had pictures of the night in Chicago, and James was excited to see his face in some of the photos. This had been a remarkable experience, and we would always share great affection for Barack Obama—politics and policies aside, he was a decent, generous, and thoughtful human being who touched our hearts and gave James hope and faith in a future when he most needed something to cling to.

*   *   *

Arriving at school on time was becoming tougher as many mornings were just too complicated. Dreadful nausea was a regular occurrence now, and James needed to vaporize just to get out of bed. We had reconfigured his room and put a table bedside that held the vaporizer, water, and his collection of pills. Before turning out the lights at night James would assemble the necessary bottles and paraphernalia so that everything would be ready when he woke up. More frequently these items would be needed during the night as well. He bought a funky desk lamp at a secondhand store that cast a soft beam which also sat bedside. He was meticulous in how he laid out his pills, water, cannabis, lighter, and vaporizer before climbing under the sheets.

The recent bout of radiation had really affected James far more than in the past, and there were now very noticeable side effects. Acupuncture was helpful (for both of us), and it was remarkable how calm and rosy cheeked he appeared after the treatments. I too was mellow and felt a deep peace afterwards. Both of us were grateful we had discovered this simple alternative to all the chemicals that had become his lifeline.

Interestingly, I was starting to carry discomfort in the same areas of my body where James's lesions were located. Apparently this phenomenon is not uncommon for parents nursing their sick children; one manifests the other's struggle.

Zometra was now a monthly infusion, and we thought in early February that James was holding his own. More frequent scans were performed to get a sense of where the lesions sat in his body. This double life we led:

attending school, making plans for college, following the new administration in Washington, and then on the flip side constantly collecting data on and monitoring this vile cancer that was slowly consuming my son's body. We had collectively shifted our focus from seeking cures to finding the greatest relief.

February 9, 2009
The week did not start as we would have hoped.

James became very nauseated in the night, and the nagging pain in his lower right side escalated to the point that he woke me and asked that we contact the on-call doctor. Fortunately it was one of his team, and Dr. Ward instructed us to head over to UCSF for an ultrasound, labs, and observation. She would call ahead and set up the tests. It was 3:30 a.m.

I wrote how easily we negotiated the city streets at that hour with a full moon to guide us to Parnassus. We felt that our little friend Putters could do this route on automatic pilot after all the trips there these past months. Upon arrival, the ER staff were wonderful and moved us quickly through the registration process. Even though the hospital staff knew us well by this time it was amazing that every visit required new paperwork; the same forms were signed countless times, insurance cards checked, disclosures read and initialled. When President Obama tried to streamline all the waste in health care, I was supportive of his plan as we had witnessed first-hand the mountains of papers accumulated. I saved much of the paperwork for my records and teased James we'd be able to wallpaper a room with them one day.

Blood work was organized and an ultrasound set for seven thirty. We showed up in the room before the technician even had time to pull up James's chart. I had a sense we were on warp speed, and while eternally grateful for their haste, I wondered why they were so focused. My old friend denial was sitting right by my side. Lying flat for the thirty-minute ultrasound was difficult, and James had to get up and walk about the room multiple times.

Dr. Dubois met us on the floor and managed to look at the results as soon as available. James was so weary and just wanted to bolt. Nausea made it difficult to take the all-important pills, and he could not face any food to help coat the stomach. The awful Catch-22. James had not been able to vaporize before leaving home in the early morning, so his agitation was heightened. It was a miserable start to his day, but somehow with the doctor's gentle nudging, James finally managed to get the drugs into his system so that the pain started to subside. This was good as we now had to head over to China Basin for a PET scan.

Finding a good vein for the contrast dye took some time, but the meds had kicked in and he thankfully could lie flat long enough for the scan to be successfully completed. The results would be available in the coming days.

James could not face school that day and ended up quietly at home, sipping ginger tea and eating a Balance bar—the limit of his food intake. Wretched does not even begin to describe the state of mind I was in. This dream was miserable, and everything was going even more terribly wrong. How could a supposedly loving God allow such anguish? I was entering a dark and angry place that questioned everything. The cruel randomness of fate was starting to make me bitter.

On February 11, we had a meeting scheduled with the oncologists at the clinic. It was incredibly difficult with two social workers in attendance this time, the ubiquitous box of tissues, and Mary taking notes. We had reached a crossroads. The lesions continued to grow and multiply. One in his liver was stretching the lining, hence the recent lower back pain. A new tumour lay in the lining of his lung. Some had appeared in his skull. The chemotherapy drugs were not working; therefore, James would cease taking them immediately. Pain management would be the focus of the oncologists' attention going forward.

James's nausea and fatigue were directly related to the cancer now, and sadly, these symptoms would only be exacerbated over time. We had to regroup and look at options:

1. Radiation could be performed on his liver as it did seem to have slowed the growth of some other lesions, but they would still remain.
2. Chemotherapy using different oral drugs could be explored.
3. James could decide to do nothing for the moment and concentrate on staying comfortable and enjoying time away from drug therapies. More emphasis would go into pain management, days with friends, and hopefully fewer side effects.

These were not choices James should have to consider. It felt like being kicked in the gut, thrown on the ground, and run over by a truck all at the same time.

The team of doctors and nurses were remarkable at being honest and compassionate, but they all knew this was a lousy hand to play. They would follow whatever plan or combination of plans James wanted. Space and quiet time was what he desired most, and we retreated from the dark building on Parnassus without making a decision.

James announced early that evening that he'd like a picnic supper, so I picked up his favourite mild chicken curry and rice from Lemongrass, our local Thai restaurant, and the two of us drove down the street to the cable car turnaround park at the Hyde Street Pier. We sat on a bench in the cool evening air, watching the sun set over the Aquatic Park, silently observing the tourists floating on and off the cable cars. The white lights of Ghirardelli Square reflected off the calm waters, and for a fleeting moment, everything seemed perfect. Life had taken a dramatically abrupt turn, yet here in this singular moment, there was the continuity of good warm food, happy tourists, jangling bells, and a peaceful evening by the water, which made everything seem, at least for a few minutes, manageable.

In the coming days and weeks James's energy would lessen, and instead of walks or outings, he would choose to go on simple car rides to sit by the Marina Green or the water at Crissy Field. Medical marijuana would be needed more and more for comfort and relief from the nausea. He would soon only be interested in eating a minimal amount of food, literally just a few bites, after vaporizing. Acupuncture became a weekly treatment while I watched his body become swollen and, in places, distended. "Comfort" and "quality of life" had become the catch phrases.

For years I had called James "Samwise Gamgee," my faithful, unconditional, and loyal friend who helped me keep my balance through difficult days. Even as I fought to change the template and as much as I wished it otherwise, James had now become Frodo carrying the burden of a dreaded ring that had been thrust upon him; it was now my role to be Samwise for his journey. Our games of chess were now becoming less frequent as he strained trying to remember the moves of some of the pieces.

Quietly we were both struggling to come to terms with this truth and how best to use the remaining time we were given.

Chapter 13

DNR

We accept the graceful falling
Of mountain cherry blossoms,
But it is much harder for us
To fall away from our own
Attachment to the world.

—Rengetsu, a Buddhist nun

James had planned a trip to Colorado to see his friend Michael over the weekend of February 14 to15, but these new developments made it impossible for him to consider a flight now. It tore him apart not to be up for the journey, but it was the best choice.

Michael decided to come to San Francisco instead over the weekend of February 21, which gave James something to look forward to. They shared a glorious time together with lots of friends flowing in and out of the gate. Peter Gabriel adored all the attention as well with endless hours of hide-and-seek.

James, Michael and Peter Gabriel

During the nights James started to need me more, and I slept on the inflatable Aerobed on the floor next to him. Within a week I realized that a chair that pulled out into a bed would be more practical. That way I could be close by but the room would not be so overwhelmed during the day.

The days were becoming more difficult and the nights troubled. I knew we needed help.

On February 17 James decided that he did not want to face any more drug therapies or radiation for the moment and instead he'd like a full-court press to bring him comfort. The next day we met with the oncologists as well as Beattie, the social worker James had grown fond of, to discuss the next steps.

Hospice care would be arranged. James could be at home, and the nurses would come to him. There would be 24/7 attention to his needs with someone available constantly at the end of the phone. The discussion was all about his comfort and quality of life, and the team would do everything possible to ensure James would continue to have the best care.

While it was devastating to sit and hear these words spoken, my companion, denial, settled in next to me, and I found myself an observer listening to words and figuring out routines that were for someone else, surely not for my James.

Deep down I knew what *hospice* meant, but this news became part of the conveyor belt of mounting grief that ran beside me. I would think about that another day. What was needed now was all that mattered; any long-term issues would be dealt with down the road. James was upbeat knowing we'd not have to make the midnight trips to the dreaded hospital, and having some new options for pain relief sounded great. He amazed us with his confidence and maturity; but perhaps he too was in denial.

Hospice would offer support services such as massage and spiritual guidance, and his drugs could even be delivered to the house as needed. I wrote on CaringBridge that having the weight of decisions lifted off my shoulders felt like Christmas (such an odd reference now). Knowing there would be professionals to lean on more consistently was a huge gift. Obviously, I was running on fumes.

Patrick, a male nurse from Hospice by the Bay, came by on Thursday morning for the preliminary intake visit. He was armed with a handbook to review, which included a number of information booklets. He also left a large binder that would be used for updating James's files whenever the nurses visited. The paperwork was extensive, and they also requested a complete list of all the drugs James was taking (or had taken). Hospice had an in-house concoction that would help ease the nausea, which was by now truly debilitating. There were so many details to process, but the relief of having other eyes and ears monitor James here at home was worth any uncertainty.

As he concluded, Patrick handed me a large plastic bag containing some vials and paperwork. He told me it was known as the end-of-life kit. DNR (Do Not Resuscitate) forms were included. Without looking at any of the contents, I shoved the bag deep to the back of my bedroom armoire's top shelf.

*　　*　　*

Paris, a friend from James's early childhood, spent the afternoon with him, and it was great to hear their laughter, as they attacked zombies, floating down the stairs. It felt as though our new "extended family" was expanding daily, but they were all medical professionals. I had come to depend on them more than family or friends, probably because we were together constantly, and I never realized just how much I would miss them over the coming months and years. I have been told since that this is a common phenomenon with patients who are so desperately ill. It has to be incredibly difficult for the doctors and nurses not to get too deeply involved in the lives of their patients; a fine line and delicate path to walk.

In the midst of these days of transition James amazed us all by applying to Emerson and Loyola Chicago. The college process was moving forward with ease, and he'd wait to see the results in the coming months. Nonsensically—yet in my state of disconnect, it made sense to me—Peter Gabriel was up to more antics and had discovered an old frying pan hidden under the kitchen tablecloth that he'd sit in for hours chewing on cooking magazines. College applications and crazy rabbits were all just part of the random landscape we now inhabited.

Hospice care became our safety net, and James had a new peacefulness knowing they were always waiting in the wings. They produced a cocktail of drugs that worked like a charm with the nausea, and his pain was diminished. Without the nagging discomfort, his mood was brighter and his energy improved. Miraculously, he was back to school each day and, with the help of marijuana, was able to relax fully in the evening, eat a little more than just Balance bars, and sleep soundly.

My anxiety lifted, and that too had an impact on James, I am sure. He knew how his illness was tearing me apart and a couple of times apologized for all the anguish. It broke my heart for him to be so worried about me, and I quickly dismissed his concern, reassuring him that it was not a burden at all to stand with him. I was just so sad that he had to go through it, and any anger I had was towards this vile cancer. I kept my grieving moments to late at night and in the morning, when he was far from sight.

Routine became more important than ever, so we did everything to ensure that James got to school on time and that he'd be comfortable for the duration of the day. The faculty were marvellous at looking out for him, checking in and sharing lunchtimes if he wanted to chat about the big-picture issues that were starting to bubble up.

Rowena was the wonderful primary hospice nurse assigned to James. He was listed as a pediatric patient because of his age, but his size placed him in the adult category for dosages, so it took some tweaking to get the right measurements for the medicines. I started keeping careful daily notes in small Moleskine journals for her to review at each visit. Hemingway carried the Moleskine brand when travelling, and James loved that his story was recorded as one of his favourite authors would have done. He continued plotting those days in Paris after graduation.

My first entry, shown below, recorded the various medicines and what times they were given to James on February 21:

> 3:30 am:
> cocktail x 1 tsp
> methadone x 3
> gabapentin x 1
>
> 10:30 am:
> cocktail
>
> Afternoon:
> gabapentin x 1
> methadone x 2
> cocktail x 1 tsp
>
> Evening:
> gabapentin x 1
> methadone x 3
> cocktail x 1 tsp
> oxycodone
> reglan x 2
>
> 21:30
> Licoderm patch on to remain overnight. Placed on his lower back pain (which targeted the liver)
> Transderm patch on the back of his ear—for nausea

The pages of these journals are full of lists of drugs that were needed to bring James comfort, many of which were given in liquid form so that they would be easier to swallow. The *cocktail* mentioned was the wonderful new hospice creation given to combat the extreme nausea. Now he had not only the methadone, oxycodone, and oxycontin but also gabapentin (for nerve pain), the cocktail, Lidoderm, Ativan, Zofran, Benadryl, and Tylenol. He also needed Zantac to help with the heartburn (a side effect from the combination of all the other drugs) as well as stool softeners to ease the horrible constipation that pain medicines exacerbate. Fortunately, I was a copious note-taker from my days of training as a nursery nurse in the United Kingdom, so the daily accounting was easy to keep and very precise. Now these notes provide an accurate window into the final weeks of James's care. We were all so focused on every moment that there was no time to reflect on what was unfolding.

James would update the journal during the nights and afternoons as he also understood the value of keeping this record for the hospice nurses. It is heartbreaking now to see his handwriting on the yellowing pages. Along with the record of drugs taken he included on the pages bittersweet insights, passing thoughts, sometimes even little jokes or music he wanted to download on his computer. On one page is a list of things he told me that he was grateful for: the taste of fresh water, the smell of summer air, peanut-butter-and-jelly sandwiches, mango and pineapple combos. He also wrote that he wanted to grow a moustache and learn how to spin pizza dough.

On February 24 James's oncologists, along with Beatie and Robin, the UCSF pediatric palliative nurse coordinator, paid a lovely house call. It was a special evening visit as they wanted to see James, check the setup and confirm that everything needed for his long-term comfort was in place. James was so touched that they would see him at home. After checking his vital signs, they enjoyed their introduction to the now-infamous Peter Gabriel, who managed to break free; it took all four of us, chasing him around the flat, with James cheering us on, to capture and put the panting rabbit back into his pen. The devotion of the doctors and support team was an incredible blessing, and I hope they all know how much they meant to James and me. I can say with all honesty that he could not have had better or more compassionate care.

> February 25th
>
> James is back to school again this week—attending every day even after waking at 4:00 one morning with a terrible bout of nausea. He is busily plotting the next task to complete, song to write and barbeque to organize. His stamina, drive and optimism leave no room for grumbling or fretting the small stuff. It is always easy to say this but quite another to live it. He is a true beacon for living large every moment. (CaringBridge)

When so inclined, James continued with outings to the cinema and walks in the neighbourhood or down at the water's edge, and I was not sure where he got his energy from. His transformation was amazing when all the medicines worked in unison, and he'd crash happily into bed each night after watching the lights on the bay from his window. He was peaceful, and all seemed right with the world again. The hospice social worker and chaplain made appointments to come by and introduce themselves. James, though not sure why he had to go through the exercise, was gracious. He claimed that his leg felt stronger, and he actually stopped using the cane some days when at home. His father stopped by one afternoon, and we looked at baby photos and shared a laugh. It was a good moment.

The hospice social worker Chris was a young man who shared James's interest in the alternative music scene. They would talk about music instead of the big picture (a.k.a. death), and Chris would tell me later that being with James taught him to take a different approach with teens who are dying. Chris thought his work was to help these young people die, but James taught him that as long as he was here, he meant to live and that Chris's work ought to encourage that story until the end. Indeed, one evening around this time, James told me, "I came here to live, not to die."

In early March, Marc came over to help set up James's room to work a little better, given the shrinking space, by installing some bedside shelves and cubbies for his vast album collection. The room had mushroomed into a wild collection of recording equipment, microphones, music players, speakers, drum kit, guitars, collection of drugs and cannabis, bed and folding loveseat; somehow it all worked, but there was even less floor space to move about in.

James was happy, and that was all that mattered. His music was evolving, and the friends continued to gather on weekends to play instruments and record the beginnings of some very interesting songs.

*   *   *

On March 11 I received a phone call from a New York number. Not sure who it could be, I was a bit hesitant as I pushed the Answer button. Much to my amazement, on the other end of the line was our favourite humourist, Lewis Black. He had called to speak with James. Six degrees of separation and serendipity came to play as Lewis's producer was a cousin of Priyanka (another wonderful mother of James's friends), and she had relayed the message that James was a huge fan. The matrix of paths continued to intersect, and again, one of the most important lessons reinforced throughout this time of turmoil was how interconnected all our lives are.

I told Lewis that I was just heading off to school to pick up James, and if he'd be willing to call back, I knew James would be *thrilled*. I bolted over the hills to school to find James waiting at the front door. We dashed home, and thirty minutes later the phone rang again.

Lewis and James chatted for almost an hour, and James, in an effort to save the conversation, turned on the Record button of his computer. The microphone, however, only picked up James's voice. While he was disappointed in the results, this recording of James sounding happy and sharing some laughs has become a much-treasured remembrance. It was as if they were old chums shooting the breeze, and Lewis wanted to make sure that we'd attend his next California performance in August. I was struck with how gracious, calm, and charming he was, given that his performance persona is frantic, loud, and sarcastic.

James felt so well during those early days of hospice care that he was hesitant to start any more treatments and risk rocking the boat. He did continue with the Zometa infusions at UCSF as they helped with the bone pain.

He was working on his senior-class presentation for his justice class and decided to focus on his cancer as he wrote about one of the goals of the Sacred Heart schools. He had written an essay (included at the end of this book), which he recorded to act as the background for his PowerPoint presentation. James decided at the next Zometa treatment to document in photos the process from parking the car through the blood draws and the IV drip. Once again, there is now a wonderful visual record of these important final days.

My fuse was becoming short, and I found myself quick to snap. I did my best not to show frustration front of James; the few times I had let my guard down, he immediately felt guilty for causing this anguish. Hastily, I would respond that it was the *cancer* that had me riled. Through all this James was becoming more patient and philosophical about the whole situation and exhibited a serene maturity while sharing his remarkable insights.

One morning, as Putters dashed over the hills to get him to school, a woman reversed out of her garage on Laguna Street without looking and narrowly missed crashing into us. My instinct was rage, and I pounded the steering wheel for her carelessness. James put his hand on my arm and said quietly, "Mama, everybody has a story."

He was right. Maybe she had just received terrible news, or she was dashing to see her sick child or someone had died, or . . . anything could have transpired, and he reminded me to give them space. I would tell this story to many over the coming years. Everyone does have a story.

The head of girl's school in Oakland would use James's powerful lesson as the theme for their next school year, encouraging the faculty and students to share their stories as a way to empower and hone their empathy skills. I now find myself saying quietly "Everyone has a story" whenever tested or frustrated by words or actions that hurt.

*　　*　　*

University acceptances had started to arrive, and James was thrilled. USF, Loyola, and Emerson had all entered the affirmative column. It was such an exciting time for him, and his spirits soared. The future was going to be bright, and he was ready to jump in with both feet.

Interestingly, I had a massage in early March, and without knowing the location of James's tumours, the masseuse could feel energy in those areas in my body. Now both acupuncture and massage had revealed my deep physical connection to James's cancer.

While we had entered a holding pattern, there was still great uncertainty surrounding the next steps, and as long as James did not want to pursue any treatments, we all agreed to follow his lead. Deep in my gut I wondered how long this situation could continue as the weekly hospice visits revealed the continued growth of the many lesions, with some starting to stretch through his skin. It was beyond agonizing. So long as James could go to school and be with his teachers and friends, he felt he had the upper hand over the cancer rather than the reverse. He wrote about this feeling of empowerment in his final essay.

*James and Anthony with guitars on the school steps- the stairs
would be painted and dedicated after his death*

I continued to work each day, but my journal was filled with worry over my sagging energy and sore back. I was coming to terms with the reality that there is only so much one can carry. What kept us both going was sleep and long periods of quiet rest on weekends; some sunny afternoons we'd put Aerobeds on the roof so we could both lie in the heat of the sun.

*   *   *

In late March, my sister came to San Francisco along with her husband and son John. The visit was pleasant, but I was aware of James's quiet mood. He did not want to do much socializing, and when I look at a photo my sister took of James and me on the roof, I am shocked at how puffy James looked—we *both* looked. I had been blind to the greyness of his skin and the extreme swelling brought on by all the toxins and drugs rattling around in his body. He was beginning to shut down. This photo is an awful reminder of how sick James was and the limited time that was left.

James experienced another bout of coughing blood one night in early April, and it was reassuring to be able to talk to a hospice nurse over the phone instead of dragging him back to the hospital. Fortunately, it was not a major attack, and he settled, rising in the morning ready to head back to school. More college acceptances arrived, and for the first time James expressed interest in perhaps attending a school in the city so that he could stay close to the doctors and home. The prospect of his illness worsening while far from home was making him feel unsure about a big move. Deferring college for a year was another option he began to explore. Living in the moment was his goal for now.

He was busy putting together an Andy Warhol look for the senior prom, and while hunting for suitable items at Molte Cose, his favourite vintage shop, he and Theresa, the owner, reminisced about all the years he had shopped there. She first knew him as a wee toddler out in his buggy, and we all felt we'd come full circle. He bought a paisley tie for the dance, and they exchanged a big hug. It would be the last time she would see him.

Othello and another Bukowski were the current books that James was reading, and Easter was fast approaching. Gabe had now taken to eating phone cords, cutting us off from the outside world. We moved forward, somehow solved problems, replaced cords, met with the hospice team, and simply carried on while James became more swollen and grey. The contrast of the commonplace with the gravity of extreme illness felt schizophrenic, and while deep inside I was hysterical, wanting to scream at the top of my lungs, I merely walked forward. Keeping things normal was the task at hand. Rather than falling apart, I filled the house with lilacs, painted eggs, and yellow daffodils.

On April 10 we awoke to one of those stunning spring days when the universe conspires to make everything perfect. The air was light and clear; the sun shone in crystal blue skies while light marshmallow clouds floated lazily by. I walked through the Marina Green to the water at Crissy Field, begging for a different outcome than the one we were facing. I cried, prayed, kicked the sand, and railed against a god that could allow this to happen.

When I returned home, James complained of numbness on the side of his face. A new lump had appeared on his temple. His left leg was swelling and felt tight; he could not put his shoes on. Even though he had managed to dodge scans and tests this past month, he asked that I contact the team. He would be willing to do an MRI and PET scan again. It was spring break, and while he enjoyed being with his friends, there were fewer occasions when he felt up to wandering out of doors. The boys would come and play music or chat in his room. They too must have started to notice his decline though no one acknowledged it.

An MRI was performed, and on April 14 we received the horrible news that yes, new lesions had appeared on James's skull and the area that had received radiation was also now *full* of new tumours. The remaining scans were cancelled as James found it terribly difficult to lie still for the MRI. Punishing him with a two-hour scan to only reveal what we already knew would be cruel. We came home to process the news and immediately called Hospice by the Bay to get help with his increasing pain. On CaringBridge I asked for prayers and love. The configuration on the chessboard was changing dramatically.

We were losing pawns, knights, and bishops.

The queens were battling it out.

Chapter 14

This Is all Bullshit

"Life is a good place to be."
—said to me April 23 by the delivery man from the medical supply
company as he dropped off an oxygen tank and suction machine

Hospice by the Bay had taken over the daily routine for James, and their goal, in conjunction with his oncologists at UCSF, was to provide full comfort and diminished pain for him going forward. With combined energies they managed to stay one step ahead of his needs, which was reassuring. Hospice had a relationship with ACE Pharmacy in the city, who also worked closely with the team. Medicines would now be delivered by ACE, who were incredibly prompt. Even in this vigil we would find serendipity as Ed, the owner of the pharmacy, was the father of one of James's classmates from elementary school. Oxygen tanks sat in the living room, and a long clear tube wound its way up the stairs to his bed. James used it consistently when resting. The suction machine and other paraphernalia were hidden near the bookcase downstairs. I could not bear to look at them.

Shockingly, James continued to go to school on the days he felt up to it and was working on a perspective essay for PBS. He wanted to complete all outstanding projects. He'd attend a few barbeques, one for the senior class at Ocean Beach (that provided a glorious photo of all the boys) and another with his close friends on the roof. He visited the school baseball team to watch them for a few minutes at Moscone Park and attended a Dan Deacon concert at the Great American Music Hall. Where he drew his stamina from, no one will never know. Perhaps it was just his spirit's desire to embrace every opportunity as he now had a deep understanding of how fleeting days are.

The next afternoon we drove down the hill to the Aquatic Park at the end of Van Ness and pulled into the parking lot. James hobbled on his cane over to the white-washed seawall. I encouraged him to smoke a joint in hopes that he might feel a bit better. He was not eating anymore. A spoonful of yoghurt or perhaps a bite of dry toast. His robust appetite had been reduced to a few nibbles, barely enough to act as sustenance. His face was full, which could be mistaken as an indication of a healthy appetite, but I know now that he was swollen and puffy because disease and drugs had taken their toll. He had no colour in his cheeks, and his eyes had started to turn dark.

We sat silently on the sea wall and watched the swimmers of the Dolphin Club circle the bay, their strokes measured and easy. I wondered, watching them with secret longing, if they were aware of a boy who was about to die. Maybe he could just try to muster one more lap. How icy the salt water would feel. Slipping into the Pacific would take more than he had in him.

We watched and longed in painful solitude. Did those tourists who wandered by laughing with their Fisherman's Wharf taffy, Boudin bread, and cheap cable car memorabilia know that the young man they passed was dying? He would not be here next week. Perhaps not even within a few days. They strolled by the last outing of a boy full of disease and his mother who was slowly dying next to him. How cruel the world of the living collides with the dying. The oblivion of the one makes the suffering of the other even more bitter.

James produced from his jacket pocket a ready rolled joint that Anthony had prepared for him. Rolling had always been an issue for James, struggling through pouches of loose tobacco and rolling papers.

I took out the digital camera from my pocket and started to shoot photos of him lighting up; his legs and cane; his new red sneakers (God, how he wanted to skateboard in them!); his new windbreaker purchased online from his favourite store; his funny peaked cap that became his final headdress. He looked so melancholy and worn. After a few deep puffs, he went to the water's edge to sit on the stone wall. Lapping waves caressed the piles of rocks below where, years ago as a little boy, he had scurried to find crabs and starfish washed up in the latest tide.

I could not speak. The moment was too heavy with every conceivable emotion. I knew he was about to leave me, and I think he knew it too. There were no words. Only quiet, vaporous, precious seconds between breaths, that is all we were given. Perhaps just watching the waves, listening to the swoosh of the swimmers, and smoking a joint is all that we are capable of.

It took a long time for us to consider returning to Putters. Perhaps we both knew that would be his last foray outside, and we needed to prolong it as long as possible. Those memories of him skateboarding and riding his bicycle as a child washed over us both. We had wandered down there years before when the TV game show *Wheel of Fortune* was filming at night. That was one memory he spoke of as we sat together on the seawall. James finished his joint, which didn't really help, and he hobbled back to the car to drive the few blocks home.

*   *   *

Headaches had become more common now for James, and the swollen leg had reduced him to wearing sandals. He was worried about not being in shoes to attend school; but Gordon, the head of school, told me through his tears that just having James walk through the door meant everything. Attending school in his robe would have been fine as well. The school community was supportive and compassionate beyond anything we could have imagined. They welcomed the palliative team to create a support plan for the young men who would be devastated by James's death. The forward planning that was essential boggled my muddled mind. I trusted all the details to be taken care of by others. My only focus now was to keep James at home, calm and peaceful, away from hospital.

The Moleskine diaries were full of pages listing the increased dosages of drugs, with even more of them being converted to liquid to make them easier to swallow. James complained of a strange clicking noise in his head. He had bouts of grogginess for longer periods, but the relief found from the heavier doses was more important. James was now more tearful, worried, and very small in spirit. Fatigue—both his and mine—was becoming overwhelming, and we'd nap whenever possible. I would be up most of the night to aid with the nausea and dispensing of drugs. The marijuana continued to ease the headaches and helped with the stomach issues, but sadly, James had no appetite now.

The fridge in James's room was a godsend as many of the new drugs needed to be refrigerated. What had recently held the lovely Christmas tree now displayed a tidy system of spoons, syringes, jugs, cups, and tissues. Black towels, sadly recommended by the hospice team, were stored under the bed. A commode now sat next to the chest of drawers as the stairs to the main floor had become treacherous for James to negotiate when groggy.

My heart was breaking, and I could not make sense of our story; my tears were impossible now to hide. In late April James remained grateful for life and clung to all that was good. Even in these final weeks, he inspired with a remarkable wisdom far beyond his years and experience. Friends and family rallied with incredible generosity of spirit, and many gifts were left on the front stoop. Meals were organized (that James would never be able to eat), and Emma and Pat became the lynchpins in keeping the community not only informed but also at bay. It was all just too overwhelming.

The hospice nurses were vigilant, and the biweekly visits were morphing into daily ones. The Hospice chaplain Steven and the social worker made more regular visits in an attempt to engage James in a dialogue surrounding death so that perhaps they could help him process any worries. It was very difficult for James to go there, and he chose instead to cling to the latest music reviews or musing upon what living a bohemian life in New York might be like since Steven had remarked how James's room was like a loft. I found talking to both of them more comforting than James did, so we'd retreat downstairs for some quiet time while James rested.

I learned that existential pain can be a factor in the final days. Simply put, it is suffering with no clear connection to physical pain. Some consider it the spirit's struggle with separation. In my own view, this was true for James.

*   *   *

The final days of April had me updating CaringBridge with gratitude for these precious days with my darling son. I don't know when I was fully aware that he was dying; it just unfolded. I did not look for it but realize now that death will find you soon enough.

The last time James played his guitar

God, how I missed his strumming guitar in the evenings and ached for his laughter to trickle once again down the stairs. Like a broken record I reminded parents to hug their children and treasure every shared moment. It was my mantra now. Listening to folks whine about school applications and their children's accomplishments (or lack thereof) were steely daggers piercing the heart. Did they not understand how lucky they were?

Doctors DuBois and Ward made another house call that brought a smile to James, and he decided to go to school the day after their visit, even if for a short while; he missed his buddies and the faculty and wanted to be near them. He would attempt a school visit again on May 1, but it lasted just an hour. He left in tears, broken and terribly weak. He would not see his beloved school again. His refuge, community, and abiding friendships had been forged there.

Driving him back home was more painful than anything I had felt in a long time.

*   *   *

The daily updates for hospice were expanding as routines changed and drug doses increased. James's weeping was more common now, sometimes without tears. It was sometimes just a whimper combined with a pain in his chest. I learned going forward that there is a physical pain when the heart breaks.

The Stuart Hall senior class traditionally go on a retreat before graduation, and James planned to attend. It would take place from May 8 to 9 with the bulk of the time spent at the Headland Institute Retreat Centre in Marin, across the Golden Gate Bridge. Sergio, the school campus minister in charge of the details, invited James and me to take a look at the site to figure out logistics for his stay.

James awoke that morning in a lot of pain, short of breath, and full of cramps. We increased the methadone to 55 mg and upped the oxycodone and lorazepam to make the journey easier. James hobbled around the site on his cane, despondent and tearful. Sergio was patient and incredibly kind. We tried to figure out how it might work, and it was decided that I would need to be there and stay overnight with the boys in case James had to come home. James was worried about keeping his meds cold, and could he use his marijuana since it was government land? The details just seemed so terribly daunting for him.

We drove home in silence and stopped at a famous spot in the Headlands, overlooking the Golden Gate Bridge. James wanted to get out and look at the city that he loved so deeply. We sat on a bench for ages, and I took a couple of photos of him with the Golden Gate Bridge in the distance. He seemed peaceful for the moment and announced he would make up his mind about the retreat in a day or two. All decisions were moment by moment now.

James staring over San Francisco Bay

Reverend Jason stopped by to visit in the early evening. We held hands, and Jason said a prayer bedside. James was quiet during the visit, and I think we both found, in our own quiet ways, some peace in the words that promised respite from our anguish.

Jason's promise that there would be comforting arms to receive him and a deep love that could transcend all his pain and suffering was the answer James needed to hear; I don't know how much I believed it.

James took a shower that evening and fell on the floor getting out, missing the toilet by centimeters. I was terrified. It was his last shower.

* * *

The drug regime changed rapidly, and by April 30 James was receiving medication every four hours, a poignant reminder for me of a baby's four-hourly feeding schedule.

This was the new plan:

6:00-7:00 a.m.
cocktail, methadone, oxycodone, lorazepam

11:00 a.m.
gabapentin, reglan, cocktail

3:00 p.m.
methadone, cocktail, reglan

7:00 p.m.
gabapentin, cocktail, lorazepam, oxycodone, reglan

11:00 p.m.
gabapentin, cocktail, methadone, reglan, stool softener

3:00 a.m. (if awake)
repeat the 11:00 p.m. routine.

James now suffered excruciating pain from constipation brought on by all the meds as well as the tumours that were playing havoc with his organs. It was horrible to watch him writhe in such agony. The hospice nurses, in conjunction with his doctors, tried every conceivable stool softener, fibre drink, liquid, suppository laxative, and eventually enemas to bring relief. I was also now very conscious of and livid with reality that every beat of James's weakening heart, was continuing to pump blood into all the lesions, providing them food so that they could go on devouring him. My all-consuming rage towards cancer, which I had carefully hidden, escalated daily.

Jim, a male hospice nurse, had joined the team, and James felt secure and comfortable with him. He was a strong and capable man with a no-nonsense approach to any given situation. Whenever I was falling apart, Jim would pick up the slack and take charge. These hospice caregivers are remarkable human beings.

Once again, the Goldsmiths kindly took charge of Peter Gabriel as caring for James demanded every ounce of my energy and focus. James shared a long tearful hug with his precious white rabbit before Peter Gabriel was collected one evening in early May.

Sleeping upstairs gave me full opportunity to share the long nights. They were becoming more painfully troubled. James would wake often and need to vaporize just to be able to take his meds. He loved the BBC DVD *Planet Earth* and would find solace watching it whenever distressed. At two or three in the morning we'd watch flocks of birds flying over the Serengeti or schools of dolphin deep in the Great Barrier Reef. That he would find some peace in these programs was a welcome and unexpected gift.

James's father came one night, which gave him time to witness and share in James's decline. I was grateful to get a few hours of sleep without my head half-cocked.

The daily notes now spilled onto three to four pages with all the rapid changes that were taking place. Breathing shifted, drugs were tweaked, often multiple times, during the day. James's mood swings were plentiful. More often than not, he was weepy in between naps.

Our focus became the taking of drugs and finding positions of comfort. These sessions could go on for hours, and he would eventually collapse onto his pillows, fatigued from all the effort.

*   *   *

I was now briefed on what death looks like.

Rowena and Jim were clear with their instructions. I had a booklet provided by the hospice, explaining the steps. It was clinical, but I did not need comforting phrases right now. I had a growing sense that there would be plenty of time to melt into grief once we had gotten through these days.

Like birth, death is a process. Both rely on one breath. A period known as *active death* precedes that final breath. The body gradually shuts down as organs stop working.

Just as it is when giving birth, the body needs to find a "position of comfort" in which to die; there might be a lot of movement and shuffling in the bed. Bleeding is possible, hence the dark towels. There will be a release of body fluids from all openings. Suction might be required. Breathing becomes troubled. There might be fever. The hands and feet turn blue as the blood stops flowing to the extremities. The body should be kept cool and not wrapped up. Offers of liquid and food should be avoided; once a person is in active death, you do not want to awaken the organs as increased pain can result. A quiet, calm room is ideal. It is believed that hearing is the last sense to go, so the dying can hear what is going on, even if seemingly unaware.

One of the greatest pieces of advice from Hospice was that very often, after the last breath is taken, the dying will shed one last tear. No one knows if it is a tear of relief or sorrow, but I was so grateful to have this information in advance and kept a carefully ironed hankie close by to catch this last tear. I am not sure why it meant so much to me, but I suppose it represented a link to the physical and that would be all that I would have left of my beloved son.

*   *   *

James turned a corner on May 2. His breathing became more agonized, and the doses of all his medicines had to be increased multiple times throughout the day. His stomach hurt, and he could sip only small amounts of liquid. You could see and feel the lesion in his distended gut.

At five the next morning James asked me to help him die.

He wanted me to compose a letter, and when I asked him what to write, he said, "Help me." I assured him I would do everything to help him find comfort, we all would, but that I could not aid his death. I could not live with that, but I promised him that Rowena, the doctors, and Jim—everyone would do all they could to make his death easier for him.

From that moment on I would absolutely understand the wish for assisted suicide when a patient can no longer go on. It felt like it was cruel and unusual punishment to prolong the suffering that was leading to the inevitable. I had never thought I could support such a stand, but now I see its merit and wish that lawmakers could engage in an intelligent debate on the matter.

My promise to James to make him comfortable and ease his horrid suffering was my only priority. The team convened on a call to create the plan for the coming hours/days. Two of James's teachers, Sergio and Ray, stopped by in the early afternoon to see him. It was terribly emotional, but James was able to have a good, hard cry which I hope brought some relief. His decline was rapid, and for the first time I wrote in the daily notes, "It is not fair to keep him here."

I called Robin as well as Hospice to see what I needed to do. I was overwhelmed by the dreadful feeling of treading in quicksand.

Phenobarbital was introduced to ease convulsions. Methadone was increased to 65 mm. Oxycodone was also increased. Since James's liver was consumed by cancer, it could not process the medicines properly, so the drugs were now administered by syringe (without a needle) orally, under his tongue. The liquid would absorb into his system much faster. We tried to space the doses out, but many had to be administered every few hours as he was in such agony.

The sensory levels in his room were kept low and quiet. James used oxygen constantly now, and the whoosh of the tank on the floor below was sometimes the only sound in the flat.

Robin suggested that it would be thoughtful for James to receive his graduation diploma while still aware. He would know that he had accomplished what he set out to do this year at school. We made the request to the head of schools, and at 3:00 p.m. on May 4, a small contingent of faculty presented James with his diploma, bedside.

It was beyond desolate. James wondered why they were doing this *now* as he was still aware that graduation day was in June. The teachers and the head were all crying while they made the presentation. James wailed and nothing could console him. I worried we had made a terrible mistake, especially as we had been warned not to agitate him. Struggling to try and make it "normal" we took some photos of his award for him. They all hugged and gave James their congratulations, promising to see one another soon. No one had the heart to say goodbye to him.

Since we already had this presentation scheduled for that afternoon, Sergio asked if some of the boys could come to see James as well. The team decided that since he was going to be stimulated and agitated, it might be better to do it all in one swoop, so a couple of mothers, Priyanka and Marcella, picked up a number of his classmates from school and shuttled them over to the house. The boys went up to his room a couple at a time so as not to overwhelm, and it was a continuation of tragic hugs and farewells.

James was especially sad to see his closest friends, the ones who had played music with and carried him these final months. The boys bravely chatted about the next barbeque and looked forward to sharing the upcoming retreat as a way to lift James's spirits. Sergio brought a cake to set out on the dining-room table so the boys could celebrate this graduation ceremony. I have no idea who served it or what else they might have had to eat or drink. I was numb.

That afternoon James received word that he had been accepted at the University of Chicago. His application had been a last-minute one after meeting President Obama. Before he fell into another sleep, James told me, "We have to tell Obama—he'd be proud."

James's diploma sat bedside so that he could see it in the coming days. He was deeply distressed that evening as to why they had given it to him early, but within twenty-four hours, he would no longer be aware of its presence.

James became feisty in the late evening and quite assertive. Thank goodness I had been warned that this is also a piece of the death puzzle. He got a bee in his bonnet that he wanted to go to the loo on the main floor and was determined to go down the stairs. It was scary as he was more sedated and extra support was needed while negotiating the steps. The night was troubled with him climbing in and out of his bed.

James started pushing me aside and told me multiple times, "You are in the way." Rowena warned that with his electrolytes all out of whack, James would become more agitated and "goofy." He could say and do things that might hurt or not make any sense. It was important to stay on task and pay attention so that he would not get hurt. She reassured me that nothing I was doing was wrong and that I must not take anything to heart.

The next afternoon two of James's friends came to visit; Michael, who had just flown in from Colorado and Andrew. James picked up immediately upon seeing them, and he got out of bed, sat on the new chair in his room, and chatted about evening plans. He was lucid and bright and seemed very much like the old James. It was a shocking transformation. He told the boys to go up the hill to ZA, their favourite pizza restaurant on Hyde Street, and he'd get dressed and walk up to meet them there. They agreed that it was a great idea and stayed a bit longer to visit. James was chipper and ready to meet them later. The boys left, and he fell back into his bed.

At six that evening, James awoke, confused and agitated once again. He did not know where he was, and sat on the chair to cry. He thought he was downstairs, then upstairs. I was once again in the way. He said goodbye and climbed back into bed. Of course he did not get dressed and walk to ZA. That suggestion of pizza with his buddies would become lovingly known as his last hurrah.

*   *   *

I was afraid now that I could not handle James at night since I was once again on my own. He was a big powerful young man, even in his current state, and if he wanted to do something, it would be tough for me to rein him in. In a bit of a desperate state, I called Marc and asked if he might come and stay with me since I was on my own and might need an extra pair of hands during the dark hours. He willingly came and sat on the stairs most of the night to be at the ready should I need him.

James awoke to say he missed school. He would be in and out of sleep for hours. While asleep he waved his arms and reached up towards the ceiling. At another time he said he was "fucking miserable" and he "had to die." During the early hours of the next day he awoke, crying without tears, and said aloud, "Half of life is a game," and then "I wanted the red ones," and "Press letter A" I will forever wonder what was going through his head.

In rereading these daily notes to write this book, I am amazed at how rapidly James slipped. I had tucked these small journals into a bag and not opened them for four years; yet the details and emotions remain ripe.

The doses of medicines were increased, and I wrote how James growled like a bear caught in a trap. "Weepy anxiety" best described his state.

On the night of May 6 Marc sat with me yet again. During the very early morning hours James was determined to go downstairs to the loo and started spitting out his medicines. I was becoming frantic as I knew how much he needed the comfort they would provide. Marc finally made a deal with James. If he would take his medicines, Marc would let him go downstairs. James agreed and swallowed the lot.

Marc, using his powerful back, draped James over his shoulders and, with my dear broken son flopped in that position, helped him down the stairs to the master bathroom. It took twenty agonizing minutes to get there. Once on the toilet, James slammed the door, and we waited patiently outside. He did not need to do anything other than assert himself, and when he was ready to leave the room, Marc helped him up. James announced groggily he wanted to climb into my bed. We escorted him to my bedroom, and then I was worried that he needed his drugs, which were all upstairs.

For the first time, I said aloud, "He needs to die in his own bed."

It was painful to watch while Marc lifted James and partially dragged him to the stairs. James attempted to walk but was terribly unsteady. Going back up the stairs took much longer. James collapsed into his bed and never asked to go downstairs again. Marc would say later that it was "a man thing" and important for James to have that moment.

In the early morning James awoke and announced, "I have stayed too long. Move over, I am trying to go." It is not uncommon for those who are dying to speak of a journey they are going on. Some ask for their passports or a suitcase. James's movement of pushing away and lifting his arms signalled his need to travel on as well. Those who have sat with the dying talk of the veil that the spirit moves between in the final hours of life. Some who are dying speak of passing through a doorway, a wall, or walking along a corridor. I was fully aware now of the unravelling of James's physical form, but where he was going and what he saw will always remain a mystery.

*   *   *

May 7 was my mother's birthday, and she had just had knee replacement surgery in Canada and was therefore unable to come to see James in these final weeks. That would always leave her heartbroken, but I am grateful now that she was spared that sorrow. Sometimes it is better to remember our loved ones as they were. There was nothing to be gained by witnessing the horror of his dying. It would have been too much for any grandparent.

James awoke in the early morning and said, "All for you, Mama. I am so sick." His eyes seemed darker and he was much weaker.

Sergio came by with Patter, James's art teacher, at eight before school to pray, perform a simple meditation, and leave a relic of the founder of the Scared Heart network as a talisman to keep by James's bed. He appeared to recognize them and stood up as they were about to leave to share a group hug. With our arms wrapped around each other's shoulders, James raised his head and uttered what would be his final words: "This is all bullshit."

Chapter 15

The Last Tear

It is all downhill, so the getting there is easy. I can't let go, but have no say in the matter now.
—Personal journal entry, 2009

A heat wave had settled over the city during the past twelve hours, making the flat very warm. The door to the roof was left open, allowing some breeze to float in, but it was really becoming unbearable. I can't recall who it was, but someone from the inner circle went to Walgreens to get a fan that was placed at the end of James's bed, and it provided blessed relief. I worried it might make him uncomfortable, forgetting that he was unconscious and therefore external discomfort, such as a possible cool breeze, was probably not even noticed. Reality was staring me in the face, and yet I still swam in the pool of denial.

The afternoon of the seventh saw an increase in all the meds. ACE had created Phenobarbitol discs that were inserted rectally. Once we got over our discomfort of the process, the drug did seem to bring James some comfort. Staying focused on this important work now was all that mattered, and any inhibitions were tossed aside.

Marc, Emma, and Pat checked in constantly and took turns sitting with me. James was resting peacefully, and while there was some moaning, he did not appear agitated. Soft classical music played in the background. The heat lessened slightly when a late-afternoon fog rolled in, but the door to the rooftop was kept ajar nonetheless.

What motivated him, I don't know, but at 6:00 p.m., James crawled out of bed, for what would be his last time, to use the commode. He collapsed back on the sheets afterwards. Shifting him up and down in bed became the activity over the coming hours. I had been warned that this would be important now as James needed to find his position of comfort in which to die.

James's father came that evening to stay over, and feeling nauseated from fatigue, I told him I must lie down on my own bed for a few hours. He stayed with James upstairs, and I collapsed fully clothed on my pillows at 2:00 a.m.

At seven I bolted upright and cried out loud, "Oh my god, you are dead!" Running up the stairs, I found James curled up in a ball at the end of the bed, which he had just wet. I barked at his father to get dry sheets and to help me clean things up. My fuse was short. Tension was palpable. Rowena arrived then and helped to hold James while the sheets were changed around him. He was sponged and left without any clothes on other than disposable underwear. Just a top sheet would suffice. Hospital-blue waterproof pads now lined the bed.

Not until all these tasks were taken care of did I fully realize that James was unconscious. He showed no signs of recognition. His skin was clammy grey, and his dark eyes were partially closed. His breath was slow and measured.

*   *   *

May 8 unfolded slowly. Hospice checked in throughout the day to take James's vital signs and to offer whatever support and encouragement might be needed for the coming hours. We were entering the final stages of active death. What did I need? I did not have a clue.

Rowena sat down with me in the living room and went through all the drugs to make sure the doses were at their peak performance. She spoke to ACE Pharmacy, who would end up delivering a couple of times that day. The team had an arsenal of ideas and solutions to help us through this awful scenario. I left it entirely up to them to direct us.

Marc came early in the morning and remained. He was wonderfully patient and strong lifting James to find better positions, sometimes climbing on to the bed, hoisting my limp son under his arms and moving him up on to his well-loved pile of pillows. Marc had never before been involved intimately with someone so ill, on the cusp of death, but he was a perfect assistant and friend through those long, sad hours.

I called Emma at the Well to say that James was dying, and she dropped everything, asked Pat to take over, and came to spend the rest of the time with us. She would sit quietly and hold my hand or leave me alone. Her ability to read my needs was amazing. Pat would be in and out with us for the afternoon and evening as well. I recall that at some point she brought food for everyone, which was appreciated as none of us had eaten since the day before.

I took time while James rested to place a call to Pacific Interment to confirm that the arrangements were in place for his cremation, whenever that might be. I had spoken to them a few days earlier to discuss the details of how the process worked. They would collect his body when directed by us and then hold him in safekeeping until the cremation ceremony. Hospice would take care of registering his death and also contact Pacific Interment after he died. It's impossible to describe the sickening misery I felt while making these plans.

James's medicines were constantly tweaked over the coming hours:

2:00 a.m. pheno 200 mg and methadone 160 mg

3:00 a.m. lorazepam 4 ml and cocktail

6:40 a.m. lorazepam and cocktail

8:00 a.m. methadone 120

8:30 a.m. pheno 300

9:10 a.m. methadone 40 mg and lorazepam 3 ml

10:10 a.m. lorazepam 4 ml.

If agitated around eleven, go back to 4 pheno 300 mg every 3 hours, lorazepam every hour, cocktail every 4 hours.

15 mls of oxycodone if *any* sign of pain

Reverend Jason stopped by midmorning and delivered the last rites. He had done this three times over the past days as James had slipped so rapidly. In time, we would find humour in the fact that James had received more blessings than anyone Jason knew. His calming presence as well as that of Reverend Jennifer was welcome anytime as we all felt completely comfortable with them.

By late morning I was feeling nervous and edgy. James looked so awful and empty. How had he gotten to this place? What had seemed improbable a year ago was now inevitable. This unravelling of his life story had occurred too quickly. Hadn't we fought this outcome every step of the way? Why were our efforts so futile? Had I failed him so completely? I did not want him to suffer any longer but dreaded letting him go. This internal struggle only amplified as the hours passed.

Sitting at the end the of the bed, looking up his broken body towards his head, I saw James as a perfect rendering of the painting by Mantegna, *Lamentation of Christ*. I massaged his cold feet. As forewarned, his extremities were turning blue. His long elegant fingers and toes lay gently atop one another, making him look like carved marble.

Marc, an accomplished photographer, took photos of his hands and feet. I was desperate to save every moment. I held James's cold hands for hours, which Marc captured on his camera. One of these pictures became the cover of the funeral program and is also included in this book. I feel there is nothing morbid about having these photos, which now have become some of my most treasured.

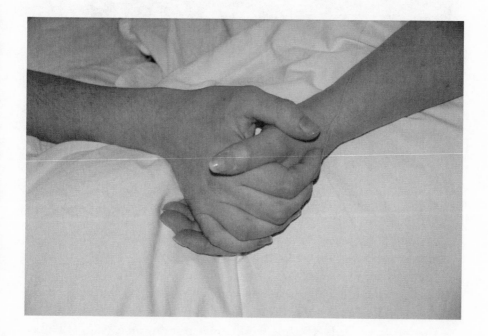

While James lay silently, it was possible to see the lesions protruding through his skin. Many of them had created deep red stretch marks; internal bleeding had begun. Dr. Dubois called to check in and said he would stop by when finished at the hospital about three that afternoon. He could not believe the dramatic shift in James since his last meeting and was very sad. He checked the heart and blood pressure and assisted with the admission of some meds. Dr. Dubois, Marc, and Jim, who had by now joined us for part of the afternoon, hovered over James to shift his body for more Phenobarbitol. What possessed me I don't know, but I took a photo of the three of them bending over the bed caring for James. It is a powerful picture filled with their urgency to care for this dying boy.

Dr Stevie, Marc and Jim caring for James May 8, 2009

You cannot see James, but their backs tell the whole story. James's doctor, his valued new friend, stayed for quite a while, holding hands and watching over him. But for the cancer James was a robust and healthy young man; the team warned that it might take a long time for his heart to give up the fight. James's spirit of survival and living big would be his legacy that day.

The subject of the DNR paperwork came up at this time, and Dr. Dubois asked if we had signed it. I had not even taken the bag from the armoire in my room. He suggested we look at the contents together.

DNR, Do Not Resuscitate, a carbon form in triplicate, will let emergency services know that this is your wish should they be called to assist. By law, paramedics have to do *all* they can to revive a patient, but by signing this form, they will not resuscitate or take actions beyond providing comfort. As a parent, I would do anything for my child, so it went against every bone in my body to put pen to paper.

The doctor gently explained that due to the many tumours in James's chest and lungs, any CPR or pushing would actually puncture the lesions, break his rib cage (due to his now fragile bones), cause extreme bleeding, and certainly exacerbate a very painful death. It was the hardest signature I ever made, but it was agreed upon and even though the decision could be revoked at any time, I prayed that it would not become an issue.

Vials of solutions used at the end of life—some to dry up mucous membranes, others to prevent seizures—were lined up and added to the collection of bedside drugs. It was all too clinical and awful, but now the time had come to make educated decisions.

The doctor gave James the biggest hug before leaving and thanked him for being in his life. It hurt us all to watch James die. This vile disease had thrust total strangers together whose lives would be forever entwined. Somewhere, buried deep inside this sorrow and loss, there would be a gift that we could acknowledge given time.

Late in the afternoon while we sat vigil, Sergio arrived with a huge envelope filled with letters for James. He climbed onto the bed, put James's head in his lap, and proceeded to read aloud every letter. Teachers, administrators, friends, his classmates, all had sent him a note filled with the most amazing sentiments, professing their love and respect. Their longing and sorrow was deep, and it was poignant and agonizing to listen to their words.

Sergio was gentle and spoke softly, reminding James who this person was or where that faculty classroom was located. He spent over two hours reading aloud these notes and then pulled out his laptop, which had a message from his classmates all shouting, "Hey, James!", "Love you, guy!", "See you soon!", You're the man!", "Get back here to play some music!" They toasted him with soda cans, a cacophony of joy and nonsense.

There was no reaction from James, but I cling to the hope that he heard them and that their words made him feel loved and peaceful. Sergio also presented his Tibetan prayer bowl for us to use. I had not rung one before, and the sound was mesmerizing. Buddhist monks use these bowls prior to their meditations to open up and cleanse the energy of any given space. We each took turns ringing the bowl, but it was Marc who took possession of it, and he would create mystical sounds for hours going forward.

James remained still, and except for a few small groans, he made no sound. The hours stretched on, and his father and I took turns lying next to him on the bed. I whispered my love in his ears and repeated over and over that it was all right for him to leave. How I found the words and strength to say this I don't know, but the palliative and hospice team had told me that often the dying will hold on for a loved one, prolonging death and their suffering. If James was lingering in any way for us, then he must be given permission to let go and find some peace.

Throughout the long, quiet afternoon I became aware of a presence. I felt that there was something at the end of James's bed and was sensitive to this new energy in the room. At the time I wondered if it was my father's spirit coming to help, but in the coming days and months, I became convinced that it was James, and when I jolted awake at seven in the morning, he had come to say goodbye. Some will think me mad, but I have always had a deep sense that the energy of the dead is powerful and can manifest in many ways. If James was there, watching over us, it brings me great solace.

Many who have experienced near death speak of the spirit leaving the body and hovering over the room. When they "return" to their bodies, they can articulate sights, sounds, and experiences that are amazing in their truthful detail. Since James was now just a body with no sign of life but for a beating heart, I am left to wonder if his spirit had indeed "shuffled off this mortal coil" and if he had found that place that mystifies all who are left behind. I will never know what is waiting until my time comes, but there were so many indications that day of larger powers that it does provoke greater thought.

The afternoon slipped into evening with the steady doses of medicines being administered and documented in the Moleskine journal. James became colder and paler, but his heart kept beating, and there was a slight pulse. Dr. Dubois had explained that his lungs might fill with fluid, which would make James's death less stressful for him. If internal bleeding occurred, it might cause greater pain. I was desperately clinging to the former as I could not bear the thought of him suffering any more.

At eleven fifteen that night, James was given another dose of pheno, and something shifted. He coughed and lurched forward, shocking us. We laid him down gently, and as had been forewarned, fluids started coming out of his mouth and nose. The suction machine was produced, and I attempted to clean out his mouth and airways, but it quickly became too much for me, so Emma and James's father took over, insisting I sit down.

The bottom fell out, and I became hysterical. A terror crashed in all around me, and through my tears, I gasped that it was time to call again for Hospice help. We were amateurs, and this was getting too huge. I picked up my mobile phone, dialled the Hospice number, and asked for a nurse to come as soon as possible.

*   *   *

There is an angel, a midwife of death. Her name is Jeanne.

The gate and outside door were left open and unlocked for her arrival. What felt like an eternity was really only about twenty minutes, and I could not have been happier to hear her measured steps as she approached the bedroom.

Jeanne was a formidable presence, solid and tranquil, soft-spoken, professional, and ethereal. She wore black and arrived carrying a large black medical bag. I recall she had soft beautiful clear skin with rosy cheeks, and she instantly reminded me of the nurse who had helped at James's birth—a no-nonsense, ruddy-faced woman who looked as if she came from rural Cornwall. The maternity nurse was all business; she knew how to get things done and took charge when others were fumbling.

Sadly, here we were again at the end of life, giving birth to death, with a dire need for someone to take charge. Immediately, Jeanne took James's vital signs, felt his body, and suctioned out his mouth and airways. She was assertive with the tube, and I realized, even more, how useless we had been. I thanked God and James that she was there. Her demeanour was amazingly serene, and she almost whispered the instructions to us.

A bowl of cold water ("Please add some ice cubes"), clean towels, and a few rags. When presented with these items, Jeanne turned her attention to those in the room, asking them to step away from the bed and sit down and then suggested that I lie down next to James. This would become the moment of greatest intimacy in my life. It was just James and me with this angel hovering over us both.

She whispered, "James has a fever, so we must cool him down."

Ice cloths were prepared in the bowl and laid on his torso. Almost immediately his temperature dropped; I could see the external thermometer drop to below 30 almost instantly. She asked me to get close and hold his head and shoulders and lean him on the pillow. When she first arrived in the room, we had shifted his body up in the bed again to open his airways. It is helpful to slightly elevate the body during these crucial minutes to ease the final breaths.

I whispered in his ear that I would miss him but somehow I would be okay. He must not stay any longer. It was time to go. I repeated over and over, "I love you."

After long hours of his strong heart beating, James's jaw dropped, and he instantly resembled a ninety-year-old man. He sucked in and gurgled, emitting the worst possible sound imaginable, the death rattle. I watched his pulse on his neck, and then a sigh escaped. I was fixated on his neck. There was no more movement.

"No! No! Please, one more breath. *Please*," I pleaded.

"James is dead," Jeanne barely whispered.

As predicted by Hospice, one large tear fell from James's right eye and rolled down his cheek. I captured it in my hankie, and it remains to this day safely wrapped in plastic and tucked in a box. The last living piece of his story was a tear.

Checkmate.

*   *   *

Truth

He died before his heart could be broken
By unrequited love
Or an unfaithful partner
Or a lie that would cut in half those two fragile chambers.

He died before his manhood could be found and exploited
No mistakes made.
No conquests to boast of
No seduction of position
Or accomplishment
To make him unbearable.

He died before all my stories were revealed
Never to know the heartache or joys
Or spectacles
That had become my shadow walk.

We were two souls colliding
Finally at a point of maturity
Where all could be shared
Without judgment or fear
Of looking foolish.
A mother and son about to embark on adulthood together.

Instead I cup your beautiful porcelain skin in my hands
How blue you are. How cold.
My now chiselled, sunken marble son so pure and simple
And free of suffering.

While your pain ends, mine is just beginning.
Its cloak waits patiently bedside
To become my mantle.

—Jean Alice Rowcliffe, March 2010

Chapter 16

Postmortem

There is no greater gift of charity you can give than helping a person to die well.

—Sogyal Rinpoche

When I am gone the cold fog will still nip your nose.
When I am gone the morning dew will still linger on the grass.
When I am gone only those who knew and loved me will be changed.
—James, 2002 (ten years old)

After death.

It had taken the same number of hours for James to die as for him to be born. The same urgency and focus had been applied to both.

We cried and held each other for the longest time. Each took turns hugging and kissing James. Surpassing all others, it was the worst moment of my life. I cannot speak for the others, but I do believe we would all be changed because of this experience. Jeanne stood quietly offering hugs but did not say anything. There are no words.

After a while she said that time of death must be established. She would choose 1:45 a.m. Did we agree to this? Lying next to James, holding his hands, which were already tightening around my fingers, I asked Jeanne if she would say a prayer. She picked up a book by Marianne Williamson that Sergio had left. Opening it she randomly picked a page, and even though I can't recall the words now, I remember thinking at that moment that they were perfect.

Extreme shock had started its slow quiet dance. Crying was the only sound in the room. Jeanne allowed us this and excused herself to make phone calls downstairs. She would proceed to register James's death, confirm with

Hospice the details and time for their records, and call the undertaker to set their wheels in motion.

It had been decided a day or two before that whenever James died we would have a visitation at the house. I, especially, did not want to see him in a coffin under yellow lights at a funeral home. Since it was hot, we could only have the body in the home for twenty-four hours max. If visitation was to be longer, there would need to be dry ice brought in, and Rowena had warned that this was a difficult option to put in place, given the circumstances.

Jeanne suggested that we prepare James, bathe and dress him while she worked downstairs. The icy bowl was emptied and replaced with warm water and olive-scented soap. Large soft towels were collected from the linen cupboard and a lovely new shirt taken from James's cupboard. In retrospect, I am amazed at how focused we were. The task of caring for James's body became bigger than acknowledging death. The shock-infused adrenaline had kicked in and would carry me for days going forward.

Each of us helped prepare James's body. We moved him to the new couch while we quickly changed seats, and he sat there appearing like a sleeping boy; it had not yet registered that he was dead, gone. His body was just a form now that we were manipulating. We wondered if we could leave him sitting and then move him in the morning back to his bed, but Jeanne assured us that rigor mortis would soon set in and moving his body later would be impossible.

It did not take long before James was clean, his hair washed and combed, lying peacefully in his bed, wearing the green plaid shirt he had just purchased. I thought of all the bath times shared over the years and how he giggled with joy, splashing and blowing bubbles.

Now his once-beaming eyes were partially open, and Jeanne suggested we put a penny on each lid to help close them over the coming hours. His hands were folded across his lower chest.

To say that partaking in these preparations was surreal is an understatement, and yet there was an element of them being truly sacred, and we felt privileged to be the ones taking care of James at the end.

*   *   *

James was dead. What did that mean? How could it be? How were we able to bathe and dress him and lay him out in bed as if an everyday occurrence? What do we do now? How did this happen? How do I ever let him leave this room, his only home? It could not be true. Couldn't this awfulness have been prevented? Something was going to change; we'd discover that all that we had been through was just a dream. In the morning I would find him awake playing his guitar and life would carry on as normal. The swirling irrational whispers that would drive me mad were beginning to seep through the cracks and circle the room.

After James was settled we set about to tidy the space and get rid of all the detritus of this horrid day. The oxygen tanks were hauled to the garage along with the suction machine, which thankfully, someone took care of cleaning to spare me that horror. Unable to look at them again, I threw away the bowls, towels, and rags that had been part of this process. At three in the morning we were stuffing all these things in bins in the garage. Attending to these new unwanted details sucked all remaining energies.

Some order was brought to the room; windows were left open and the fan running to keep the room cool. Jeanne asked to see all the medicines and scooped them up into her custody in a large plastic bag. Most of them were controlled substances and as such had to be accounted for, a fact that had totally eluded me. She arranged with Pacific Interment to arrive at eight o'clock that evening, after the visitation, to take James to Emeryville to await cremation.

Emma and Marc left around three thirty in the morning. James's father slept on the Aerobed that seemed to be permanently set up in the dining room. I stumbled to the back of the flat and was confronted by the rooms that had become dumping grounds this past week. Things that had been tossed into the office were piled up: mail in bundles and papers strewn about the place, stacks of laundry (what was clean? dirty?). It was a disaster. I closed the door on the mess and turned to my bedroom where all of James's blankets, comforters, and pillows had been gathered. Somehow I cut a path to my bed and collapsed numb in a heap, once again fully clothed.

Before closing my eyes I managed to post on CaringBridge the awful message that James had died.

May 9
Grief is the price of love.

By nine o'clock in the morning the senior class retreat was under way, with the young men out in Marin fields working on building fences. They knew by now that James had died, and it was a miserable day for them with many unable to stop crying. In striving to find peace with this, some of the boys and faculty had decided that the only way James could attend the class retreat was as a spirit since his body would not carry him there. It reminded us of President Obama's grandmother's death just before the election—her way of being able to attend as well. This belief eased some of the deep sorrow for many of the boys going forward that day, and it was profoundly moving that these young men already had a bourgeoning understanding of the spiritual.

To be expected, my sleep was troubled. Wild images and memories collided into one another. Fatigue exacerbated my ability to process any of what had transpired, and I awoke in a cold sweat, having dozed for just a few hours. I raced upstairs, but sadly nothing had changed. James still lay there, quietly in his bed., hands folded, eyes partially closed. He had a slight smile on his lips—had that been there a few hours ago? The smell of a warm dawn filtered into the room. Damn. It was *all* true. I could feel a void expanding around me with every second that passed.

Emma and Pat somehow arrived midmorning, arms full of flowers, to set out vases in James's room and around the flat. They were both exhausted and yet willing still to scoop me up and take charge of all the details that needed to be attended to. This gift can never be fully acknowledged—they were beyond remarkable.

As I showered and dressed, they took my address book and compiled names and numbers of folks to be notified. The visitation would take place in the afternoon between 3:00 and 5:00 p.m. Having zero idea what to do or how to organize any of this, others thankfully stepped in to orchestrate. Furniture was shifted around the flat and extra chairs set in the bedroom. Who did this and brought the coffee, made tea, baked treats, and fed the mourners, I have no idea.

This was all just taken care of, and I will always be so grateful. Community shows its strength and compassion during these difficult times. Marc and Pat stood as gatekeepers at the front door to make sure only close friends came to visit. I was aware that since there were so many following James's story on the blog, the visitation could become a circus, and I did not want just anyone wandering in. Even though a public moment, I was desperate to maintain some privacy.

At 3:00 p.m. the steady pace of footsteps started to ascend the steep flight of stairs to the flat. Because the upper bedroom was small, only a few would go up at a time to say goodbye to James, allowing an intensely intimate moment for all. Rowena was the first to arrive, and she sat next to me, mostly in silence. We both marvelled at how handsome James looked, and with his hair bushed back, you would never know that he had lost a big patch on the top of his head; some of the protruding tumours were hidden. He looked tranquil and beautiful, and I was so relieved that we had decided to keep him at home.

James adored this place. His bedroom was his sanctuary. He hated the hospital, and being able to spend his final days and hours in the place that brought him such joy was a blessing. He died surrounded by the things he loved, listening to music in his room, smelling the evening air on a hot night, hearing the foghorn blaring by the bridge, even the crazy parrots of Telegraph Hill serenaded during the final hours. As awful as death is, James had been given as good a death as we could muster, and I cling to the thought that his spirit was happy and content to have been allowed the gift of his own space for his last tear.

I started to ponder that afternoon about how much nicer it was to die at home versus a clinical hospital. Witnessing death is awful and it will hurt, wherever it occurs. Somehow the thought of being in a generic sterile setting surrounded by beeping machines that eventually flatline seems to add another layer of horror to the finale. Of course, we don't always get the choice of how or where we will die, and as I sat there next to my beloved son I became overwhelmed by a difficult sorrow realizing how awful it must be for parents whose child dies due to an accidental or violent death. How *devastating* not to be able to hold them and say goodbye. Even with my profound loss, I felt incredible gratitude.

If death at home is an option for the family, I would like to see us advocate and provide more support services for it. It used to be this way. The large wooden tables in rural kitchens were especially built for birth and laying out of the dead. It was expected that dying at home was a ritual that the community participated in. I cannot mandate that one is better than the other, but after this intensely intimate experience with James, I felt relieved that he could be at home, and I think deep down he was grateful too. We spared him those hours after death in the dreaded basement corridors of UCSF, wheeled out on a shrouded gurney by a stranger in a dark suit. I had managed, at least, to keep that promise.

*   *   *

The day wore on, and I have no recollection of who came to say farewell. It was a sea of faces, and while I might have appeared social, it was all a façade. In all honesty and without wanting to appear rude, I don't know who I spoke with or acknowledged.

The only group I do recall was James's classmates. The teachers made it possible for any of the boys who wanted to leave the retreat to come back to the city and pay their last respects to do so. A bus was made available to transport them. A steady stream of young men came to James's bedside, and their sorrow was beyond agonizing. For most, this was their first viewing of a dead body, and knowing it was their friend made it even more painful. It was a difficult and harrowing experience, but I was so proud of them to have the courage and deep affection to say goodbye. I know this has stayed with many of the young men to this day, and they share with me the certainty that James continues to be an influence from afar.

After most of the people had left and only a few remained behind I was suddenly aware of the time. At 8:00 p.m. the undertaker was going to arrive to collect James. I was not ready to let him go. In fact, I was adamant that he was going to stay. Rowena sat me down and firmly explained that James had to be collected. We did not have ice for him, and it was too hot. Tomorrow would be Mother's Day, and "You cannot have your dead son here on Mother's Day." She was right, I suppose, but letting go of him that evening was more dire than I could have imagined.

The bell rang promptly, and up the stairs they came with a collapsible stretcher. They were a middle-aged African American couple (could they be married?), very solemn and polite. I could not bear to watch the proceedings, and Marc escorted them upstairs to the bedroom. As they ascended the stairs, I begged that they not put James in a body bag, but California law said they had to. This triggered some powerful tears. Everything started tumbling again all around me.

Marc assisted them upstairs, and then to spare me the thumping sound of the stretcher coming down, he offered to help carry it. Within a few minutes, they had all the details attended to, and James's body, now very much dead weight, shrouded in the burgundy-coloured bag, was very slowly carried down the stairs. In total, there were over thirty-nine steps that they had to traverse, and I know it was incredibly difficult; in every sense of the word the weight was amplified. The assembled few watched, cried, and followed them out onto the street. That Marc was the one to help carry James on the final descent felt right somehow since he had been so instrumental in helping James climb the stairs to the main floor just a few days earlier. A man thing.

The evening was cool after the heat of the day and the sky crystal clear. Not always possible, I could see stars above Polk Street. These strangers pushed my precious shrouded son into the back of a van, closed the doors, gave me their card, and asked me to call the company in the morning to discuss further details. Pat held my shaking body while the van pulled away slowly and drove down the hill towards to the Maritime Museum. I walked into the middle of the street and watched until it was gone from sight. How could I let them take James from me? I became hysterical. Who were they? Where was he going? I had just allowed total strangers to steal my son. Oh, God, no! I continued to spiral into madness.

*   *   *

I was told after the retreat that James's presence was everywhere with the young men. The boys talked of him and reminisced while Keaton played James's acoustic guitar around the beach campfire. Candlelit paper lanterns were set free over the ocean while the boys meditated.

Sergio, a vocal proponent for the value of ritual in our lives, made sure that the boys had a way to express their gratitude and sorrow in multiple ways during the retreat. The boys collectively painted a large white bowl that was then smashed and each took a piece of the ceramic, wrapped it in wire, and manipulated it into a necklace. Sergio gave me a crafted necklace in the coming days. This ritual of painting and breaking the bowl has now become an important component of the senior retreat for each graduating class.

Apparently, one of the most powerful moments of the retreat occurred in the early evening. Sergio had taken another Tibetan prayer bowl to share with the boys during a service of remembrance. These heavy bowls are made of solid brass and are, I would think, pretty indestructible. Just as Sergio was about to begin, the bowl fell to the earth, splitting in two. It was not a hard fall or sufficient enough impact to have caused the break. All assembled decided that James had sent the message that he was indeed there with them.

The two pieces of the broken bowl were incorporated into James's funeral service and now have a place of honour at the school.

On Monday, May 11, I met with the undertakers on Folsom Street to discuss the next steps. The death certificate had to be signed and arrangements for the cremation set in motion. Doris accompanied me and took me out to lunch afterwards. Again, sadly, I have few recollections of any of this day and depend on my journal to remind me of the details. The cremation was set for 1:00 p.m. on Thursday. The memorial for James would be held at Grace Cathedral on Saturday, May 16, and his ashes would be ready for collection on the Friday to be incorporated into the service.

A day or two after James's death, I asked Marc to bring his camera to photograph James's bed. After his body was removed the sheets had stayed as they were, and they looked like a swoosh of draped marble. The bed would stay like this, frozen in time, for months.

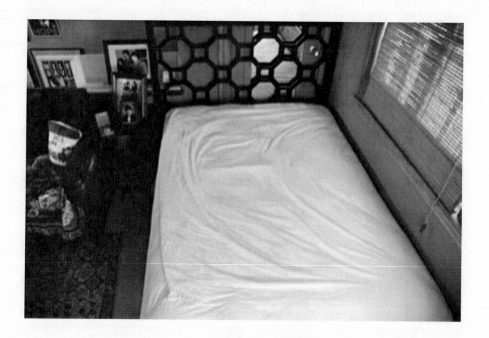

James's empty bed

Planning the memorial service took a few afternoons with the ministers. When I realized that James was not going to survive, I had started to listen to hymns at night on the computer. As if being guided, I tried to have many details in place, or at least considered, so that the bulk of these decisions would not have to be negotiated after he had died.

What motivated me, I will never know, but it was a huge help during that first week. I had a list of over sixty songs that felt appropriate, and eventually they were whittled down to the ones that became part of the service. A couple of mothers with graphic design backgrounds from the Village Well community kindly helped produce the program for the service, and one of the fathers generously donated the printing of them.

Lori, the computer teacher at school, offered to put together the slide show of photos that would be shown during the reception. She had many of the young men helping to edit and choose the background music, and it ended up a beautiful presentation of James's short life. So many kind souls stepped in and did what was needed to ease us through those impossible days of transition. I felt deep gratitude even as my all-consuming sorrow escalated.

On May 18, I wrote on CaringBridge that grief, replacing denial, would now be my silent constant companion, and with slow deliberate steps, we would work to negotiate the path that lay ahead. The conveyor belt that ran alongside me was now groaning under the weight of all that I had piled on it, unable to process when James was so ill. There would be nothing now but time to sift through the layers.

*　　*　　*

Cremation

Thankfully, James's father and I had already agreed that our sweet son would be cremated. Not to have another major decision to tackle at this time was enormously helpful. My meeting with Pacific Interment felt dreamlike. They were professional yet detached from emotion. They had important work to do, and that was their only focus. I wondered how they could do this day in and day out but accepted their demeanour and carried on. Papers were presented, including the death certificate. Signing this hurt even more than the DNR forms, something I did not think possible.

The layers of sorrow just kept piling up. It was decided that the cremation would take place in Emeryville on Thursday. We would have the small chapel and opportunity for a viewing beforehand. James's ashes would be delivered to this office on Friday, and we could collect them in the late morning. Trading my son's body to receive a box of ash—it was all so incredibly erroneous.

*　　*　　*

On the evening before the cremation, the school's sports-award dinner took place. The award for Most Improved Player for the baseball team, the one that James had received just a year ago, was now renamed in his memory. It was the beginning of many emotional gatherings that would honour and remember James not only now, but also in the future.

I sent out an e-mail inviting a short list of those who had been so important to James at the end of his life to attend an intimate cremation ceremony. Emma, Pat, Marc, Sergio, and Ray accepted, and I asked each one to bring a small special gift to tuck in around James's body to help send him on his way.

The crematorium was across the Bay Bridge, near Oakland, in a depressed part of Emeryville. Nothing externally would show signs of it being anything other than a warehouse. The entry had the requisite potted plants and low-maintenance ferns, with double glass doors that lead into a small carpeted foyer. John, my contact over the phone, met us and led us down a long corridor to a large room with a high A-frame ceiling. About ten rows of pews were set in place.

We walked down the centre aisle to the front, where James was resting in a large white sheet in a simple box. He looked so peaceful and beautiful. Free of pain. The slight smile had remained on his lips. I reached in to kiss his head and felt his hands. His chest was solid and his body icy cold. Silently we stood and prayed, cried and then individually put our gifts in around him.

Emma had brought a small gift box containing a tuna melt sandwich (a favourite of James that she made for him whenever he visited as a toddler to play with her son). Pat included a book of Irish poetry and guitar strings. From Sergio came a glow-in-the-dark rosary and prayer card from the Sacred Heart community while Ray brought copies of James's powerful writings from this year's Justice class, including his final essay. To help pay the journeyman, Marc gave James the two-dollar bill from his wallet that his own father had given him when leaving home as a young man.

As for me, I placed next to my beloved boy a map of the constellations, his recent *Thrasher* magazine, my personal love letter, and a white rose. He still held in his hand the piece of blankie I had given him just after he died. Sergio and Ray each said a short prayer aloud and a few words of love. I had brought my scissors and small bag to cut some hair to keep but could not do it. One of the others stepped forward to do the cutting for me. I was inconsolable.

After some quiet time, the mortician joined us and asked if we were ready, and I agreed. He wrapped the sheet around James and wheeled the rolling stand through a large steel door that opened automatically, revealing an enormous industrial room with a number of massive furnaces. One was rumbling.

John positioned James in front of the furnace, and I followed him. The space inside the furnace was empty, but huge flames leapt at the far end. John asked if I would like to participate in the next step, and I stood at the top end and slowly pushed the box into the furnace. A door slid down, and James was gone.

Finally, I had gotten the upper hand on this vile disease. It could no longer consume my darling son. I looked up to the dingy ceiling and shouted angrily, "Fuck cancer!"

*   *   *

We gathered in the main room, stunned and empty. Everyone who has gone through such an experience knows the hollow feeling that envelops, and you wonder if taking the next step is even possible. After time we realized we needed food, and we asked John where we might get a bite nearby. He said the only place for us to go would be Rudy's Never Fail Café a few blocks away. Rudy's is a funky café that we assumed must be loved by bikers. It was set on a corner with all the grit one would imagine.

Inside we found a boisterous diner with huge menus serving every combination of foods and drink. It was a perfect retro restaurant. We sat at a long series of tables on vinyl chairs. The table tops were boxes filled with eclectic toys, books, and junk coated with clear plastic. It managed to make us laugh, and we agreed collectively, "James would love this." Above the bar I noticed a black chalkboard on which was written in white chalk, "There is only infinity." This would become the first of many messages that would remind me that James might indeed be very present and I'd better pay attention.

We ate tuna-melt sandwiches and some drank Bloody Marys. Later I discovered that Rudy's had been featured on the Food Channel's *Diners, Drive-ins, and Dives*, a program James loved to watch.

*   *   *

I did not expect this, but planning the memorial, designing the funeral programs, helping with the slide show, and organizing refreshments kept me detached from my grief—in fact, detached from everything. Clearly, these details kept me distracted while running on adrenaline. What swirled around me was an anesthetic fog that numbed the pain and kept me in what I now think of as a drugged state. I was not taking anything medicinal; my core just shut down on its own, preventing me from feeling very much of anything. Others who have shared with me their early days after the death of a loved one also describe this feeling. It may be the only way that the spirit, mind, and body can get through these incredibly difficult hours.

The funeral memorial for James was held at eleven o'clock on Saturday, May 16, at Grace Cathedral, Nob Hill. Family and friends gathered from far away. Flowers arrived for the altars, and cascading white arrangements, created by the school's secretary, framed the transepts. Unable to fathom the scale of the day, I had no idea that there were one thousand people in attendance. Apparently the cathedral was packed.

It was a beautiful and incredibly moving service. The eulogies reminded us of all the gifts and great love that James shared with us so generously. His classmates participated, and his godfather flew in from the United Kingdom to read some of James's poems. The hymns were perfect and the readings powerful. Reverend Jason gave us permission to be angry at God. We sang, railed at the universe for taking James too soon, and Marc rang the Tibetan bowl to silence the space.

Afterwards, the large crowd gathered in the courtyard under blazing sunshine to visit and partake of refreshments prepared by old friends and chefs Bruce and David. They had chosen plaid tablecloths in honour of James's love of plaid shirts. It was all too poignant, perfect, and still incredibly *wrong*. I could not accept that this was the final celebration for my son who deserved a lifetime of parties and events. The queue of tearful faces and hugs seemed endless, and in the heat I felt like fainting. Special days were now going to be relegated to moments gone. I was entering the world of the past tense, a concept that was soon to become one of the most difficult to grasp.

As a casual way for the boys to say goodbye after the memorial service, a barbeque was planned—by whom, I don't know now—at Crissy Field. Each friend of James was given a small handful of ash, which they gently placed in the salty water of the bay. They ate, romped in the waves, cried, and shared hugs. James would not have wanted anything different, and it was a perfect ending to a very long week for us all.

Barbeque at Crissy Field after James's Memorial service

*　　*　　*

While James still had strength, weeks before his death, we wandered to the local secondhand store, on the prowl for more fun shirts. At the Town School shop at Polk and Pacific, James found a lovely eight-inch-square brass box. It was two inches deep and had a flip lid; the lining was blue velvet. James immediately decided it would be great for his pot drawer to hold the special blends he had collected. At $2 it was an easy purchase.

Knowing how much James liked the box made it the only choice to hold his ashes. The committal of ashes is a powerful service, and on June 5, James was placed in a lovely columbarium on the grounds of St. Mary the Virgin in San Francisco. The Village Well was housed in the church's compound, and ironically, the columbarium was in the process of being built when the Well was in the early days of development.

Reverend Jennifer performed the intimate and poignant ceremony in the garden. Not all of James's ashes were interred; some were given to his father, and I also received a box. Some ashes were placed on the blue velvet lining, and then the box was gently wrapped in the white katas scarf that Sergio had presented. The niche was left open for the box to be placed inside, and once the front granite piece was engraved, it would cover the opening.

My ashes will one day rest next to James's.

Keaton and Michael with James' boxed ashes wrapped in white scarf before being placed in final resting place

*   *   *

Graduation

The senior-class graduation was held the afternoon of June 6 in the outdoor courtyard of the school. My brother Bill had come to the city to share in the service at St. Mary's as well as the graduation which I hoped to attend. I had multiple copies of the photo of James with Obama to give to each of the graduates and faculty of the school: his farewell gift to them all. The graduation speeches were heart-warming, and James was listed in the program as a graduate. His photo now hung with the rest of the class in the school's foyer. Awards were presented, and the last one, the highest honour for any of the graduates, was given to the student who best exemplified the spirit and heart of the school. For his bravery, courage, and tenacity, it was a unanimous decision by students and faculty that James receive this award. An overwhelming moment and terribly difficult to receive, but James's father and I managed to stumble on to the stage while all assembled stood.

This school, that James instinctively *knew* he needed to attend years earlier, had become his home and community of unconditional support and love. They gave him permission to find his voice and guided him every step of the way on the lonely path he had to walk. This village of strong and deeply loving friendships provided each of these young men a place where they could nurture and share their strengths and vulnerabilities. James had indeed been blessed to have participated in this treasured circle.

Chapter 17

Signs

Nature continues to provide its ordered rhythm even during my daily unravelling.

—personal journal entry, July 2009

In the days that followed May 9, I became aware of a small bird that sang the most amazing song outside my bedroom window. It was a song unlike any other I had heard, and I would race up to the roof to try and find it, to no avail. This songbird would begin to appear at the strangest of times and wildest of places, and yet I could not see it.

Others heard it with me, so I knew it was not fantasy; they too could not locate it. Every time it sang its magical tune, I would think of James and so clung to the belief that this was his way of reaching me. Equally surprising, on certain evenings when at home, I could smell James passing by. It was fleeting but very distinct. During a quiet morning just after his death, I heard a few notes chime from the glockenspiel up in his room.

One evening it felt as though there were hands on my back, but no one was there. My journal entries from those days, while starting to fill with the beginning expressions of a powerful grief, also mentioned quirky circumstances and odd gifts from nature.

Within days of James's death, in the centre of the fountain in the courtyard of St. Mary's and the Village Well, a wild iris started to bloom amongst the lily pads. This had never happened before, and those who had been involved with the church for decades had never seen one there. Whenever James and I were out in the country and we'd stumble across a wild iris, I would make sure he stopped to look at the glorious colours and also take a deep whiff as the scent is quite intoxicating.

211

Many of us interpreted the appearance of this iris as a sign from James. It reached its full bloom the day of his inurnment in the columbarium and would only bloom that one time. It never appeared again. A friend wrote to tell me that the iris represents faith, hope, and wisdom; purple is the colour of highly evolved souls. I started to cling to these signs as treasured indicators that James must be watching over us.

Wild iris in the fountain

*   *   *

In the early summer, President Obama sent a letter to James acknowledging all the challenges he was facing. He admired James's strength and hoped that he could draw on the power of hope, determination, perseverance, and faith, finding strength and comfort in those principles, as he had done. After his Make-a-Wish adventure James had sent a thank-you to the White House acknowledging all that the President had done for him.

Sadly, President Obama did not know that James had died. I sent a letter back to the White House informing him of the sad news of James's death and included the funeral program, also mentioning that James had been accepted to the University of Chicago and that he had wanted President Obama to know this in his final days.

A few months later I would receive the following letter from the White House:

August 3, 2009

Dear Jean,

I was so sorry to hear about the passing of your son James. He continues to offer hope to those who knew him well or for only a brief time. I was humbled by his courage and tenacity in the face of such tremendous challenges.

It is a credit to your strength that his final days were peaceful. Although words cannot ease the pain of such a loss, I trust that his spirit will continue to serve as a guiding force in your life and for all those he touched. I appreciate your kind note. Please know that Michelle and I will continue to pray for you and your family at this difficult time.

Sincerely,
Barack Obama

I will always hold precious the sentiments of that letter and also have an abiding respect and admiration for President Obama. He proved the cynics wrong and poured his heart and soul into governing America. History will be the judge of his time on earth, but I know that he deeply touched James, his friends, and the many who shared the "dream wish" around the world. Obama gave us all a chance to believe in the power of hope even when there was little to cling to.

Before the end of the school year, the senior art class always worked together on a group project. This year's class decided to design a permanent installation "Moving On," which would be created on the school's outdoor stairs at the back of the art room, where James and Anthony rested while playing their guitars. The students painted the face of each step to represent a flowing stream with rocks and goldfish woven into the tapestry. The shadow of James and Anthony playing their guitars was painted on the top step, and it became an exquisite piece of art.

Patter, the art teacher, and Sergio orchestrated a very moving dedication ceremony in which the young men participated. Sergio had each of the boys hold some oil and anoint a step of their choosing after which he performed a ritual smudging. Some of James's ashes were incorporated into the final paint that was used to outline his shadow on the top step. Powerful in its simplicity, we all cried and said a prayer. Some of the boys even laughed as they thought of how embarrassed James would be by all this crazy emotion; he'd certainly conjure up some witty comment to diffuse the serious tone.

The dedication of the stairs painted by the students at SHHS

In the coming months the community would also plant trees at the front of the school and dedicate the one closest to the gate for James. His ashes were sprinkled into the soil, and during that ritual, when all was most quiet, the mystical unseen bird started singing hysterically from a nearby rooftop.

The underlying message of all of these signs was to pay attention, which would become my mantra going forward. Many of those who mourn have shared with me their longing to have some sort of signal from their dead child, partner, or parent. My constant reminder is to just be still. The more you seek, the less you find. Let the messengers come to you instead of engaging in a quest. It is so easy to become swept up in all the uncertainties instead of allowing things to unfold in their own way. I don't think James's spirit has been any more generous than others with his nudging and messages; I have just promised to remain mindful and listen.

*   *   *

Peter Gabriel was now my faithful companion, and together we cobbled some sort of daily routine together. He continued to enjoy sitting in the old frying pan under the kitchen table, and we'd curl up together in the evenings watching television, wondering where James had gone. Peter remained frisky and chewed on everything he could find, and his excitement when I came into the kitchen was a glimmer of light in the midst of very dark days.

*   *   *

The grief mantle was settling upon my shoulders, and sadness was everywhere. The shock that had buffered me in the early days was slipping away. My anesthetic fog was lifting, revealing the horror of what had transpired. Nothing was protecting me anymore; my newly exposed nerve endings were raw, and I was experiencing a very real physical pain. My need to withdraw and retreat became a big piece of the daily ritual. People asked me how I was. "Fine," I would reply; taking breaths, and that was it.

By mid-June, Peter Gabriel had taken to standing on his hind legs in the cage, reaching up with his forepaws, indicating he wanted out. He did this whenever James had walked into the room, and I asked Peter if he wanted James. I would let him out to hop around the flat but thought it odd that this reaching was becoming more common.

On Sunday, June 28, I went in to the kitchen to make my morning tea and found Peter Gabriel dead in the small nest in his pen. Initially I thought he was sleeping but when I saw a quiet chest, I knew he was gone. Hysterically I called Emma and through the tears heard her say she'd be right over. Within minutes she and her husband arrived to collect Peter. In warp speed, they took down the pen, towels, bedding, and bowls; everything was removed.

I was devastated. Horrible shock slammed into me once again. How could this be? He was so young and healthy! Rabbits live for decades, or so I had been warned. James was so devoted to this little fellow, and we had given him constant love. How? Why? Yet another death.

"Enough, God!" I screamed through my tears.

Within two months of James's death, Peter Gabriel was also cremated, and his ashes now sit in a special box, waiting for the day when we will all be reunited in the columbarium.

Once I calmed down and could begin to ponder the great why, I was reminded of how often of late Peter had been standing on his hind legs, reaching up. Perhaps James *had* come to visit him, and they decided that being reunited was better than being apart. I don't pretend to know how any of this works, but I feel now, after many years, a hopefulness that they are indeed together in some form or place. Pets are deeply attached to their owners, and I have heard of many such parallel deaths when a pet dies soon after its human companion.

As the days and months passed, signs that James was somehow all right would become more common, and I was grateful to have kept a running account of his quirky visits. While I dismissed them in the early days of grief as part of my descent into madness, I see them now as punctuations that remind me the spirit *is* powerful, omnipresent, and yes, perhaps it can even transcend that last tear.

Section 3

Slow Descent into Madness

Chapter 18

Grief Bearer

Slow Descent into Madness

No one told me it would hurt this much.

The day to day minutia
Becomes an unbearable task to negotiate.
How can putting two feet next to the bed take every ounce?
Don't even think about washing,
oh god the gooey oozes of shampoo
Running down my back disgust.
Soap might slip and need picking up.
The smell of steam and lather on my broken body
Nauseates.

Pounding water beats down with violent rhythm—
What do you mean it is only a trickle, on gentle?
No, the towels are too rough on my skin
Even with Downy, they scratch.

Shower walls prop me up
I stand under the faucet adorned with its hanging altar of plastic
bottles filled with uncertain elixirs.
This is my personal cathedral.
But Madonna and child are nowhere to be found.

Here is
Where I come to pour my soul's broken gasps
And let tears mix with water to carry the residue of
A head, once sane
And heart, once full
Now both scraped raw by death's scythe.

—Jean Alice Rowcliffe 2009

Death is like hitting a wall.
Grief is the pain from hitting the wall.
Mourning is coming to terms with the pain from hitting that wall.

—Jean Alice Rowcliffe

Unsolicited

You slipped silently through the door,
when held open to allow the shrouded stretcher to ease out.
I did not see you standing next to me as the undistinguished hearse pulled
away,
down the street out of view.

We did not collide that first night
but when I awoke, there you were
propped up next to me.
You had climbed in
Over piles of pillows and blankets, from his stripped bed
That lay in a heap on the floor—
No one could bring themselves to sort out the folds of fabric that once encased
that beautiful, broken body.

Your blank ashen face
that mirrored mine, in a troubled silent way,
stared back at me.
"We live together now,"
you whispered, after some time.

But I did not invite you in.
We had no period of courting or easy seduction
Nothing prepared me for your arrival.
This new rough-hewn terrain forged from incredible loss
Was supposed to be all I needed to negotiate.

Relationship was not predicted
or expected.
But here you are.
Bold.
Already effortlessly, growing comfortable in your new surroundings.
Oozing into the cracks of my life.

You join me in the shower causing tears to mix with water
So much so that I can't tell them apart.
As I walk down the neighbourhood streets
You prod me with that incessant prickly finger.

"There, that was the spot when he first fell."
"This is the scrape from his grinding skateboard."
"You asked about the afterlife on this pavement square."
"Remember that first coffee at this café table?"
"My, my . . . You won't share that again."
"How empty you look."
"Can you sit with all that pain?"

Over and over your strident insights and proclamations
Taunt and drain.
Will you ever shut up?

And just when I think I have gotten rid of you in my own specially devised
divorce proceedings,
You show up again.
All calm and resolute.
"You can't get rid of me that easily."

Like a couple who stay together through a shared relationship of disdain
You and I will grow old together.

I can't bring myself to file the papers
Or find a lawyer to argue my defense
it all just falls on deaf ears.

Crafting the agreement takes more energy than I can muster and I don't have
the vocabulary that could articulate how painful your presence has become
Besides, the fee would be prohibitive.
So we just stay together.

Sharing the same bed,
And dining in silence
We watch the news and listen to the radio
Maybe even find a song we like, from time to time.
The seasons flow one into another and years pass
without purpose and any need for memory.

One day I shall curl up in that final fetal
And you will be next to me
Spindly arms wrapped tight around my chest.

My uninvited companion
Our marriage complete
And story told.

—Jean Alice Rowcliffe, October 2011

Grief is a universal phenomenon that we will all share. Death and loss
are the great equalizers. No one can escape its grasp, and everyone will reach
the same conclusion. Copious amounts of wealth, good luck, bad fortune,
uncertain health or robust days, friendships, lovers, partners, enemies—all the
extroverted or introverted escapades of life cannot dodge this inevitable. We
are all dying.

Just as there are a plethora of causes of death and the manner in which we
live, I have discovered there are different types of grief. We all experience many
losses in our lives, and the sorrow associated with each loss is unique to that
individual. Even within a family, when all have endured the same death of a
member, each person connected to that story will experience his or her grief
and mourning in their own personal way.

Some losses are expected, especially when the dying have reached an age that we would consider a good run with a life well lived and hopefully rich in experiences. If the dying have suffered near the end of their life, there is often a relief attached to grief, which has its own dynamic. Other deaths are a total surprise and leave us stunned for a long period, before the grieving process can even begin.

We will, in our lifetimes, experience many types of loss, but I do feel there will be one or two *profound* deaths that will knock us off our stride. No one knows what will be the cause of death for the parent, lover, spouse, friend or, God forbid, child, but this loss will strip you to your core, leaving you shaken and deeply changed in every possible way. You will feel weak and nauseated, kicked in the gut, and incapable of going on. Each step forward saps all your energy. Life loses its meaning, and you have no focus. Your belief structure is stripped bare. It hurts to breathe. You are stunned and broken, in a state of disconnect and disbelief that lingers what feels like will last forever. Your life is dramatically changed, and *nothing* is as it was. *Why was I not taken instead of them?* A terrible fear that you will forget your loved one over time consumes, returning you regretfully to square one.

Losing James was my profound loss. Others have died leaving a great void in my life, but their memories eventually started to float in and out of days with ease. Somehow I thought that when I knew James was dying, his memory would be the same, and negotiating the landscape would continue much as before: however, nothing could be further from the truth.

Since the days following James's death were consumed by all the minutia of his cremation, memorial service, and arrival of guests from out of town, the individual details became the focus of any given day, and that swirling anesthetic fog provided numbness with odd bursts of energy. My mind, spirit, and body collectively shut down sufficiently to let me move forward, and an internal survival mechanism kept me from feeling too much. I entered a safe zone that was controlled with detachment from any given moment, person, and emotion.

I am sure this is why I have so little memory of those early weeks. I wrote that perhaps it was nature's way of preserving and preventing those who are left behind from jumping off a bridge. This adrenalin overdrive keeps you on task and giving what becomes your standard response to "How are you doing?", the proverbial, "All right."

I now have fleeting recollections of meeting with the ministers and teachers to make plans. Flowers arrived. I attended a warehouse cremation in Emeryville. The heavy box of ash was later collected from somewhere south of

Market Street. How did they get there again? How did I collect them? For the first week after May 9 dear Pat and Emma took it upon themselves to sleep at my house each night, alternating evenings between them. They did not want to leave me alone. I recall seeing the inflatable Aerobed set out in the sitting room with flannel sheets, pillows, and a comforter piled on top, but how and when they came and went, I have no recollection of now. They did make me eat one meal a day; they insisted on this. What I consumed and where we ate, I don't know.

An insufferable creature of habit, I showered and dressed, fixed my hair and makeup, but the other day-to-day occurrences unfurled with no connection to me. Some days I went through the exercise of getting ready, only to curl up in the fetal position back on top of my bed, unable to do anything else. That would be my accomplishment for the day.

Tears flowed endlessly, and I awoke every morning with a drenched pillow. Condolences poured in, and the cards and e-mails rapidly became overwhelming. I thanked the universe that the CaringBridge site was there to hold on to the many messages as I could not face them on a daily basis. The outpouring of love for James was a huge gift, and at no time was I ungrateful. It just felt like a tsunami that I had no control over, and I am aware that I failed miserably at responding to all the greetings. One begins to trust that most people will understand or perhaps even know how difficult the days were, and they did not expect a response. All of the cards and letters have been lovingly saved, and one day I will be able to go through the boxes that house them.

Many have wondered why I became so removed and cloistered. The truth is, this became the only way I could tackle each new day. Buffering myself from the world and the paralyzing grief was how I survived. It all just hurt too much. Profound grief is manifested in many ways, and acute physical pain is one element that no one warned me about.

As I soon discovered, there are many layers of mourning that no one warns you about. In an attempt to comfort me, people wanted to hug or stroke my arm and hand, and I would withdraw instantly. Every nerve ending was raw, and touch was often the most painful thing of all. It took well over a year for me to be comfortable with any physical contact. Friends had given me gifts of wonderful massages, but the early ones were so difficult that I would lie on the massage bed and weep uncontrollably.

Thankfully the masseuses were gifted healers and understood my plight, and some just gently held my sore limbs while I wept. There are many unexpected angels that you will discover on this journey.

Within weeks of James's death, I began to crave two soothing elements: water and heat. Long showers with hot water pounding my back allowed me to weep in silence. Morning and night, the shower was my only place of refuge. Bewilderment became my daily state of mind, and I found myself saying out loud, incessantly at times, "How could this be?"

"How will I not see you again?"

"How, how, how?"

*   *   *

C. S. Lewis, in his wonderful book *A Grief Observed*, writes about his profound grief after the death of his wife. There are so many insights that I carry with me, but the following was one that spoke particularly to those early days:

> "No one ever told me that grief felt so like fear. I am not afraid, but the sensation is like being afraid. The same fluttering in the stomach, the same restlessness, the yawning. I keep on swallowing. At other times it feels like being mildly drunk, or concussed. There is a sort of invisible blanket between the world and me. I find it hard to take in what anyone says. Or perhaps, hard to want to take it in. It is so uninteresting. Yet I want others to be about me. I dread the moments when the house is empty. If only they would talk to one another and not to me."

Frail is a wonderful word. It sums up what I felt leading up to James's death and have continued to feel for these ensuing years. The days before the memorial service, I was in a state of shock, and I let the shifting fog carry me. So many who have experienced profound loss speak of "somehow finding a way to just keep going," and this was my truth. It did not bring me satisfaction or sense of accomplishment. I doubted ever being able to feel those sentiments again. All the hundreds who attended the service were deeply compassionate and loving, yet I have so few memories of that day. Who did I shake hands with? What did I say? How long did we stand there? I was not prepared for the forgetfulness or how vague I would become.

One day we were short of supplies at work, and I volunteered to go to Safeway to pick up the few items. I arrived in the car park, unsure why I had come there. I wandered the aisles, totally blank and had to call Emma to remind me what I was supposed to be buying. Milk, juice, tea, and sugar.

Such a simple list, and yet I had no connection to the task whatsoever. At the time it reminded me of how forgetful I became during pregnancy and realized that my hormones were probably just as jumbled now by all these new raw emotions encompassing grief.

Another truth that I was not warned about was loneliness. There is a solo-ness that can't be explained or replaced by activities or being with others. It is greater than just "being alone." This grief loneliness is layered and reminds one of how vulnerable you are at every moment. You not only miss your loved one's daily presence, but also, beyond that, there is a hollowness that reverberates and you doubt that the empty space will ever be filled. You feel guilty, a failure, and useless, all while grappling with a sense of having no purpose. *Why bother?* This becomes an easy place to escape to when tackling anything that seems too large. The lack of purpose fueled by this loneliness becomes a harrowing reality.

The following reality, that many parents who have lost a child have shared with me, was also my truth. We find ourselves rethinking the events that have just transpired and convince ourselves that this waking life is the dream or, in so many cases, the horrid nightmare. If we could just have a deep untroubled sleep, we'd all awaken in the morning and find our children still here. James would be climbing the stairs, getting off the bus, skateboarding in the garage, greeting me in the kitchen or at the front door with his beaming smile and big bear hug. If I could just *somehow* get through this day and sleep soundly, I would shake this and life *would* return to the way it was. Did he not deserve that? Did I not deserve that? Surely it would come to pass. I just needed to work harder at making it happen. Within a few weeks, a stealthy madness was starting to envelop me, but having the photos from the day of James's death reminded me that yes, what I was experiencing right now, this was the real story and nothing was going to change that.

Years ago, as a rebellious teen, I visited an undertaker in my hometown to debate the merit of funerals. Surely they were a barbaric ritual that we had embraced without thinking. With patience and humour, he led me through the process of embalming, burial, and the value of gathering collectively to grieve. He said that, especially with the death of a child, it was important to have a service and *see* the dead child as there was a madness that would descend and often parents would begin to wonder if in fact their child had indeed died. Having the stark image of the reality of their child's death or seeing them laid out or in a coffin would actually be more beneficial for the grieving parents than not. Gathering in a group to say farewell would also make their mourning more complete as it gave everyone a chance share their sorrow. If a service is not held, the bereaved are then reminded with each meeting of someone else who did not get to say goodbye. Never could I have imagined that this would be important advice that I would accept in my life, but now my sacred photos of James in his final hours placed that truth squarely in front of me.

*   *   *

Driving was impossible. The all-consuming distraction of my grief made me incredibly vulnerable and dangerous. One afternoon, soon after James's death, I undertook an almost-suicidal four-minute drive to the Walgreens at the corner of Broadway. I ran the red light at Union Street and all the subsequent stop signs on Polk. Once Pat and Emma discovered this, they quickly set up a system of drivers who would get me from point A to B, and all I needed to do was to send an e-mail or make a phone call, and a volunteer driver would miraculously arrive at the front door. This became an incredible gift for the coming months, and I can't recommend it enough for those who are recently bereaved.

*   *   *

My anguish was becoming unbearably crippling. A dark melancholy had descended and enveloped me. I *knew* that James could not have lingered any longer, enduring that terrible suffering housed in his broken body, yet all logic was lost and I tried valiantly to conjure up a new outcome. Chapters in my journals were dedicated to the wish that I could just run away, become invisible, push the rewind button, or at least live in silence.

One day, months after James's death, while walking on Union Street, I prayed to the universe to give me something tangible that I could share with others to articulate how prickly I felt. I had not found the words to express the feeling of being under the control of this outside force. It had not been invited into my life, but there it was, dictating and orchestrating every move. Some people attempted to penetrate my bubble, and they looked shocked when I told them just how sad, hurt, and angry I felt, causing them to beat a hasty retreat. The emptiness became my shroud. I felt a constant longing to be invisible and sit quietly with my pain.

As I crossed Broderick Street, a water puddle on the sidewalk caught my eye. It looked like some sort of troll creature with short spindly arms and spiky skin, holding a wreath in one hand. Garishly ugly and frighteningly Orc-like, it looked *exactly* as I felt and was stunning in its perfection. I took a photo on my phone and then watched it evaporate in the August sun. That image has remained the most perfect illustration of how I felt for that first year, and one day I would like to paint it on a large canvas.

"Prickly" grief troll found in a sidewalk puddle on Union Street.

Rowena from Hospice and Robin from UCSF were bricks in the early days, calling to check in and provide support as best they could. I will always hold on to a phrase that Rowena shared with me. Another mother who had lost a child told her that it felt as though she now lived on "an island of pain" with a massive sea surrounding her. I felt that no one understood what my island was like and how excruciating the pain of living on it had become. I did not want to venture off the island for fear of the depth of water, and the unknown horizon was too foreboding.

They also warned me that it is usually after two or three months when one really starts to grapple with the depth and lasting pain of loss. Folks who were once so engaged with your story of disease and death have returned to and carried on with their "normal" lives. You are left alone for greater periods and have to face the inevitable truth of what has just transpired.

Joan Didion, in her powerful book *The Year of Magical Thinking*, describes the vortex that she grappled with after the death of her husband. I called it the tumbling dominos or looking into a mirror that goes on endlessly. Once you make a step over the line into a memory, longing, or question, you are suddenly swept away and engulfed in the endless spinning, tumbling, or whatever you choose your metaphor to be. There is no going back.

The swirling becomes all consuming, spitting you out when complete. Initially it was impossible to control this tidal wave, but in time I started to recognize the triggers that caused it and I became proficient at dodging them. Driving miles out of my way to avoid the old playgrounds or baseball diamonds was the norm. Walking to the local shops might become a convoluted route, so I could dodge favourite corners. Plotting my journey became an important element of each day.

James's friends gathered faithfully to celebrate his birthday with a barbeque on June 13. Their thoughtfulness and willingness to share their love and grief so openly for him was very dear. We met in Golden Gate Park in a quiet dale in Sharon Meadow. A couple of the guys confessed they had not paid attention when James planned barbeques in the past, and so they fumbled with all the details to pull this one together.

Jokes and stories were exchanged, candles lit, and we sang "Happy Birthday" around an ice cream cake. How had he been so robust just twelve months ago? In such a short span of time James was reduced to ash and the void was huge. I returned home that evening and collapsed on the floor of the shower, convinced I would never be able to celebrate a birthday again, and I prayed to the universe to *please* spare me.

*　　*　　*

As the months progressed the grief burden was starting to take its toll. My posture shifted, and I walked hunched over. Excess weight stuck to me as my body entered survival mode. When I look at images of myself during that time, I see how heavy every part of my being had become. Probably six months after James's death, I felt like the sorrow was going to kill me, and thoughts of ending it all became overwhelming. There was no light at the end of that dark tunnel, and the thought of continuing like this for the rest of my days was impossible to imagine. I kept the suicide prevention number close by in case I found myself willing to take a handful of pills.

Another shout went up to the universe to please, please help me. I needed something to aid me in the lugging of this story. Bereavement was all-consuming, and I could not carry any more. For every step forward, I felt that I was taking two steps back. This is when the "Grief-bearer" entered my life. Thankfully, I have always had a vivid imagination, and there were small punctuations of it resurfacing during these months.

One foggy afternoon while walking along Polk Street, I felt the presence of an older Edwardian man next to me. In my mind he was thin, to the point of gaunt, and erect; he wore a black tailcoat and floor-length overcoat, white shirt, cravat, and pristine top hat. The flowing black ribbon down the back told me he was an undertaker. We never spoke, but I somehow understood that whenever I needed to hand over some of my grief, his arms were ready and waiting. No package proved to be too heavy. Some days it felt as though I presented him a steamer trunk of sorrows, but he willingly picked it up or dragged it along beside us. He always kept pace and did not need acknowledgement.

One day I visualized him in the backseat of the car staring forward, expressionless, holding a number of sorrow packages in his lap. Be the load small or massive, he remained steadfast and impartial, and we forged a quiet, humble relationship. Having a safe place to put my grief became all important. Rather than trying to dodge and get rid of it or "move on" (as many told me to do), I understood the need to acknowledge and honour *all* my emotions, including the doubt, insecurities, and deep sorrow that were with me every day. Having someone, even a phantom, to help me carry my weighty load made this time of transition bearable. Even now, four years later, I can conjure him up, and while he does not need to carry as often for me, the bond remains strong.

$$*\qquad*\qquad*$$

Someday

Someday, the quiet gasp will not escape when I open the bathroom cabinet
and find the toothbrush and razor
Waiting patiently.
Do they wonder what happened?
Where are the hands that used us every day?
The teeth to clean?
Stubble to scrape?
No more.

Someday, the shoes left at the door will be worn again.
By someone else.

Someday I will remove the almost-empty shampoo bottles from the
shower
And the favourite soap
Now like wood in its dish.

Someday, the sight of Za
Or a music store
Or the school intersection
Or soccer field
Or baseball diamond
Or skateboard scrapings on a curb
Or a guitar pick
Or notepad
Or Bukowski novel
Or half-finished canvases,
Will not make me cringe and want to hide, all the while craving one more
look.

Someday, there will no longer be the solicitations
For airline credit card offers
Or applications for summer college programs
Or surveys
Or requests for donations to the cancer society
Or Thrasher magazines,
Arrive in the mail.

Someday, my pillow will not be wet upon waking
From the silent tears shed in the night.
Did I cry out, my heart pounding?
I can smell him hovering over my bed,
Still.

Someday Beethoven
Or Mozart
Or the Beatles
Or Spoon
Or Fleet Foxes
Or Lewis Black
Or Andrew Reynolds
Won't make me resent that they could go on.
While he was just finding his voice.

Someday I will not carry multiple hankies, his hankies, in my bag
When facing a new day.
With wads of tissues filling my pockets
Or dark glasses, even when cloudy
To hide puffy eyes and streaked mascara.

Someday I will wipe the screen of this laptop
And remove all the smudges and fingerprints
That were once his.
The only impression left of his hand,
Now ash.

Someday, I am told,
It won't be a struggle to breathe
Or dread to walk into an empty home
Or find baby booties, wrapped with blue ribbon, in with my scarves
Or stumble upon an unfinished poem
Or look to the window—maybe he will get off this next bus,
Or find a wish list, or a journal
Or a song in the process of being composed
Or his watch, bus transfer and glasses
All tossed casually in a drawer.

Someday, sitting alone in the evening
I won't find myself repeating over and over
"How can this be?"
Or
'When will I see you again?"
Or
"This is so fucked up."
So I am told.

Someday,
But not today.

—Jean Alice Rowcliffe, January 2010

Chapter 19

Are You Up for This Today?

Grief fills the room up of my absent child,
Lies in his bed, walks up and down with me,
Puts on his pretty looks, repeats his words,
Remembers me of all his gracious parts,
Stuffs out his vacant garments with his form;
Then have I reason to be fond of grief.
—Shakespeare, King John, *act III, scene IV*

For many months, I left James's room as it was on the night of his death. Even the way the sheet on his bed had shifted after his body was removed was saved. The pictures, candles, dried petals all stayed in exactly the same place. His hats, glasses, photos—some things remained in that position until I moved. When he died, I had not realized how powerful the urge would become to preserve and leave things where he last placed them. His tweed cap and wooden cane sat at the front door of the flat where he set them the last time he ascended the stairs. The smell of his hair miraculously remains fresh inside the cap.

I inherited James's Mac laptop, which we had purchased in the final year of his life. His writings, music collection, and silly nonsense photos and fun with his friends are carefully preserved in various files. Soon after I started using the laptop, I realized the screen was covered in fingerprints and smudges. These were James's last fingerprints, and I would dissolve into a weeping mess, just turning the machine on. Never had I imagined the acute sorrow that this type of remembrance might conjure. Everything related to him became a precious treasure that I didn't want to tamper with. It took me over two years to finally pluck up the courage to clean the screen, but the top-left corner remains untouched to this day. When I need a gentle reminder of my sweet boy, I can turn off the screen's light and see his fingerprints there. Fleetingly, he is with me.

It was perhaps eighteen months after James's death (I had no sense of passing time) that I walked into his room and realized it had all just become too painful and a shift was needed. I have no idea what inspired or nudged me, but my fractured energy went into sorting, boxing, and trying to figure out how to live in this different space. I was still struggling to acknowledge he was not coming home again and had quietly been saving his things (just as Joan Didion describes) *in case he might need them again.*

Some parents find it impossible to touch anything in the room of their deceased child, leaving it as a museum of sorts. Some parents gut the space immediately after death and remove any sign and reminder of their loss. There is no right or wrong way to go forth, and each parent and family will follow their own hearts when it comes to their child. One of the most hurtful things anyone can say to a grieving parent is to suggest that *you* might know what is best for them. We can't begin to know what a parent feels. Even now, with my firsthand experience, I would never assume to suggest to another parent what they should do. We are all here just to support them in whatever they decide, and that is the best we can do.

What had been James's bedroom as a baby and toddler on the main floor of the flat had been transformed into a makeshift office and catch-all during his illness. This room now needed to be emptied and made ready for something else. For months I had avoided the space by keeping the door closed. The memories poured out with such ease washing and twisting me around that I had to keep the door bolted to protect myself from the raging river that would so easily consume. Somehow, given time, I found the energy and was able to box up the things that I needed to save but could not face at that moment. Many boxes were stored in my garage, in other rooms, or under tables, and Emma kindly took stacks to her garage and attic for safekeeping until I was ready for them. I did not have to make major decisions about their future. Just having the things in a safe place opened me up to considering other possibilities. If others are willing to help carry this burden of mourning, let them. Often the smallest gestures bring the most peace.

*   *   *

Hospice by the Bay provided many gifts during this time, and one of the greatest was the ability to see a bereavement counsellor for my first year of mourning. There is so much that I would like to do to support this wonderful organization and wish they did not have to scramble incessantly for funding. A nonprofit that does so much to help the dying and bereaved should be on the radar of all benefactors who want to make a difference. My debt and gratitude for all Hospice services remains steadfast. That James had a good death and that I am still standing is a reflection of their devotion and understanding.

Rowena set up the initial appointment for me at the Marin office in Larkspur. I can't recall much of that first meeting, except for lots of crying and bewilderment that I needed to be there. Returning to the city across the Golden Gate Bridge was another miraculous undertaking as I was a mess. Somehow, I made it home in one piece. It was decided at that initial meeting that I would meet weekly with Carol, who was the senior bereavement coordinator for HBTB. Their San Francisco office on Van Ness at Jackson was a simple five-minute drive from home. It could not have been easier.

I soon found myself counting down the days to see Carol. She had an amazing presence, and her ability to listen and ask the right questions, combined with a lack of judgment or need to "solve," was so appreciated. She would sit quietly across from me and allow me to share what I needed, or not, with her hands cupped on her lap. During our visits she assured me that she was going to hold safely whatever I wanted to put in that invisible bowl. It could be my rage, tears, sorrow, jealousy, frustration, silence, fear of living, fear of intimacy, impossible future—everything was welcome, and over time I would start to visualize the "bowl" in my own hands, even away from her office. It became a powerfully healing metaphor to focus on, and I have suggested to others in this same situation to find a way to hold their sorrow. We need to honour all the emotions and insights experienced during our mourning, and finding an authentic place to put grief is essential.

Only when the pain is acknowledged, embraced, and eventually honoured can one start to let go of its power over you. Pounding the message that you should just get over it is counterintuitive. Those who said that to me tore my heart in half as it just invalidated all that I was working to understand. Carol had written the foreword to and consulted on a marvellous book called, very simply, *Grieving for Dummies,* which I highly recommend for every household. It is concise and goes through the various stages of grief, what works, what doesn't, what to say and what not to say, how to support the bereaved in thoughtful ways and how to live with grief when it is thrust upon you. She, along with others who walk this path, introduced me to many helpful books, which are included in the reading list at the end of *The Last Tear.* Reading

Grieving for Dummies in the early months helped enormously in reminding me that what I was going through was universal.

Everything in my life had been turned upside down, and I did not know how I would ever set things straight. What I once believed in no longer had merit. My coping mechanisms had all shut down. Dealing with one task felt insurmountable on any given day; never mind multitasking. I was floating on a vast ocean in a ship without a skipper or rudder. Carol assured me that it would make sense one day but I had to remain true to where I was at any given moment. Not getting bogged down in trying to solve my problem was a huge weekly reminder. Understanding the process would be multi-layered, and not rushing towards a preset outcome was one of her many insightful lessons.

My work with families was becoming more difficult. I walked into a space each day where my role was to be supportive and nurturing, all the while feeling deeply broken. I had nothing left to give, and those who wanted the most from me, I fear received the least. I fantasized about stacking shelves at Safeway, delivering mail, gardening, or working in a library—any sort of Zen work that would require me to use my hands but not my heart would be perfect.

One afternoon some mothers came into the office and proceeded to bombard me with pictures of their children and their recent escapades. I felt as if I had been thrown against the window, their energy was so huge and overwhelming. One of them looked disappointed in my reaction, and she asked me what I needed. "*What was wrong?*" She knew the story of James's death, so her question left me befuddled. Without hesitation and editing I said, "I need my son back, but that's not going to happen." She immediately retreated with the other mother, both probably a bit shaken. I sat quietly and cried at the desk, feeling guilty and angry at myself for being so bold; why couldn't I bury my feelings enough to indulge them,? After all they meant no harm. It was at that moment that I decided to make sure to include the following in this book.

"Are you up for this today?"

If that simple question was asked before instigating a conversation, it would make it so much easier for the bereaved. You would then be able to respond yes or no. Maybe it is not a good moment or maybe it is something that can be shared, but permission needs to be granted. As I shared this notion with other parents, they all responded enthusiastically, "Yes!" They too had felt bushwhacked when others had barged in to their lives. When feelings are hurt, things become overly complicated. Ask this question graciously and accept the answer graciously. You will find a time to be together again, if not now. Don't push. Be patient.

The bereaved parent often finds being around children and hearing family stories very difficult, and one should never assume that your story will somehow be the "boost" that is needed. In this world where boundaries are rapidly evaporating and technology insists that we be in everyone's business 24/7, I think it would serve us all well to remember that sometimes space is needed and it is okay to step back and be silent. Let the bereaved tell you what they want and when they want to. This is an important piece of mourning that is often overlooked, and I think it is one of the most helpful.

I shared with Carol this story of my rage at self for being so blunt, and she reminded me that this is common and also important. In 1969, Elisabeth Kübler-Ross wrote a book, *The Five Stages of Grief*, which has become a template for those working with the terminally ill, dying, and bereaved. These stages—denial, anger, bargaining, depression, and acceptance—don't follow any set pattern, but the more I explored her writings, the more relief I felt in knowing that I was not going mad or intentionally hurting others. My denial and rage tinged with depression had certainly been in the forefront of my emotions for many months. These feelings would come and go as time passed, with depression settling in for the longest period. I doubted ever finding "acceptance" and decided to not even put that on the list. I was too busy coming to grips with a life that had abruptly changed course. What motivated and sustained no longer existed. The bewilderment surrounding this empty grease board of my life without James only escalated.

I swore that I'd never get close to anyone again. The thought of losing someone I might care for, God forbid love, was impossible. A conscious decision was made to float through my remaining years removed and detached. I would stay polite but retreat as needed to my newly formed and increasingly comfortable bubble. Pulling up the drawbridge around a relationship was doable. This would be the key to my survival. Dodging the pain by not opening my heart was a perfect solution for the future. Robin spoke of one day reengaging with the world, and I told her it sounded like total rubbish.

*   *   *

Hospice by the Bay and UCSF hosted memorial services each year. I attended, taking James's graduation photo to add to their Remembrance Table and was shocked by the number of children who had died recently. The table top was groaning with pictures of smiling faces from the very young to teenaged. Rows of chairs were filled with ashen-faced families. Sniffling provided the background to the poems, prayers, and short meditations. Being surrounded by others who were in the same boat only reminded me of the fact that we had all become members of a fraternity that we did not want to join.

Enrollment was forced upon us, and no paperwork was needed, beyond the death certificate. We would pay dues for the rest of our lives and continuing membership was guaranteed. While comforting on one level to know I was not alone, it only reinforced just how much I loathed this new reality, and I ached for James to be alive and our lives to be whole once again.

In August, four months after James's death, Make-a-Wish Foundation chose Stuart Hall High School and James as "heroes" in their annual acknowledgement of those who had helped the organization. The school had been very successful with their spring fundraising drive. I wrote on CaringBridge of how great the young men had been in supporting this cause, but it also reminded me that these new graduates were packing their bags and getting ready to head off to their various colleges and future plans. Many of them had stopped by the flat to pick up some items of James's clothing to take with them. I am glad they felt comfortable to invite themselves over or just to show up and ring the doorbell. Sweaters, scarves, hats would all become a part of their wardrobes, and while it broke my heart to see them carry the items out the door, I am able now to enjoy the thought that there is still life for James vicariously through these clothes. Some of their mothers have shared with me that they see their sons wearing the outfits with pride, and they treat them carefully so as to make them last.

During the first Christmas break without James, a group of the lads invited themselves over for a pizza night and sleepover. They smoked some of the remaining marijuana on the roof in memory of their friend. The reality of lost relationships was haunting me. James would never know the thrill of falling in love or the sorrow of a broken heart. That he was robbed of the complete spectrum of the human condition hurt me more than even my loss, and I struggled in my weekly sessions with Carol to try and make peace. There was no solution to be found, and I just had to quietly work through the mire. I may never make peace with all that he lost, but I try to cling to what he had gained by being authentic and living well during the time he had.

*　　*　　*

Odd gifts started showing up in the same spot on the front stoop: a white rose, pinecone, polished stone. Birds continued to be a favourite messenger, and there were countless rare sightings of unusual birds appearing everywhere. Friends would send e-mails or photos with their "visitors," and each one convinced me that James was well and, dare I think, happy with his playfulness.

One moment that was particularly powerful for me occurred while sitting in a black cab in London, England, stuck in traffic on Knightsbridge, heading towards Hyde Park Corner. On the lap of a passenger in the minivan next to me, I spotted the most enormous falcon I had ever seen. It turned its head and stared at me through the window without flinching. We locked eyes for a long time and stayed fixed on one another until the traffic jolted forward. That moment of kismet produced a calm that washed over me, and every time I think of that chance meeting, I feel James's presence.

A recent reminder of serendipity occurred in 2012 when I took my aging mother to London for a week's visit. Pushing her wheelchair along Hyde Park's South Carriage Drive, running parallel to Knightsbridge, we literally stumbled upon a young man with a falcon on his arm. With the Mandarin Hotel standing between us and Knightsbridge, it was the *exact* spot where I had seen the falcon in the car three years earlier. The falconer was there on that afternoon to chase the pigeons from the exclusive apartments that now dot the perimeter of Hyde Park. What appeared to be a chance meeting that made us smile reminded me that the universe is powerful, and I could hear sweet James whisper, "Pay attention, Mama."

Chapter 20

Address Book

Even names in my address book no longer represent connections. It is all muddled and uncertain. Everything is upended.

—personal journal entry, 2009

Final Scraps

Did you know that tossing the deck of cards, bus transfer, Albuterol puffer, button, pennies, sunflower seeds and Bic pen
In the side pocket of your ragged sports bag
Would one day reduce me to tears and open that never-healing wound?
With the gentlest of touch I carefully lift them,
This precious archaeological find,
And set them gingerly on the wooden floor.

I sit on the top step in the hallway, and look at these new-found treasures with a melancholy that
Cannot be described.
Your hand was the last to touch them.
What baseball practice was this?
March 2007, so the bus transfer tells me.
A crumpled, sticky name tag for St. Anthony's Kitchen, folded in half.
Stuck together.
Volunteer/Visitor.
"The James" you had written on it to identify you to the group.
Community Service. That must have been it.

Of course you would call yourself "THE James," your ability to poke holes in everything we take so seriously, jangling our notions of what is correct.
Find some humour in this please!
I hear you plead.

2007, sophomore year. No idea of the mutant genes that were multiplying at an exaggerated speed inside that youthful, strong body.
The diner sign was glowing bright.
We could not turn off the switch in time.
Consumed you would be.
That was your fate.

Now, mine is to sit and peel away every layer of your fleeting life with these random discoveries that become golden nuggets and bitter pills, all one and the same,
living in fear of the day that I won't find anything more.
The frozen moments will be discovered, catalogued, boxed,
Reminding me that the clock has stopped.
That is it.
Done. The play is finished. The cast have all gone home.

How random our acts are on any given day and yet when we can't do any more, each of those singular moments will become the gasp for someone left behind.

Who will fondle my yellowed pieces of papers, wrinkled hankies, bits of twisted string and coins and be reduced to tears knowing these were the last things I touched?
Is that person in my life? Or do they not exist?
That reality hurts just as much as being the one to carry your final scraps.

—Jean A. Rowcliffe, July 4, 2010

Profound loss changes everything in your life. What you thought mattered, what motivated and sustained you, who was important, and what that relationship represented are all questioned. You struggle to validate what was once real and now has become a vapour. As I worked with Carol, many layers of struggle surfaced that I had not anticipated. Old relationships became a recurring theme as the months passed.

Somehow, I had become detached from people that I used to know and cared deeply for prior to James's death. It was not as if they did anything to alienate me or that I could articulate a reason behind this distancing, but it troubled me deeply and, frankly, became a bigger burden than just managing my grief. Some had left subtle messages that they were disappointed and hurt by this, which only compounded my guilt and remorse, making it even harder for me to reach out to them.

I found that the more that people needed me, the more I retreated. Some of those who had once been very close to me became separated by my self-imposed vast ocean of uncertainty. Not being able to articulate what was going on, I remained quiet and distant, and this, of course, only conjured up more guilt and thoughts that I had become a terrible friend. How could I appear such an ungrateful person to those who had been so kind?

I was deeply confused and troubled, and during an afternoon session when I shared this horrible turmoil with Carol, she gave me the greatest sense of peace by quoting a line written by novelist Anne Lamott on the death of her mother: "Death rewrites your address book." These five simple words summed up my new reality.

After death, a remarkable shift in tides surrounding friends and family takes place. Those who you thought would be there are nowhere to be seen while others come up from the rear to fill the vacancies. New friendships are placed on the table while old ones might evaporate. There is no rhyme or reason for this, but it is so common that it needs to be noted. Why I felt such a distance for so long with many from the past I cannot explain; many others who walk the grief path have shared the same truth with me over these past years. Perhaps this is one of those awful universal axioms attached to grief that we just don't want to talk about.

Now almost four years later, I feel a little insight has surfaced; perhaps being with these old friends and relationships just hurt me too much. They had been such an intrinsic piece of my life with James that perhaps I felt subconsciously being with them might only amplify my loss and longing, that a reminder of past days would only reinforce my fear that there would be no future. Some, I know, wished that I would be able to help them carry their grief and make sense of all this, which I was totally incapable of doing. I don't have the answer, and none of the experts seem to either, so I can only hope that those who feel abandoned by me will find peace, and perhaps one day we shall cross paths again without any tension.

Some folks had started to say, as a bizarre way of greeting me, "We miss the old Jean." I know they meant well, but once again, it made me feel inadequate as I did not know what I should do to conjure up that woman again. "I miss her too," was all I could reply. The person now residing in these bones feels very different from the one before, and this forced journey of discovery has been difficult for me. Relationship needs and desires had changed, and I became very aware that I could no longer deliver to many friends and acquaintances what they expected or wanted from me. Small inklings of who I used to be would surface from time to time, but there was no reliability that she'd come to stay permanently. Feelings of guilt and confusion had created an impenetrable wall. Dealing with the expectations of others while trying to sort out my own cornucopia of issues became overwhelming, causing me to retreat further.

Putting pressure on a grieving parent to assume the old persona is an unfair expectation, and if you want to be a good friend, take your clues from more subtle messages. In the end, those who could sit quietly with me while expecting nothing in return brought the greatest peace.

Do you Really Want To Know?

What a mumbled, fumbling world of humans
I now inhabit.
"How am I doing?" is the constant question
Pleading eyes, hoping not to hear the truth.

Do you really want to know?
How dark my dreams are as I
Wander the night sky searching for a new morning outcome.
The same story with every rising.
Repeated longing as I lay my head down.

Solo meals served on a tray
With cloth napkin at my side continuing the rituals in a false, disjointed
sort of way.

Waiting for the door to open
To hear the slow, measured steps
On the never-ending stairs—
Your last journey taken in a body bag
On a cold, unbending stretcher.

You were supposed to leave with bags in hand
Starting out to tackle life as a man,
Not covered in a shroud, carried by strangers.

Do you really want to know?
How that last breath is relived over and over and over and over.
Each visit to that graphic, horrid, messy moment
Longing for a new outcome.
"Are you over this yet?"

Does looking at my pale and weary face
Remind them that they, too, live close to that edge
Where a mutant gene might devour their child, soulmate or self?

So I am asked . . .
But really they want to say, "Get over this"
Be done with sorrow.
Don't remind me how fragile, thin time is.

So I am left exposed, raw
Craving one authentic person
Who will not ask, but rather offer me some tea
Or a branch of blossom
And send me back to my quiet solitude
That asks no questions
And demands no answer.

—Jean Alice Rowcliffe, March 1, 2010

*   *   *

Mourning becomes another job. Just like a challenging new career, it is time-consuming, takes all your focus, and leaves you drained at the end of the day. You crave the things that will give you a little boost to tackle the next steps. It even has its own uniform: basic black.

I struggled with balancing the truth that life going forward would be something quite different than what I had hoped for. I was living in a world with two clocks.

There was a time before James died when life was easily tracked and recorded. I had all the tangible pieces to construct a story, and it was an honest portrayal of who he was and how we were all connected in that tale. It was a perfect puzzle where the edges were straight and the picture easy to decipher. The clock ticked in measured time.

Then suddenly I was presented with a broken, jumbled, and messy jigsaw that made no sense. I had zero idea how to reconstruct the thing that was handed to me. Without asking permission, or making the choice, I was now responsible for this new puzzle but felt I had none of the necessary skills to perform the task. The clock ticked and bonged when it wanted to. I was there merely to respond or not, depending on any given day.

These two clocks had no relation to one another, and yet they were profoundly real and now had become dynamic parts of my life. Trying to make sense of these two measures of time became an ongoing struggle that continues to engage me to this day. How to hold on to the past and all the richness of that story while coming to terms with this new one, attempting to remain comfortable with both, has taken much quiet introspection. The recurring theme of detaching from everything and everyone filled pages of my journal; this was my way of trying to find balance.

While struggling with all these changes, I was reassured by Carol that this need to detach is a common phenomenon that many parents (and others who are living with profound loss) experience during this time of transition. It is interesting how many couples separate or divorce after the death of a child as the strain of negotiating this ever-changing landscape becomes too difficult. Partners often expect the other one to be at the same place they are and become unhappy, even bitter, that they can't share equally.

If one spouse shuts down, the other feels abandoned. Intimacy becomes an issue, and the couple grows apart, living on their "islands of pain." Grief counsellors can help negotiate this maze, but the couple must be willing to seek help—something else that can be tough if it is seen as a sign of weakness.

Contrary to what some thought, I was actually very happy *not* to be in a relationship as there was no one expecting me to be there on a daily basis to prop them up or pretend that life was the same as before. Being solo gave me permission to immerse myself fully in all the emotions I was experiencing at any given time, and I do believe that I am stronger and healthier now due to the fact that I processed my grief so completely every day.

I have the deepest respect for parents who have to process their grief while raising other children in the family. Each family member will have their own personal struggles, and trying to balance that, on top of living life as close to normal for the siblings of the dead child, adds a dynamic I cannot imagine. Following through on special holidays and birthdays for the other children must be excruciating.

Special days still (and may always) pierce my heart. I was indulged in that there was no pretence or expectation to make believe for a partner's sake that things were hunky-dory. I was able to say that "it sucked," and that truth became liberating over time.

Another reality I had not anticipated was the potent grief surrounding loss of the medical community. James and I saw more of his doctors and the UCSF team than anyone else that year. They had become our extended family. Knowing they were available anytime day or night forged a special bond, and it was inevitable that we would become close. I am forever grateful to those who have stayed in touch but know how difficult it must be for them. They have to set careful boundaries; otherwise, they would be sucked into the dark hole of continuously grieving families, and that would not be healthy. They are now and will always remain special souls who shared the most difficult of days with us. James loved them for their devoted care, and I treasure their many gifts of wisdom.

* * *

A year after James died, a woman who knew our story asked me point blank, "Are you over this yet?" I was incredulous. How did she assume to know what goalposts I was supposed to be reaching? I did not know what I was supposed to be *over*. Was I just expected to dismiss the final years as trite? Did she not understand how empty my life had become? Was my sorrow so palpable and disagreeable to others? Days were terribly complicated and confused. That my grief had become such a burden for others was a shock to me.

Interestingly, many other parents have confessed that similar things had been said to them at the most unexpected times. We all acknowledge that it throws us off our stride. The struggle of attempting to find balance with our daily lives, while colliding into those who don't understand, will perhaps always be a reality that we need to confront. In hindsight, it is not surprising that around the time of this pointed question, I suffered an attack of vertigo.

One Saturday morning I stood up and fell over. I clung to the wall to prop myself up and ended up at the local emergency room to figure out what to do. After a few hours of observation, the doctors prescribed Meclizine and assured me this was quite normal and I should not worry. It might happen again in my life, and I should pay attention. Literally, I had been knocked off balance in every way possible, which only reinforced that I should not doubt the power of loss.

*   *   *

Over these past years, I have become emboldened in what I will and won't accept. Having experienced the bottom rung of the ladder, there is very little, if anything, that will disappoint me now, and I have accepted the realization that I am not here to gain the approval of others. "What's the worst that can happen?" is my response to the unknown.

I probably swear too much (James would be proud) as I have no nurses telling me to watch my tongue. I try to speak my truth plainly and without editing. Since necessity dictates that I reinvent myself, old patterns have been given permission to fall away, and I embrace new ones that come along. My grief made me extremely bitter and angry for a very long time, but slowly an internal emery board surfaced to buff off some of those rough edges allowing me to trust my vulnerability. Opening my fragile heart again, the one thing I vowed never to do, has slowly become a reality. I may always struggle with trust.

I crave simple days. Social outings can still be daunting and exhausting. Being anonymous appeals greatly; hence, visits to places unknown are easy. Grief grabs at the most unexpected moments, and sometimes the most insignificant thing causes the greatest sorrow.

What I have entered now is a time of discovery; the "new normal." No one knows what their new normal will be and each person's experience is unique. Detached engagement allows one to be present but not fully immersed in all the emotions of that moment. You hope the guilt and fear will dissipate, and in time the burden does. It's okay and actually incredibly brave to say, "There are no words." "No" becomes empowering, and you learn to use it with authority whenever boundaries need to be set.

*   *   *

I continue to find James in boxes, photos, music, and mementos. My gasp is still audible with each discovery, and I ache to hear his voice, the guitar strum, his laugh, and nonsense banter. Often as I fall asleep, I see him walking into my room with his big ebullient smile as he did on Saturday mornings, calling out, "Hey, Mama, what's up today?"

Many times I have said that I would give everything for just one more hour with him, but understand now that the fantasy will have to be sufficient. I struggle with the truth that there is nothing more to our personal story, and I'll need to be careful with what is left as there is no replacement plan. His life story is carefully bubble-wrapped and carried with me now, and as I unfold things gently to admire or reflect upon, I understand this is the best one can hope for.

Yes, there is a comfort in knowing that James does live on through his friends and those he touched in his short years, but the void is potent and nothing will ever fully complete the circle we started.

James' friends celebrate his 19th birthday

James's friends celebrate his 20th birthday

Section 4

Retreat from the Precipice

Chapter 21

The Only Way Out Is Through

I can gaze out now,
With these new eyes
on a view that blinds me.

— *James, "Coastline" poem, 2006*

The day that James died my life, a perfectly constructed puzzle, was tossed into the air and the pieces left to scatter at will. Nothing was connected and the picture destroyed, yet all the pieces were still there, just in an ad hoc fashion littering the landscape. It would require days, months, years for me to scrounge around on hands and knees, gathering up the pieces trying to make sense of how they might become whole again. Some pieces had lost their connecting tab, others were bent. How would the border be defined? It would actually become a new puzzle picture, composed of old pieces that had to be manipulated and eventually reconfigured.

— *Jean Alice Rowcliffe, 2012*

His death is fast-approaching and part of me wants James to die to end his wretched suffering . . . I might then be able to completely let go, but I am also terrified that I might not find myself again.

— *Personal journal entry, May 6, 2009*

In the early days following James's death, a dialogue, often dictated by others, began, and the recurring theme was how best to make me feel happy and less pained or troubled. The words spoken would hopefully bring comfort and solace, perhaps some sort of magical healing balm that one could rub on and make everything all right. I know they came from a place of love and profound caring, but unwittingly the words only punctuated my sorrow. How these well-intentioned people could not understand had me perplexed, rattled, and insecure on what felt like a daily basis.

There are no words to make it better. Nothing will erase the hollowness that sits in the freshly broken heart. Anguish becomes the new normal, at least for the moment. I had no interest in trying to make anything better, and that suggested task, on top of my incredible sorrow, made everything feel impossibly overwhelming. Since nothing made sense any longer, I would leave healing as an undertaking best left for others to contemplate.

I now inhabited a place of incessant reacting. The thought of ever being proactive again was as alien as a trip to Mars. There was no path to follow or blueprint to memorize. Isolation was palpable, and I felt, perhaps incorrectly, that so few could truly understand what I was going through.

Why do I have to be happy? Why is this constantly presented as the only option? How can others presume to know what is best for me? Why can't I just be where I am right now? Totally detached from reality, it did feel as though I was going mad.

* * *

During the first two years of mourning, I became a recluse, in every sense of the word. Showing up for work and putting on a plastic smile was doable some days; on others I just wanted to hide in a closet, and the office closet did become my refuge from time to time when I needed to be invisible.

Unexpectedly—but now, I suppose, not really surprisingly—my work at the Village Well taxed me more than anticipated, and it became more difficult to interact with parents and young children. Every day, just walking through the gate, I was reminded of what I had lost.

To those who knew me best, I would say it felt like a poultice of salt and vinegar being rubbed into all the ragged edges of the chasm that once held a complete heart. I was astounded some days that it kept on beating.

Many journal entries from those early years after James's death were filled with descriptions of overwhelming brokenness and desolation. Would it ever hurt less? My breathing had become shallow gasps. Pain was everywhere. Disconnection from surroundings was a daily occurrence. I vowed never to get close to anyone again. Promising to shut down my heart and never allow myself to care deeply would surely spare me any future anguish.

The threat of loss and even more sorrow was all-consuming. Volumes were dedicated to receiving this gothic dialogue of dark sorrow, uncertainty, rage, and isolation. It all seemed impossible, yet as I now re-explore these journals, there were occasionally small glimmers of a sense that for some reason I was left on this earth for a purpose. James had died way too young and been robbed of a larger story, but somehow I had to carry on.

"Time will heal." If I heard this once, I heard it a thousand times. It became a grating saccharine message of goodwill that felt disingenuous in its simplicity. Heal. How could anyone know what I needed or how I would recuperate from this free fall? It felt too bold for others to make the assumption that they knew what I was going through and what was going to be the cure. Time. Just an arbitrary measure that others place upon moments and anyway, I had lost all sense of it.

I began to resent others for trying to dictate the way I was supposed to walk this path of grief, and their assumptions made me angry. How could they know better than me what I needed at any given moment? I had not expected this reaction, and it frightened me. Hospice had warned me that once the shock of James's death had subsided, my bottled-up emotions and frustrations over the course of his illness would need to be released.

For most of my life, I had been very happy-go-lucky, willing to make it up as I went along, and this deep anger was something new and scary. My travels and work experiences all just fell into place, and I often joked about sailing through life by the seat of my pants. I would show up in a foreign country and find work, establish and grow friendships; explore and become knowledgeable about the terrain. I had a willingness to let things work themselves out and adapt accordingly. It was a skill I never took for granted and felt grateful to possess.

Suddenly, I was confronted by this new landscape that I knew nothing about and, worst still, had no desire to explore. It had been thrust upon me, and there wasn't an escape plan in place. Unlike the past, I had not saved up to buy a ticket here, nor did I want to stay. This path to an unknown destination was agonizing, but that sadly was the new reality. Not even my prior willingness to make it up as I went along or sail through the moments could help me grasp this one. The twists and turns were often excruciating.

The reason for being here was certainly not one I had chosen, and the emotions attached felt insurmountable.

*   *   *

At the end of a year, my grief sessions with Carol came to a close, and she thoughtfully suggested that I join a group for bereaved parents, led by Dr. Nancy Iverson, a well-respected San Francisco pediatrician. Nancy had found that the long-term support needed by grieving parents was not always available and that the insights of others going through the same thing was often the greatest help, even surpassing what the professional healthcare providers could offer.

Nancy held the support groups in her home near the Opera House in San Francisco. I was a tad daunted when I arrived for the first evening meeting. Greeted at the door by a small plaque inscribed with the Hawaiian salutation *Mahalo*, I was immediately struck by the intimate nature of the gathering. There was no organized structure as to who would speak, what would be shared, or who might be there since at any gathering the mix of parents would shift and change. Some had only recently lost a child. Others had suffered this tragedy three to five years earlier. One family had been attending for over ten years. I rapidly learned that this grief story was going to be with me forever, and as harsh as that realization was, it did bring a modicum of comfort to know I was not alone.

Since the evenings followed no pattern, we were each invited to share our stories and where we found ourselves at that moment.

On that first evening, there was a couple whose four-month old baby had just died at a day care. The rawness of their emotions reminded me how unbelievably difficult those early days are, and my heart broke for them. I shared the story of James through many tears and was glad to have brought his graduation photo to circulate. They all commented on how handsome he looked and also what ancient wise eyes he had. I soon discovered that when looking at the face of a now-dead child, we perceive an almost sacred aura about them and we don't see them in the same light as we do the living.

Those in mourning understand that this moment in time, frozen on film, is one of the greatest prized possessions we carry. There will be no more photos, works of art, writings, or presents. It has all come to an end. There was an unexpected relief in the shared simplicity of that truth. I attended Nancy's group on a regular bimonthly basis and found myself looking forward to the meetings more and more. Sometimes, we might share memories of our children; other times we might delve into one particular aspect of grief. I recall especially bringing my frustration and bewilderment to one gathering.

It was during the period when I had discovered that there was little I wanted to share with some people, many of whom had once been close to James and me. It was difficult to articulate, and the continuing struggle troubled me greatly, especially as some of these people were making subtle digs that I had disappointed them, making me think I was doing it all wrong. Thankfully, other parents in the group shared the same feelings, and we agreed collectively that yes, as Carol had said, death does rewrite your address book.

Some parents, who had been attending for a longer period, had acquired a calm and confidence in carrying their grief burden, and I found myself jealously wondering how did they did it; was it authentic? Nancy was marvellous in her ability to prod us to go a little bit deeper with each visit, and I valued enormously, just as with Carol, her lack of judgment or desire to solve or 'fix". Being true to the moment and accepting all the anguish, rage, sorrow, and emptiness was valid. It felt liberating to be in a setting where I did not need to explain myself or my actions. There truly was no right or wrong way to walk this shared path. She introduced me to the simple concept "Of course," which would stay with me going forward.

Of course it would be difficult to get out of bed some days. *Of course* we would feel hurt by those who might say inappropriate things. *Of course* I would struggle with being authentic. *Of course* I would not want to be close to anyone again. *Of course* missing James would be all-consuming. "Of course" explained, validated, and interestingly liberated me from the suppositions of those not walking the same path.

Some lives intersect for the long haul while others are more fleeting. The imagery of parallel and intertwining pathways had always been a core belief of mine, but I had totally abandoned this hypothesis in the early days after James died. Attending Nancy's group allowed that conjecture to return and helped to influence my interactions moving forward, a major factor in my retreat from the edge.

*   *   *

I have always been interested in the faith journey of humankind and must confess I have not found one religion to answer all my questions. I suppose I am one of those "spiritual but not religious" souls that seem to have become their own demographic. I do have a sense of a higher power, and whatever we choose to call it is left to our personal interpretations. Since moving to California in the mid-1980s, I became exposed to many more religious philosophies and found myself particularly interested in the teachings of the Buddha. There is one story that stayed with me and illustrates my slow re-entry into life:

> Legend has it that a man was clinging to a cliff edge, when the Buddha walked by. The man yelled out for the Buddha to save him and the Buddha replied, "Let go." The man did not and so Buddha carried on walking the winding path.
>
> Soon afterwards some disciples walked by the man clinging to the edge and again he shouted out to be saved. Again, he was told to let go but refused and so they also continued on the path.
>
> The poor man was struggling terribly now when one last disciple came along. Once more the clinging man pleaded to be saved and this time the disciple knelt down and said quietly to him, "How can you be saved, if you don't let go and trust that you will be caught?"

Attending this group for broken parents, I began to realize that I was the one clinging to the edge and the exercise of holding on had become all-consuming. Even though years earlier I had promised James that I would never leave him, my grasping on to his memory through resentment, anger, and sorrow was not what he would have wanted. Unless I was willing to trust and let go, I would never be saved.

Slowly, through my journal entries, I started to plot new potential pathways, allowing myself the luxury to contemplate ones that did not revolve around the survival and struggle issues that had become my story for too long. Running a nonprofit during incredibly difficult financial times for the country was, in hindsight, an additional burden. The incessant need to fundraise and be the face of the organization meant that I was living an almost schizophrenic life. While appearing in public brave, stoic, and omnipotent in my capacity to give, underneath the surface I was crumbling, intensely sad, and horribly uncertain. The fatigue from this exercise started to take its toll. I was pale, puffy, and numb. Sorrow survival, as I called it, had become my modus operandi, and the task of working to keep everything ticking over came at great personal expense.

*　　*　　*

In the spring of 2011, I opened myself up to exploring an opportunity of a house exchange in France with the parents of dear friends. My travel had been limited after James's death to a few trips to Canada to see my mother and family as well as a wedding in the United Kingdom. Beyond that I had stayed bound to the story (and grief) of San Francisco.

Polk Street was my nest, and I retreated every evening to a distant corner of the flat, curling up on a sofa in the study, literally, the furthest spot away from the outside world. Then, almost miraculously, the thought of some time in a house abroad started to appeal. Acknowledging how I dreaded the yearly anniversary suffering on Mother's Day, I made a vow to always be in new surroundings on May 9 as well as June 13, James's birthday. My goal was to somehow replenish my spirit, or at least escape the triggers, on the darkest of days.

The prior year I had spent the dreaded anniversary at the Abbey of New Clairvaux, near Chico, in northern California. While there was no interaction with the monks, who follow the Cistercian tradition, I found incredible peace in their world of solitude and prayer. Over 600 acres of vineyards and orchards provided harmony, and the opportunity to sit completely with my grief, without any distraction from the outside world, was cathartic.

Cloister, New Clairvaux

Monastic life revolved around work, prayer, and silence. While I longed for the simplicity of such an existence, I returned to the city oddly empowered. This retreat in nature began a tradition of scattering some of James's ash in special places; he now resides in a number of magical spots on the planet.

The house exchange had come out of the blue, and of course I now realize the power of unsolicited opportunity. The dates for the exchange fell close to the wedding of the Duke and Duchess of Cambridge, so I decided to travel to London to be there for the celebrations as I had in 1981 for the wedding of Prince Charles and Lady Diana. Those who know my story of royal service will understand the appeal of being in London to share in this day, a full-circle moment, if you will.

I was apprehensive and unsure what to expect on this trip, but for the first time since before James was diagnosed, I felt a tiny surge of willingness to open up to an adventure and see where it might take me. As I boarded the plane, I was aware that the overwhelming weight of James not being able to share in this experience did not make me cry. Safely packed away in my suitcase was a soft silk pouch holding some of his ashes to be sprinkled on foreign soil. I missed him terribly, but my breathing was easier and I felt less raw. It would be a lie to say that I don't ache to send him off on an adventure again. That longing will always be with me until the day I die. No amount of time will erase the desire to share more with your loved one; you just learn to live with that desire.

During this trip to London I was reacquainted with some old friends—one in particular—I had known thirty years before, and there was a subtle shift and willingness on my part to return to those days and share stories once again. Prior to this point, any reflections beyond the days of illness, death, and mourning had been impossible. My numbness had left me unable to connect to anything in life beyond sorrow. Sharing stories and recalling simpler days from decades ago was a gift I had not anticipated.

Cautiously, I contemplated the possibility of opening my heart again and maybe, as Robin had predicted, even reengaging in life.

I spoke to James incessantly and asked for his guidance while sprinkling ashes in the Thames, the Round Pond, and special gardens, a few fingers full at a time.

As had been foretold by the palliative and hospice team, my willingness to re-enter life had eventually come but in my own time and way. No one can orchestrate this scenario, and that is one of the most valuable lessons I want to share with you. It only reinforces how intensely personal and private the mourning of a profound loss will be, and reengaging in daily life is a choice that one comes to only when ready. For some it is almost immediately after death; others might take months or years. For me, it has been a slow process that has taken over three years, and even now I still have many moments when I need to retreat from the world and find solitude. Not unlike a turtle I come in and out of my shell with great ease. One is not warned how lengthy this process of discovery can be, and again I stress that it is essential to listen to your gut and trust those instincts, which are rarely, if ever, wrong.

* * *

The homeowners from France were concerned that I not make the trip on my own as their ancient stone house in the small remote village was dark and I might find it lonely. Knowing it was the anniversary of James's death, they were especially concerned that I not be travel on my own; hence, two of my San Francisco friends joined me there. We met up in London and, after some pleasant days walking the city, flew to Bordeaux, picked up the rental car, and headed into the bucolic rolling countryside to explore village life for a week.

We arrived in Eyrenville late on May 8 and groped about in the dark trying to find the door that fit the ancient eight-inch forged-iron key. In our quest I jiggled a few of the neighbour's doors, and I am sure they wondered what in God's name was going on, but we finally found the right one, and the five-foot-high oak door opened onto a lovely three-storey home filled with eclectic furnishings and stories.

The owners had warned in advance that a possible visit from Reginald, the resident bat, might be in the cards, and sure enough, as we wandered the house to get our bearings, Reginald swooped down from a wooden beam, causing the three of us to run in circles screaming and flapping like banshees. By now we knew the neighbours would be well and truly baffled by these new village residents, but the screaming soon turned to laughter and we were crying from our hysterics. It was the first time in years that I laughed with such gusto that it hurt.

Once calm and settled into my little iron bed in the garden room, I remembered that this was the eve of the second anniversary of James's death and somehow the universe had provided me laughter instead of endless tears. I think that night was when I started to grasp that I truly might be able to turn a corner with my suffering.

On May 9 we drove into the river town of Bergerac to have lunch and explore the sights. In our wanderings we were confronted by a very bold bleached-blonde waitress who insisted, in her broken English, that we sit at her outdoor table under the gaze of Cyrano. Being quite willing to be bullied by a local, we accepted her "invitation" and found a table under an oversized white umbrella. Lunch consisted of bountiful salads, including the freshest of goat cheese and garden oranges, produced with incredible speed.

While dining in this village square, a lovely, hitherto unfamiliar ease washed over me. I watched children frolic in the fountain, parents buy ice cream, white-haired matrons in ridiculous sun hats walk their lap dogs, and for the first time in what seemed forever, it did not hurt. I was able to engage in the moment without connection to the powerful emotions of past memories or resentment. I would contemplate and begin to embrace more completely that afternoon my new interpretation of detached engagement.

After lunch we wandered into the ancient church that towered over us, and once again the synchronicity of moments that we are all destined to experience was revealed. I wandered off on my own as the memories of May 9 suddenly became potent and the surge of tears began. Under the transept sat a long altar table with the most glorious bouquet of Casablanca lilies, freshly arranged and deeply fragrant. "My favourite," I whispered and felt a humbling gratitude that those would be the flowers on display today, of all days. Nearby stood a statue of the Madonna holding the baby Jesus on her hip, and I was struck by their gentle expressions; none of the pleading sorrow so commonly attached to their story was present here—only a mother's calm and her baby's love shone through. Sitting on the table at the base of the statue was a single long white taper. No other tapers candles were there, just this one, and a small glowing votive. Something compelled me to light the taper, and I did without hesitation, placing it in a holder in the folds of the statue.

Sitting on the front pew I wept uncontrollably and without reserve. Months of sorrow spilled onto the stone floor beneath me as I prayed for James and myself. Loss, longing, and the ensuing suffering of both; life's unfairness and also the magic of moments that remind us we are not alone (at that point, even kindnesses made me weep) all swirled generously around me. I don't know how long I sat there, but over time I felt my friend's hand touch my shoulder and their eyes were also glistening; they had just found a brochure in English telling the history of the church, the Chapel of St. James.

Somehow we had missed the name when entering.

As we approached the back of the church, about to depart, we noticed tiny white footprints that had been placed in a line down the centre aisle leading to the altar. They were traced outlines of a child's foot, and in the centre of each foot was printed the message, "Il fait route avec nous" (He is travelling with us). Tears started flowing once again. While I had felt small hints over the past year this new discernment was huge. What I had felt prior to this moment was just a small crack in the window but now once again we both agreed I had been given a sign. Overwhelming in its simplicity but powerful in its truth, I was being reminded that James was a quiet partner for me as I walked what I felt was a solitary path. He would always be with me. Even in a far-flung village in France, I was jolted into the reality that he *had* become a piece of everything and could help open the door; suddenly it was flung wide open. Things changed dramatically for me on that day, and it was the true beginning of my retreat from the edge.

Child's footprint on the floor of the Chapel of St. James in Bergerac, France

*   *   *

From childhood, I had an acute, sensitive, and some said remarkable sense of smell. Perfumes, aftershaves, baking smells from open windows, green fields, laundry soap on passersby, gardens—everything had a distinctive aroma, and I loved the way this excited my other senses.

When James died, these senses became numb, and I had not fully realized how much I missed them. Interestingly, others who have shared their grief stories with me also tell of losing their senses (both literally and figuratively), and many struggle with hearing or seeing fully. It makes sense. Powerful grief knocks one off stride in so many different ways. My earlier bout of vertigo and loss of smell only reinforced that my core had been totally unhinged. In hindsight, it makes perfect sense.

During the days following the visit to Bergerac, I noticed an awakening of my sense of smell. As I walked the quiet fields on cool evenings, I could savour the dryness of the soil, and trailing roses suddenly had their distinctive scent once more. Even my old favourite, dripping blue wisteria that hung over the front door of the house, produced its subtle evening aroma, reminding me of how much joy this flower had brought me over the years.

Village neighbours baking bread or smoking meat at the local farm became part of this reawakened symphony of sensations. Not only was my sense of smell rekindled but so too were taste and the ability to see colour and texture more fully. Until this moment, I had not fully acknowledged how completely numb I had become.

As positive as this all sounds, I want to warn you, it was not a sudden bolt or a switch that was turned on but rather a methodical process. I use the metaphor of a slow-motion film documenting the opening of a flower. It is a gradual and uniquely personal experience. There are no quick fixes here, and one is foolish to think that just making the decision to reengage will suffice. Body, mind, and spirit all need to be in sync, and it does take time. The beginning is just that—a beginning. Triggers will continue to haunt and taunt. Time and patience will still be cards in the deck that must be played out. For me, there was a bourgeoning sense of liberation in knowing that a life, once again rich in all experiences, might just be possible.

While in Bordeaux, on the final days of our visit, I felt a sudden urge to have something done with my hair. Since James's illness I had not done anything for me. There was an abandonment of vanity or caring for self. Everything had been poured into him, and now my mourning sucked all remaining interest and energy. My clothing had remained the same, basic boring black. My complexion was pale and sallow, and my hair, left untouched, grew into an unruly mess.

Along with a plethora of *macaron* shops, Bordeaux seems to be abundant in hair salons. I wandered into one to see if they might be able to take an impromptu appointment. They had an opening in an hour and a half, so I put my name on the list. As I walked out, there was an overwhelming urge to do it now, before I could talk myself out of it. A few blocks away I stopped at another salon and asked in rudimentary French for an appointment. When the receptionist replied, "Oui" without returning to cancel the other appointment, I headed to the swivel chair, undid the raggedy bun, and waited for the stylist to take a look. She made no effort to conceal her horror while brushing out the mess, lifting the layers to see if there was something salvageable; under her breath I heard many a "Mon Dieu!" My friend waited, patiently reading a *Hello* magazine and shooting me the occasional thumbs-up as a way to keep me tied to the chair.

After multiple shampoos, conditioning treatments, and massages, she clutched industrial shears to begin the process. I could sense her disdain and that of the stylish salon patrons as the withered locks carpeted the floor by my feet.

Somehow from somewhere I plucked up the courage to explain, in very broken French, that I was in mourning, having lost my son, my only child. The atmosphere of judgment in the room came to a grinding halt, and all the women started to cry. Each one in her own way tried to make me feel better with a smile or pleading look of "Please forgive me."

Being honest with them had opened their hearts, and all the issues of my being the Canadian tourist, a broken mess of a woman in black with ugly hair, evaporated, and we became mothers in a salon in France, sharing in relative silence, a tragic story: the worst of nightmares for us all.

Two and a half hours later I walked out onto the cobblestones with the softest head of hair I had ever possessed. It was wonderfully cut to a length never tried before, and I felt, for the first time in ages, beautiful. My friends both loved the look, and we marvelled collectively at how long it had taken me to come to a place of caring for me.

Much shifted for me on that special afternoon, and the shedding of old dead hair became an allegory for the layers that I needed to lose, not only to heal myself but also to set James free. We dined in the local square that evening while musicians played folk songs, and for the first time in years I cried tears of joy for having come to this moment in time.

That night, true to form, I had a powerful dream. The setting was simple with James sitting across from me at a small wooden table, not unlike the outdoor café tables in the village. He looked robust and healthy, just as he had on his sixteenth birthday. As we sat together, James looked deeply into my eyes and told me point-blank that I had to release him. Unwittingly, my grief was the anchor that kept him earthbound and unable to move on to other things. Never had I stopped to think that my actions might still have an impact on him, but in this dream state, it made perfect sense. We are all so intrinsically intertwined and bound that *"of course"* the dead and living must continue their connection. Everything in nature is dictated by the cycle of life, death, and rebirth. Why would the human world stray from that guiding principle? James had stayed close by, held and carried me, sat with me, manipulated the elements, all in his effort to bring me peace and reminders that he was okay. It was now up to me to trust that and also find a way to make peace with this new reality. I needed to set him free.

I awoke very early and felt slightly rattled, more by the honesty of James's words than his dream-induced presence. After being haunted by his deathbed image, I was struck by how handsome and complete James looked once again, and it brought me great joy.

Breakfast service at the hotel began at 6:00 a.m. on the upper floor, and I showered, dressed, and walked empty corridors to the dining room. Sitting solo, watching the sunrise with a pot of strong tea, I surveyed the port of Bordeaux, trying to digest all that had transpired in the past twenty-four hours. The return flight to Heathrow would leave at noon, and I was suddenly overwhelmed by anxiety. Could I hold on to all the goodness of this trip? How would I be able to cling to these insights and sensations, my rebirth and new discoveries and lessons? It felt daunting and overwhelming, but my journal once again became the safe place to plot my course of action and save the words that tumbled so freely once again.

Somehow, I had managed to negotiate that once all-consuming darkness and felt hopeful that there might indeed be light and warmth ready and waiting to embrace me. I was not totally confident, but I had certainly made great strides, and the old Buddha saying that "the only way out is through" rang more true than at any other time in my life.

> Now that you live here in my chest
> Anywhere we sit is a mountaintop.
> What used to be pain is a lovely bench
> Where we can rest under the roses.
>
> —Rumi

Chapter 22

Stepping off the Grid

O heart, o heart you are broken in part, now what must I do to save you.

—James, 2008

Every blade in the field—every leaf in the forest,
Lays down its life in its season, as beautifully as it was taken up.
—Henry David Thoreau

I don't know what I am supposed to do, but I do know what I will do no longer.
—Jean Alice Rowcliffe, March 2012

*   *   *

Such a lot has transpired since my last entry in this journal. I now keep two separate journals; one is just for my travels as I felt it important to hold those realizations in their own place. This trip was indeed transformative on so many levels and I have returned to San Francisco less heavy, lighter in heart and spirit; perhaps I am more able to detach from the grief story here.

—Personal journal entry, May 20, 2011

This was the beginning of the new chapter in a journal that would document the coming months. The time abroad had shifted my outlook and presented the ability to question and grapple with the notion that change might be something to embrace and perhaps even become my new reality.

Profound grief is universal. We will all share in it at some point in our lives. My profound grief had shaken me to my core, and I had become a different person, someone I did not know. This new woman who had been carved out of a slab of bereavement marble was dark and angry, hollow and full of anguished resentment. Being in France on a fresh and unexplored landscape where I shared no history, when every day unfolded as it should, where no one knew my story (free of expectations) provided an opportunity to let go of some well-worn patterns. I began, slowly, to trust once again.

What I was about to trust, I did not have a clue, but I was willing to accept that I did not have to manipulate every moment to make it worthwhile. I surrendered again to my childhood belief that the universe would provide what I needed at any given time.

* * *

Returning to San Francisco proved a challenge. Clinging desperately to the desire of allowing days to unfold effortlessly clashed with the reality of running a business, paying the bills, providing for myself, and once again dealing with the daily triggers of my life without James.

Sadly, I quickly became once again, unbalanced. Every day my decision-making process was being taxed and the struggle to hold on to what I knew to be my personal truth, compared to how I was living, started to consume and trouble me. That comfortable old pattern of retreating into my own space continued to be the only way I could tackle the day-to-day, and I found myself again a recluse.

"Miss Jean," the omnipotent giver/caretaker of others, kicked into high gear within just days of my return to the city, and I resented my inability to set boundaries. I have always been a prolific dreamer of vivid, even colourful escapades during the night. Since my childhood, dreams have provided a way for me to process my feelings, and for decades I have kept dedicated dream journals. Thankfully, James continued to be a regular night time visitor upon my return to San Francisco, and there began a number of recurring dreams during the following months, one of which was particularly potent.

In what seemed to be now a favourite setting, James was sitting across from me at an ancient table. In this dream, he held a massive dusty leather Victorian ledger, the front of which was heavily embossed, but I could not decipher the wording. In my sleep state I marvelled at how easily James held it, given its size. Had he not been weak such a short time ago? How had he regained his strength? Thoughts are so easily unclouded in the middle of the night.

On the pages of this tome were written the names of all the people I had saved, touched, or worked with during the decades of my life. Lists of families and children, individuals and places, it seemed to go on endlessly. James, silently and without expression, turned the many pages. The final leaf was empty, except for my name written in the centre of the page in beautiful oversized calligraphy. He turned to look at me, and though no words were spoken, I understood what the message was: "It is your time, Mama."

Silently, James was giving me permission to do something I had hitherto thought impossible: save myself.

Yes, I was weary of the struggle and sorrow, and that was certainly recorded on countless journal entries, but I could not see a way to shift the paradigm. How was I going to receive what the cosmos might conjure up for me when my vision was so blurred and energy blocked? How could I save myself when saving others had been my mission for most of my adult life? Did I deserve this tempting salvation? I suppose that was at the core of much of my struggle.

On June 12, 2011, the eve of James's twentieth birthday, powerful feelings of anguish and emptiness once again became overwhelming. Immediately the dreaded buttons of uncertainty were pushed. I had nothing to hold on to, especially no sense of future. Lacking purpose or ability to have a story continue through my child was the thrust of this drowning sorrow. Even with the healing I had experienced a month earlier, this death saga and mourning would forever haunt me. Nothing was clear, and the next steps felt impossible.

The prior year, during his birthday anniversary, I had travelled to Hawaii armed with new journals, faithful to the promise of being somewhere new on this eve. Enviously, I watched families frolic in the water, couples cling to one another, diners enjoy the breathtaking sunsets over bottles of champagne, all the while telling myself to be at peace and let go of my desire to have someone to share all this glorious beauty with. Even though my spirit was bruised from colliding into these sights, there was, a subtle shift taking place.

While in Hawaii, on the anniversary of James's birth, I had gifted myself with a massage. That morning the beaches had been closed due to a shark sighting. When I mentioned this news to the masseur, he told me that this was a fortuitous sign as sharks in Hawaiian legend are visitors from the afterlife. As the sun set that evening, I took some of James's ashes to sprinkle in the ocean along a lonely stretch of shoreline. At that moment, I saw two shark fins pass slowly in front of me, which brought me incredible happiness.

Now, a year later, while feeling distraught and heavy, I reflected on those Hawaiian memories and felt grateful for the experience and proud that I had followed my gut, and stepped away. Unwittingly, each of these steps had been bringing me closer to a peaceful place of total transition.

June 13 started with floods of tears, and that omnipresent fear of slowly descending into madness bubbled up once again. As if James knew he needed to send some signals my way, a number of odd physical manifestations occurred over the next two days. I would credit these manipulated moments as his way of reminding me to stay alert and be willing to embrace change and maybe even, as he would tease, "lighten up!"

1. A dear friend in the United Kingdom has a glorious garden frequented by many breeds of birds. On June 13, sitting in the middle of the lawn was a bird he had never spotted before. Even while taunted by blackbirds, the bird sat focused, looking straight in the window without budging from his spot, as if to make sure he was seen. Referring to his bird compendium, my friend discovered that it was a Mistlethrush. "Extremely rare," according to the book, with sightings "most uncommon." Once the bird knew he had been seen through the window, it strutted about the garden, taking its time to explore and enjoy a leisurely splash in the pond. After another long stare in the window, it swooshed up into the sky. This bird has not appeared again.

2. I had lost a pearl earring at work days before and was concerned that no one find it, especially a child, who might try to swallow it. I had looked everywhere and had the staff searching as well. It was nowhere to be found, and I struggled to make peace with the thought that it was gone, and trusted that no one would be harmed by it. Late in the day on June 13, I passed by a poster in the office, and whatever motivated me to look at it I'll never know, but there in the top left corner was the pearl, acting as a pushpin. I smiled and shared its discovery with the office, and collectively we all said, "James!"

3. The evening of June 12, I found some quarters in the dryer lint, and how they got there I will never know. Interestingly, that afternoon, I had said out loud that I needed more quarters to pay for parking meters as I had run out. Saving parking quarters was an ongoing pastime for James and me.

4. Robin, the palliative coordinator, sent an e-mail at that time to say she had been awakened for the past days with the loudest bird chorus she had ever heard; and she marvelled at where it was coming from. Knowing how James had enjoyed the bird metaphor, we both

agreed this might be another of his visits. She also confessed to asking James for help parking when visiting patients (parking is an ongoing nightmare in San Francisco), and she had been successful *every* time since James died.

5. Marc had gone to a birthday party on June 13 at a club in San Francisco. It was a casual evening, and he wore a sports jacket. Apparently there were no gifts or birthday cake at the gathering. It was just to be a few drinks with friends in a bar. When Marc got home, he was taking off his jacket, and something nudged him to check the pockets. Buried in one was a small purple birthday candle, striped in green. It had not been lit, nor had he ever seen it before. It was quirky and unlike anything Marc might have picked up. He too immediately thought of James and placed the candle on a shelf in his bookcase along with other special mementos collected in James's memory.

6. On the morning of his birthday, June 13, on the step outside the flat, where many quirky "James" items had been left since his death (a pinecone, white rose, a heart-shaped rock, to name a few), there was a glass filled with water. It was one of those heavy bistro glasses often used for juice or wine, and it had a slice of lime and pink blossom floating in it. Who left it there? And why? In any case, it brought me the greatest smile and a chuckle, especially as James knew I did not like lime in my water. Without missing a beat, I thought of him and how this gesture was so in keeping with his sense of humour.

Skateboarders had started to scoot down Polk Street, with some of them out on the street well after midnight. Friends started to leave messages, saying they could hear skateboarders everywhere they went. It felt as though James was playing with all the elements to remind us, but especially me, that he was fine, happy, and enjoying being, at last, *free*.

The message I took away from these days was to pay attention, Jean. There was much shifting going on, and I must stay alert and keep my mind uncluttered. I was becoming aware of an evolution, and while unable to articulate fully what it might look like, the transition towards saving myself that James had predicted in my dream had begun.

*   *   *

As I shared these tales with others who had experienced great loss, they told me of the moments when they, too, felt a shift in their mourning. For each of us it had been an intensely private journey, and we all agreed that there is absolutely no blueprint to follow. You can't instigate the change. No amount of manipulation will bring it to fruition. The ebb and flow will continue, but somehow one starts to put a little more into the living cup where the scale had been tipped profoundly by the weight of the death cup. Only then does one feel capable and confident enough to consider stepping more completely back into life.

Through my writings, I wondered if it was the need for our own survival that kicks in, and somehow there is a unification of body, spirit, and mind that says, "Enough, we can't do this anymore." Interestingly, it seems to be around the third year when the fog starts to lift for many, but again, I would never assume that this is written in stone. It might take decades, but there does come a point when you can consider stepping more fully into the day-to-day functions of life, and things do become a bit easier.

This is not to say one is "healed." To look for that outcome is foolish. I describe it as "a willingness to sit with death and allow it to become a companion instead of fighting it constantly." This unwelcome death has destroyed your life so completely, but discovering a place of union where grief is present, but not the ringleader in every decision or response, is perhaps all one can hope for.

I knew that James would always be with me in some form, yet the desire to share with and watch him grow to be a man continued to make me sad. The empty feeling that I am solo and will not have a child to share my senior years with is difficult. It would be a lie to say anything else. The loss of purpose and ache for physical contact with James remained a desperate longing, yet even in the midst of all this, I began to feel that a new path might just be possible, but it would require dramatic change.

*   *   *

San Francisco was becoming a place of great burden. "Grief whores," as I called them, hung out at every corner tempting me as I passed by:

"Hey, Jean, remember when James skated here?"

"Remember when you carried him home when sleepy?"

"Remember when you laughed so hard it made him cry?'

"Look, there are his initials in the once-wet cement."

"Here's that favourite bread you both loved."

"Oh, look, this is where you bought the Christmas tree each year."

"Here is where he took his last steps on the sidewalk before he couldn't walk anymore."

"Remember how painful it was to watch him climb the stairs for the last time . . . It took over half an hour, didn't it?"

This incessant, noisy babble haunted me every time I stepped out through the gate, and even though I thought it was bringing me comfort to be in the city, it was actually having the opposite effect.

During September of 2011, I returned to Canada to spend a couple of weeks with my niece in Northern Ontario while my brother and his wife had their annual retreat. The explosion of autumn colours set against the teal waters of Georgian Bay jolted my senses. I was overwhelmed by beauty. I wrote and quietly spent time surveying the glorious scenery, and for the first time since James died, I felt not just awe but also deep gratitude for nature. I was aware, once again, of my awakening.

On September 9, the twenty-eighth month of the anniversary of his death (yes, I kept a running record of this anniversary in my diary), I treated myself to breakfast in a small café by the water. It was simple and very quiet, but I was shocked by the overwhelming peace in that moment. I had not felt such serenity since being in Europe, and I was startled by an epiphany that perhaps I could start over. Maybe this never-ending loop could cease and a new dialogue might be possible. There were no bells, whistles, and crashing symbols, just a gentle nudge that told me, you *can* step away. Life could be easier. People do this all the time. Maybe I could move? Perhaps I was finally willing to accept that, yes, I deserved this.

*   *   *

Without knowing it, December 2011 would be my last Christmas season in San Francisco. Once again, I made the conscious decision not to get a tree. A few branches of holly, evergreen, and poinsettia made their way into some of the rooms. I placed our favourite Aromatique potpourri, the Smell of Christmas, in the basket at the bottom of the stairwell. James and I loved how it scented the front entry with intoxicating cinnamon, orange, and winter spices. All his friends knew about the basket, and each boy at some time over the years had shared with me that the smell of our foyer always made them think of the holidays. A few stopped by during this season just to get a whiff and fill their lungs once again. Through this simple gesture, James was alive for them too.

Many dear friends invited me to join them for meals or celebrations, but I did not yet feel strong enough for special family reunions. Getting through the day was my hope, and whatever it took to make this happen would suffice. I did not want gifts, nor was I able to give them. Sending greeting cards proved to be daunting, and so I decided an e-mailed New Year's message would be the plan. Listening to my instincts, trusting and doing what I felt to be right had become empowering. It simply boiled down to being true to my heart, a skill that was being gently honed again after years of doubt.

Dear friends were London bound and asked me to join them. It was an incredibly perfect scenario, and as we landed on Christmas Day, it allowed my annual "dodge" to be fully effective. The Christmas holiday may always be tough, and I now accept that creating a new one, rather than attempting to replicate the past, is okay. Maybe one day I'll be able to have a tree again; maybe not. There is no judgment attached to whatever decision is reached, and I accept that process can change from moment to moment. Living authentically with each second is what I can strive for now.

London was wonderful and once again, special friends stepped in to fill the empty spaces as needed while still allowing me the requisite quiet times on my own. Cathedrals and small churches provided refuge for tears and a forum to question God's wisdom in taking James when so young. I did not retreat from looking at decorated evergreens and white lights. Engaging in the scenery but remaining detached from the powerful emotions that had plunged me into deep despair a year earlier was now possible.

During this time away, I began to seriously ponder the possibility of stepping away from my life in San Francisco for a few months in an effort to figure out what the next steps should be. I wrote that I did not know what I was supposed to do, but I did know what I did not want to do, and that was perhaps a good starting point. Suffering did not have to be the script that I would follow, even though I had it perfectly memorized.

*　　*　　*

The work at the Village Well was continuing with the efforts of the staff I had trained, and since fundraising had been less successful, given the lousy economy of 2011, I thought it might help the organization for me to draw less salary, step away, and see how it would carry on without my daily presence. Continuing to oversee from afar but stepping off the grid was my new goal. My hands were getting close to letting go of the edge.

In late January 2012, I headed back to Canada to spend time with my aging mother. At eighty-five, she was independent and able to live alone in her home but was confined to days in a wheelchair, which had its obvious limitations. She was delighted to have some company, and without any expectations on my part, being close to a neutral home and hearth allowed me to unravel the threads of sorrow that had woven a very heavy cloak. There was a safe place to put my nurturing, a reality I never thought I'd be able to explore again, and the bruises around my heart slowly started to hurt less. My mother also had a place to put her nurturing, and together we found a corner of unexpected gentle healing.

Sweet James continued to visit me in dreams, and on one night in particular, he sat me down at yet another table, looked me straight in the eye, and said, "Mama, you can leave. You can do this. It will be okay."

I awoke with a jolt yet felt a profound calm wash over me. Over tea with my mother the next day, I asked her what she might think of me moving back to Canada, for the short term. Stepping away, shedding the stress, and allowing myself time to slowly figure things out was the message James had sent me in the night. My mother was thrilled with the idea and confessed that secretly she had hoped I might come to this decision. Watching her daughter slip and stumble, lugging the weight of grief had troubled her deeply.

Pay attention.

The message was clear, and I wrote to the board to express my desire to step down from the daily role of executive director. An e-mail to my landlady, telling her my intentions to wrap up the nest and move things back to Canada, was sent within days. The necessary notices and transfer of papers was executed, and miraculously, the attachment to the grief story was suddenly lightened. I was not troubled nor was there struggle attached to this new decision. It was quite remarkable. A possible beginning was about to emerge from a sea of endings.

We all know that when something is meant to be, the pieces fall into place with ease, and this was certainly the case with this rather dramatic—some would say drastic—decision. A Canadian team of movers, who had just completed a trek to Arizona, were available to pack and transport my possessions within a few weeks, and so I returned to California to begin packing up my home of over twenty-one years.

The first few days were incredibly painful as cupboards were opened and boxes unearthed that I had left frozen in time when James died. Tears were plentiful. My sorrow at times ran very deep, but I did not believe that I was making a mistake. I held true to my new mantra: "I don't know what I am going to do, but I do know what I can no longer do." Throwing my hands up into the air, letting go, and stepping off the grid was the new resolution. I would trust the Buddha net to catch me and place my feet where I was supposed to land for this next chapter.

Within three weeks, my home was packed. Movers arrived on April 11, and less than two days later, the stuffed eighty-foot truck, with our beloved Putters also on board, was heading down Polk Street towards Van Ness Avenue. A cross continent adventure was about to unfold with Ontario, Canada, as the final destination.

Slowly climbing the stairs into the empty flat after the movers' departure opened the floodgates that had been carefully guarded. I could not release my emotions when overseeing the mammoth undertaking of the packing, but now I stood in the hushed, empty space that echoed loss. Shadows of picture frames dotted the walls. Dings on doorways and chipped paint revealed a busy life that had now ceased to exist. Like the final breaths from James, the flat exhaled and slowly died.

The story had ended. The last tears could now be shed. I had not anticipated how deeply heartbroken I would feel at this moment, and I curled up on the floor and wept for what seemed hours. Every sadness and joy had its particular power, and the purging of the culmination of those stories left me incredibly weak. I had not moved house since before James was born; hence, this Polk Street address had been home for such important chapters in both our lives. Once more, a powerful farewell to take ownership of, in this a long line of partings. How many more did I have to experience? I felt nauseated.

Sergio called to check in on me, and I blurted out in rage, "I don't even have a place to sit with my tears!" All the chairs were gone, and after years of taking pride in creating a cozy, inviting home, there was nothing hospitable in the space. I felt desperate having only steps to sit on.

Once again, Sergio promptly took charge of a remedy and arrived within an hour with a desk and chair that he borrowed from the school. He lugged it up stairs and placed it in the middle of the empty sitting room. I now would have a place to sit and write. It was perfect in its loving simplicity. In solitude, I wrote a thank-you letter to our home, acknowledging all it had graciously shared over the years.

Being totally caught up in the logistics of the move, I had put no thought towards where I would sleep that night. Somehow, my disconnect due to packing and moving had erased any forward planning, but I now desperately needed a bed to collapse into.

Someone suggested a hotel on the wharf, an easy and quick solution. Interestingly, I had no desire to stay with friends. I needed to be anonymous. Cutting the cord was about to become the next task, and that would require thoughtful privacy.

En route down the road to Fisherman's Wharf, I was not sure if there would be a room since it was the height of the tourist season, but sure enough, there was one available, which I booked on the spot and promptly moved in with my heavy suitcase. There were a couple of days left in the city to sort out the final pieces of my life, and they unfolded with relative ease. The inevitable giveaways of favourite books, a few art pieces, leftover food, and supplies allowed a few old friends the chance to say farewell to the flat and me.

*   *   *

On April 15 a small farewell picnic for families and friends had been organized by the communities of the Village Well and St. Mary the Virgin. I had not wanted a big affair, and they honoured that request with a simple gathering at Ft. Miley near Land's End. All appropriate now in hindsight, as we stood at the furthest corner of the city with the Pacific crashing below. There was nowhere else to go but out onto the horizon.

Unbeknownst to Jennifer, who took charge of the picnic, there were a series of World War II bunkers nestled into this landscape that James and I had discovered years earlier. It had become a favourite hidden spot for skateboarding, and James made me promise not to tell anyone about it since he wanted to keep it special—his own private skating Nirvana.

While trying to find a location for the picnic, this site was the only one available through the Parks and Recreation services, and Jennifer booked it, without knowing the story of James's attachment, to that spot. Even now, on this my last day in the city, playful James was ever present in orchestrating those magical chess pieces around the board.

During the picnic, some young men were skateboarding nearby, and one in particular wore a plaid shirt and tweed cap, and for a fleeting moment, I swore it was my precious son doing brazen kick flips much too close to the edge.

Sergio asked to do a farewell smudging of the flat. It was to be done as the very last thing before I locked the door, handed in the key, and drove to the airport. Devotion to the importance of ritual is a cornerstone of his life's work, and never doubting his sincerity, I fully embraced the suggestion. As had become the case throughout this transition, the right people were there at the right time, and only five of us gathered on the roof, after the farewell picnic, to start the slow process of saying goodbye, burning sage and closing doors. Tears flowed generously as we progressed in silence from room to room.

There was no plan or time limit. I lingered as long as needed in every space. Memories collided with one another. A few stories were exchanged. Mason, one of James's close friends from school, reminisced about the barbeques and crazy evenings crammed in the upstairs room. Mason would take the picnic table and chairs so that the buddies could continue to have outdoor meals, in honour of James, at his country cottage in Sonoma.

I was the last to descend the deep stairwell, and the vision of James being carried down on that dreaded cold stretcher played out, in slow motion, ahead of me. We both had now come to the end of our chapter here on Polk Street and San Francisco. It was heartbreaking, and yet it had to come full circle for me to save not only his memory but my story as well.

Now there was no blueprint to follow. This well-trodden grid was about to evaporate, and it was up to me to invest in a new map. While daunting, it was the first time in years that the future did not feel insurmountable. Grief would continue be a component but not the guiding principle. Given this new freedom, perhaps James and I would be able to expand our individual horizons and maybe even share more completely.

Salvation had morphed into rebirth.

* * *

There are constant bookends that prop us up. Life and death are the major supports, but within those boundaries are smaller equally strong divisions that punctuate the timeline. James's life in San Francisco had been rich in experiences and friendships. He was deeply loved and also knew how to love deeply. I was blessed to have been his mother and cherish every moment that we shared. His illness and death, while a cruel and brutal reality, has taught me to treasure even more the fragility of days, and I work towards living authentically every moment. There is a renewed strength in being honest.

Following James's example, I have no room for pettiness or ego. I am slowly reconstructing my life around empty spaces that no longer echo. Shadow imprints don't leave me afraid. I fill the solitude with ease and remain mindfully aware of all messages that cross my path.

"Choose your burdens wisely."

James wrote this in the final months of his life and wanted it tattooed on his wrist. Wearing my cloak of denial, ignoring how gravely ill he was, I expressed concern that the toxic ink might make him sick and so convinced him not to go forward with it. After his death, I thought about having it tattooed on my body but, being totally squeamish with needles, never found the courage.

In James's honour, a couple of his close friends have had it tattooed, with Sam's being the most powerful as it sits boldly on his upper back between his shoulders. The day he came to show me, I was speechless. Sam said he wanted to always carry James with him, and this seemed the best way to do that. James is now a permanent piece of his body and reminds that every encounter, even fleeting ones, leaves something behind.

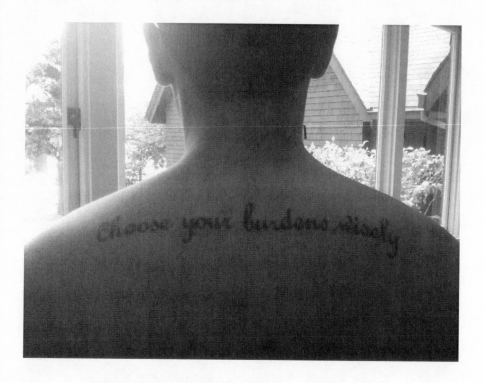

"Choose Your burdens wisely" Sam's tattoo

*　　*　　*

Time passes.

I can now be with young children, hold and hug them and not feel my heart break. Sharing the lives of other people's families is less of a struggle. It would be dishonest to say there are not moments of acute sorrow, but that is to be expected and honoured. I tell others sharing this same path that our love and loss makes these moments inevitable and it would not be right to profess a lack of sentiment or feeling. Grief truly is the price of loving deeply.

Yes, we move on. Take steps. Smell and touch and stay connected to the living in part to bring peace to those loved ones who watch over us. Who will I haunt?—now guides me in the relationships I choose to nurture and ask that friends don't send me flowers when I am dead. Share them now, while alive, so that they can be fully enjoyed. James wrote, in his final essay referring to Plato's *Republic*, of seeing his life with disease through new eyes.

Like my son, I have now also been gifted with seeing life anew, shifting from the darkness to a lighter place with gentle healing. With gratitude, we share this together now.

Chapter 23

What They Don't Tell You

There is only one road map, you are holding it.
—Thrasher magazine

It is through the unfulfilled that we become full.
—Jean Alice Rowcliffe

Death and profound grief are universal. Everyone will suffer this reality during their lifetime. It is incomprehensible not to be broken when the ones you love die. That is a fact of life. To have your child die only magnifies this brokenness. Acute anguish will sit just under the skin with jealousy and unexpected resentment part of the visceral mix. The slightest prick or scratch will unleash its full wrath. Why and how will become the questions that haunt, perhaps for the rest of your life. Triggers lie everywhere, and you will never know when something might open the floodgate.

Our children are our future. While this truth has become a cliché used by everyone, from politicians to educators, for parents their children *are* their lifeline and link to future. Almost everything we parents do, work, and struggle for is to benefit our children. They are our branches, both literally and figuratively, and to have one die represents the loss of a limb. I had not realized beforehand just how painful that would be. It does feel as though a body part has been removed. Doctors speak of the phantom pain of an amputee, and this is how James's death affected me. Everything around screams that he should still be here, but the excruciatingly painful truth is that he is gone. The death of a child goes against all the laws of nature. Parents are not meant to bury their children. It is our worst nightmare, and I do believe the deepest sorrow to carry. We will go on, but we are forever changed.

*　　*　　*

We don't do death well. I realized this in the very early days after James died. Prior to his death, a powerful energy of dread swirled about. None of us wanted this outcome, yet we were totally helpless in changing the inevitable. Just as the tsunami of his diagnosis and failed treatments overwhelmed, so too did the wave that carried James to his death, and all those who loved him clung desperately to the sides.

Even when James's body was ravaged by cancer and it was very clear that he was going to die, there were many, through their love, who were adamant that I continue to seek a cure. The doctors had to do more. Manifesting and white light had to pour more generously over James. Perhaps we were just not doing it enough. If we changed his diet or the soap he used to bathe with or the laundry liquid or the temperature of the house or offered him better massage or fed him copious amounts of homeopathic teas or flew him to Switzerland for a new drug trial, maybe, just maybe, the outcome would be different.

Sadly, what the suggestions of well-meaning and deeply loving friends did not realize, James wanted to die. He had come to the end of his struggle, weary of the pain, vomiting, and drugs. His lack of reason and numbed senses combined with the inability to move or eat (two things that had brought him such joy) had all become too overwhelming. His spirit was broken, and even the medical marijuana—that gift that helped bring such blessed relief—had ceased to work.

The day James asked me to help him die was his plea for permission to leave his broken body. It then became the task for those close to him to give him a peaceful death free of pain and hopefully full of grace. To let him go with our love and blessings, while perhaps not realizing just how much we would become the broken ones, was a selfless giving that in my gut I know he appreciated.

James died when he was ready. We did not speed the process or make the decision for him. He was nurtured, loved, and held, and as free from pain and suffering as we could muster. He hated the hospital and was able to remain at home, in his bed, supported by the mountain of pillows he adored. We were all embarking on an unknown journey, and it was our work now to honour his desire to move on. As everything we knew was grinding to a halt, there was also this profound juxtaposition of energy and movement pushing forward.

I had not expected this to be such a powerful force with death. We can't run from or numb the pain of this moment. It is going to hurt terribly. Nothing can sanitize the inevitable outcome. If we are able to support the dying with our patient, supportive presence, I know it is a wonderful final expression of our love, and I do believe this provides the gift of a good death.

I now have a deep understanding that many who are very ill, and know their time has come, are capable of making the decision to leave their broken bodies when they are ready. It is amazing how many stories I have heard of those who die when a loved one leaves the room, steps out to the bathroom, or goes to answer the phone. It is as if the dying want to spare their loved ones the anguish of that last breath, their last tear.

As tragic as it was, James allowing me to share in his final moments remains one of the greatest blessings in my life. Grief and mourning would become the next chapter, but that was not important during those sacred hours. James begged to be at home, in his bed, away from the beeping machines, horrid pillows, and plastic sheets. With the help of Hospice, we were able to honour that request. In the end, a good death was all James wanted, and I pray it is what he received.

*　*　*

We are all dying. This is not a morbid proclamation but the truth of our very existence. Every child is presented with a birth notice, but tucked in their back pocket sits the death certificate. These two documents will be the bookends of this new life. None of us knows how the story will unfold, but we will each walk our personal path from beginning to end, with all the highs and lows that will become our legacy.

Since this universal story of death is shared by us all, you would think that we would talk about it more. Prepare for it. Try to understand the full scope of what it means, share our emotions and fears surrounding it; but there is a disconnect, certainly in Western culture, that I now find fascinating. Death is not a cold or influenza that will go away. We can't magic up a homeopathic solution or tincture to spare us from its grasp. No amount of money, accomplishments, success, or failure will divert us from this shared outcome.

Having now experienced fully James's death, I find it remarkable how many try to run away from and dodge the inevitable. God forbid that we discuss or plan. Fear of this unknown clouds our perspective.

I am convinced we do ourselves a great disservice by not embracing our dying as completely as we do our living. We are all phantoms-in-waiting, as I like to call us now. It is through the decision of fully accepting and making peace with our death that we open ourselves to living more completely.

James, through his example, reminded us of this, and perhaps it was his ability to squeeze the juice out of every moment that he continues to inspire years after his death. He understood that to live fully, he had to acknowledge that death was always there, waiting in the wings. While never giving power to death, his actions and decisions were based on the fact the he knew life was way too short. Even as a young child he would make proclamations about the gift of life and power of personal energy. At the time I thought it remarkable and "very James," but now in hindsight, I wonder if deep inside he had a sense that his was a precious and precariously short journey.

Why is it that those who die too soon have such powerful insights? One hears this time and again from families whose children are snatched due to illness or accidents. Astonishingly, they have a sense of their mortality and live, determined to make every moment count. Many of them have been able to articulate through their words and example the gift of living authentically and without pettiness. They leave us inspired and willing to sadly acknowledge that only the good die young.

One of the great lessons James left with us is that we all get to choose the option of how we'll share our days. Death sits there quietly reminding us that time is limited, but James's legacy teaches us that thoughts and actions do have profound consequences, and we all get the opportunity, every day, to pursue paths that brings the greatest joy through personal growth and loving relationships.

The tale is always greater than the conclusion, and each breath we are given is just another moment of that next chapter, waiting to be written. This intensely powerful chapter with James has proved my childhood notion to be true:

Moving pieces around the chess board is more perfect than reaching checkmate.

*   *   *

There are countless accounts of death and living with grief, but this is my personal story. I vowed in the early days after James died to create a list, based on my own perspective, of what works and what doesn't. While this compilation is due to the death of my child, many of the emotions and painful discoveries are common for all those who mourn.

I hope providing these will help in some way.

*

Death. Say the word. You cannot soften the pain and make it feel better. I found that when people said "loss" or "passed away," it diminished the truth of what had happened. It can't be sugar coated. To "lose" someone makes it sound as though they will be found, and it feels strangely disingenuous. "Passed away" again sounds too poetic. Death is death. Look at it. Say it. Sit with it. Only then can you be honest about what it has done to you. It has changed you. Changed everything. Your life story now includes a powerful death story. There is no sandpaper to smooth this rough edge. Death is death.

*

Never make assumptions that you know what is best. Those suffering through profound loss and the ensuing grief need nothing but unconditional support, and any outside judgment makes them feel less capable than they already are. Don't present them with a list of what they should do.

*

Journal your feelings, insights, memories. These will become a wonderful lifeline to the past. I can relive every moment through my writings, keeping all the memories alive and fresh. These are especially helpful if you have medical issues to deal with before death. The notes will be invaluable for doctors and the hospice, but they also provide a record for you. As awful as it was to open the journals from the end of James's life to provide the facts for this book, I am eternally grateful to have them now.

*

Sudden death must be beyond anything imagined. I had time to prepare for James's death, and even still, it crippled me. To have no time to prepare, say goodbye, make peace, or even hold your loved one has to be beyond excruciating and would only amplify all the emotions and issues that I have listed. Extra patience, nurturing with unconditional support and love is needed for the bereaved given this horrible scenario.

*

If you have a friend (preferably with a medical background), bring them along to take notes during the hospital visits. The influx of information compounded by your desperation might make you incapable of absorbing details. Mary provided a wonderful gift by taking notes and transcribing them into lay terms to read after the doctor's meetings.

*

This death has affected all of you, and patience is essential now in your dealings with those who are grieving. How you grieve may be different from everyone else. Comparisons of others or the "best" or "worst" way to grieve is a futile waste of energy.

*

Accept that when the bereaved say that they are fine, it is probably the furthest thing from the truth. It is just the easiest thing to say. It will satisfy others and buffers them from going into every detail of their brokenness. The conveyor belt of sorrow is running silently beside them, and the heaviness of acknowledging this truthfully or explaining themselves is just too overwhelmingly complicated. "Fine" will have to suffice, and it does for a very long time; maybe forever.

*

Be prepared to be overcome with terrible guilt. You might feel totally responsible for the illness and death of your loved one, assuming you had a much larger role than is true. This guilt will subside, but it is real, and you need to acknowledge it as part of the unravelling of a life you could not and were not meant to save.

*

"Why was I left?" This is another haunting question that may plague you for a long time. If it was a sudden or dramatic death, the issues surrounding this question appear to be more potent. There does not seem to be any quick fix for this dilemma; you will just need to sit with it, and given time, it does lessen its hold and you will, one day make decisions that are not based on remorse.

*

Grief and mourning are essential. I almost hate to use the word *process* as it tends to make the assumption that you are working towards a specific, orchestrated ending, which of course is not the case. There is no set outcome. This is a journey with grief as your new uninvited companion. The destination is unknown. You must, however, walk the path that is presented each day, accepting that this mantle of sorrow will be constantly with you. One day, however, the mantle won't weigh as much.

*

Sometimes just getting out of bed is the best you can do. There will be days when you feel paralyzed, and it takes every ounce of energy to place your two feet on the floor; that will seem a major accomplishment. Don't expect more of yourself on those days. Just let it be. You are now one of the walking wounded.

*

"Be gentle with yourself." Every time you feel broken, stressed, pulled, and unable to cope, say this mantra. Write it on a note and post it on a mirror, cupboard door, carry it in your bag or pocket, anywhere so that it can be a daily reminder.

*

It is okay to curl up in a ball on the floor or in bed and weep. Give yourself permission to take these moments when they come. You must allow yourself to grieve fully; otherwise your grief sits there, perhaps becoming buried. If you don't grieve now, it will surface down the road in some other guise. Burying grief can make you sick, invite addictions, or become your motivation in relationships that might be self-destructive. Long-term depression is often based on unresolved grief surrounding profound loss.

*

Be honest about where you are and what you feel at any given moment. Share with others if asked but only if you want to. Patience is needed now by all who surround you. It's okay to be where you are. Thoughts of suicide are common. You are not alone with this reality. Find the suicide support group or hotline in your community. Write the number down and keep it next to your bed. The middle of the night is often the worst, and having someone to call who will listen and guide you through the dark hours can be a life saver.

There were many times when the thought of leaving all this seemed very appealing to me, especially when the weight of loneliness became unbearable. It was the thought of how I would hurt those who loved James and me deeply that kept me from doing anything drastic. I did not want to give them the burden that they had somehow failed me in my hour of need. It would not have been anyone's failing that drove me to this, just my desire to end the pain.

*

Anger and jealousy will be abundant. These emotions bubble up at any time, and you won't know why. Be prepared for this, and don't fight it. I believe that if you don't experience this fully, it will become a bitterness that consumes your very DNA. Be prepared that for the hurt you might experience on seeing babies in strollers, families riding bicycles on Sunday afternoons, birthday party trappings, and gift cards at the store. Special anniversaries and holidays revolving around family may drive you to distraction. I had not realized just how much it would hurt to see children thriving and growing in the early days of my mourning.

I was terribly jealous of young men and women falling in love and getting into mischief. Why them? Why not James? This questioning is such an important aspect of the grief path, and I feel blessed that I could indulge myself in that slice of sorrow. I do believe now that it aided me in my healing. To not acknowledge this is dangerous. It is a dark and powerful part of our soul that is revealed, and it may startle both your sensibilities and those of others'. As a result, you may lose friends for a time, but those who are loyal and understanding will come back into your life or the universe will provide others to fill their space. This is all part of grief's elusive ebb and flow.

*

Learn how to sit with death. You cannot run from this inevitability, and those who were able to be silent with me, without any expectations of where I should be or how I should act, were the most comforting.

*

You don't have to fill up the empty space with noise or busy-ness. Take your lead from where you are on any given day. It will change constantly. Your needs might change at any moment. What felt good yesterday may be purgatory today. Maybe you could share today, but tomorrow feels like an impossibility you can't face. This is all perfectly normal.

*

Your life has been changed forever. You are changed forever. Yes, it will go on, but in another way. This will be the new normal that you will hear much about. Only you can discover it; be mindful and patient as it unfolds. It will take time. Perhaps a very long time.

*

It is shocking how many marriages end after the death of a child. One statistic has it at 80 percent. Everyone grieves differently and at their own pace. This can place a huge strain on a couple as often there is an expectation for partners to be at the same place, at the same time. This is just not possible. Be honest with your partner as to what your needs are, and listen to them. Take time to be solo. Try to support and nurture each other as best you can while still taking care of yourself. It is tough as there is no template to follow. Seek professional help if you feel overwhelmed. There are many who can help you negotiate these rough waters. It is not a sign of weakness or inability to cope, to seek help.

*

Be mindful of the body language of those who are grieving. They may very well not want to be touched or hugged. Sometimes it all just hurts too much.

*

Don't assume that stories of your family will heal. All too often, to the grieving parent especially, this is the proverbial salt in the wound. You have what was once most precious. Thoughtful exchange is needed now.

*

It is unfair to ask those in mourning to help you make sense of this death. Find a professional, go to your spiritual leader, talk to others, but don't put that task on the grieving parent. It adds to their anguished sense of self and inability not to be able to help you as well. Remember, the bereaved are even more perplexed than you and are often just taking one step at a time. That may be the best they can offer the world.

*

It is okay to say you don't know what to say. I actually found that to be the most honest response, and those who could express their sorrow through silence honoured James's memory and my suffering.

*

Don't ever say to a grieving parent, "I understand your loss" as no one—even those who have also experienced the death of a child—can fully know the depth of another's sorrow.

*

Never say, "Well, at least you had your child for X amount of time." I am still stunned that some people, even other parents, said that to me. It is cruel beyond measure and accomplishes nothing.

*

Faith is rattled during this time, so don't assume that this was God's plan and that your child is happier now in that heavenly realm. Why does God get him and I don't? What did I do to make me so undeserving? You can see how the flip side of this can hurt. If your faith brings you comfort, that is good, but don't assume that your spiritual path is the universal panacea. Grieving parents often speak of a deep anger towards God (I certainly felt it for some time) and question everything they once believed.

Their journey to explore faith will be personal and private. Respect that.

*

"We are given only what we can handle." If I heard that one more time in the days and months after James died, I was going to scream. Again, the flip side to this is, if I had been less capable, would James have been saved? Did I set myself up for this by working hard, being stoic? Maybe I should have been more pathetic and incapable. If that would have kept James here, then all would have been perfect. The notion of handling what we are given to make us noble falls flat.

*

Don't take offence if your offer to help is not accepted. Often it goes straight over the head of the bereaved. When asked what I needed, half the time I did not know what that might be; indeed, I might not have even heard the question. Fog and uncertainty are very real and overwhelming.

*

Be prepared. Triggers are everywhere, and you never know when they will jump up and bite you. I think of them as monkeys lurking at corners, ready to pounce on your back when you least expect. Learning how to live with this will take time and patience. You will become proficient at dodging triggers in time. Taking the long way home, avoiding the stores and restaurants you used to frequent, turning off the phone in the evening, perhaps even stepping off the grid—all of these strategies may become intrinsic to your survival.

*

You are totally numb during the early days after death. Even though functioning (often on adrenaline), be prepared for the bottom to fall out, and be gentle with yourself when this does happens.

*

It is very common in the early days of mourning to have people compliment you on how strong and stoic you are being, often before even asking how you are. You are numb, and many assume this is a sign of strength. I found it difficult to listen to these compliments of being strong as I was slowly crumbling and felt that so few understood my plight. Over time it started to feel like others were transferring *their* need for me to be strong to dodge the inevitable truth of my deep sorrow.

This inability of others to look at death and mourning honestly became very real during these moments, and I struggled for years with the paradox.

*

The second year after death hurts even more. No one would dare share this when you are first embarking on the grief path as it sounds cruel beyond measure. The truth is, the second year is more painful, perhaps in part because the numbness has worn off and all the daily triggers become more potent. People around you have gotten on with their lives; some may have even forgotten your story, leaving you feeling more solitary and isolated. Be prepared to take extra steps to nurture yourself as year number two presents itself. Remember throughout all this that you are not alone.

*

Create some sort of "grief-carrier" to help you with the burden. I had my fantasy Edwardian undertaker who walked alongside me. Conjure up some sort of energy (it can take any form), omnipresent and non-judgmental, to which you can actively assign the duty of carrying the sorrow when it becomes too much.

*

Cultivate a routine of nurturing that brings you some comfort. Massage, being in water, walking, listening to music, solo stillness, going to church, sitting in silence—all are valid and necessary. Whatever you need, be honest about it and factor that into your days. The old you is dramatically changed, maybe even gone, and caring for the broken puzzle pieces while nursing and discovering the new you is essential. It is okay to be selfish.

*

Create a place of remembrance in your home. It can be a shrine, collection of photos, favourite object loved by your child. Whatever speaks to you as a memory, put it in a safe place, one that you can easily see. I created multiple shrines for James, and his photo was placed in every room. It brings me great comfort to have him close by wherever I sit, eat, write, or lay my head down; this continues to be true years after his death.

*

Sharing stories is a delicate process. You will know when the time is right, so don't be afraid to tell stories and recollections of your loved one. Say their name. They stay alive through this exchange, not only to you but also to others who loved them as well. It will make you sad, and tears will flow but far better to acknowledge their on-going presence than to place them on a shelf to become dusty and forgotten. Also remember to give yourself permission on the days when you don't feel like sharing. You get to control the dialogue.

*

As a friend of the bereaved, ask before sharing your own stories or memories, and do not take offense if the grieving parent is unable to engage with you at the same time.

*

Try to get daily exercise. It really saved my head and heart to be physical every day. You may start with small efforts, but try to build up over time. Walking outdoors is a super beginning. Maybe the gym or a pool will become a destination, whatever you need to keep your head clear and heart pumping, do it. Interestingly, James is always more present after a good workout; it is as if I have cleared the cobwebs for him to be there next to me more completely.

*

You may add or lose weight as grief affects everyone differently. I put on many pounds; I called it my grief weight, and it took me a long time to shed it. Interestingly, it became a metaphor for all that I carried, and it was not until the third year after James died that I began to feel the shift. When I stepped off the grid, the weight started to drop.

*

Family and old friends may or may not provide solace. Sometimes there is a dramatic shift in the relationships you need during mourning. It is not as if anyone has done something wrong, but you may find new friends coming in to your life that will fill a void you did not know even existed. Be kind with yourself and others. Let it unfold in its own way. Don't be offended if there is a change in the relationships you once shared. There is no rhyme or reason to this, but it is very common. Death does rewrite your address book.

*

Fatigue is acute, especially in the early months after death. If you have been a caregiver or keeping a long vigil, there will be added fatigue on top of this. Get plenty of sleep, and take naps if possible during the day. Sleep deprivation is one of the most debilitating phenomenon during this time.

*

Drink lots of water. You need every ounce to flush out all the toxins that have accumulated due to stress and haphazard eating. Water provides balance. It goes without saying that steering clear of alcohol is advised.

*

Remember to eat one good meal each day, especially in the early days after the death of your loved one. It is too easy to slip into snacking, which can become an unhealthy pattern. I was so grateful for my friends to make sure I had one meal with good protein at lunchtime. It did help me keep going, even though I resisted it some days.

*

Try to eat a balanced diet as much as possible. You may not have an appetite for a long time. Your sense of smell and taste may be numb. You may find that you do not enjoy foods that once brought pleasure. Simple, bland menus may appeal for months at a time.

*

Anniversaries and special days will be tough. Plan accordingly. You may want to celebrate the memory of your loved one, or you may need to dodge the day and try to ignore it entirely. That reality might shift from year to year. There is no correct way to do this, just be honest with where you are at any given time.

*

Turn off the phone, and don't respond to e-mails and messages when you need to be still. Don't feel obliged to be current with everyone. It is okay to step away. Be in touch when you feel strong enough. A site like CaringBridge, where you can update through a blog, is a huge tool.

*

Let go of expectations of how life will be. This is now a flower opening in slow motion as it is intended to, and you need to be mindful of the changes and careful not to judge, especially yourself.

*

"Are you up for this today?" As a compassionate friend, ask this before entering the space of the bereaved. They may or may not want company. It is much less hurtful for all concerned to ask delicately before marching in and taking over. It may sound trivial, but to one who is in the early stages of mourning, every moment can seem terribly fragile.

*

Find a local support group. Compassionate Friends, Hospice, and Well Spring are a few agencies that I know of, but there may well be many choices in your community. Sharing your story in a safe environment is incredibly helpful, and if you feel less isolated, then this is an important step to take. You can attend meetings and not share. There should not be pressure on you to participate. You will join in when ready, but being in the circle might help you articulate your feelings down the road. *You are not alone on this journey.*

*

Be prepared one day to feel a bit better, even lighter. This may well be accompanied by some guilt as you question if you love less or are forgetting your loved one, but it is, in fact, an important part of this journey. I recall the days when I started to feel less anguish and my breathing became more normal. I felt unbelievable guilt that I might be failing to honour James. With help from my support system, I patiently accepted that James was still very much with me. He needed me to be less burdened by grief and wanted me to find some happiness through reengaging in life. A wise sage said to me during this transition, "Reverse the table and see yourself as dead. Would you not want James to feel better and suffer less should you be watching over him?"

Those words guided me in my evaluation of this new path I was walking.

*

Find a friend or two to act as your gatekeepers. There will be an outpouring of love in the early days, and the arrival of flowers, meals, tributes, books, etc., at your door can quickly overwhelm. Let these friends be the conduit for others to ask what you might need. Update them daily, and they can delegate chores or needs to those who are waiting to help you. Emma and Pat were instrumental in this for me, something I will be forever grateful for.

*

Find someone to drive! I had not realized how unsafe I was on the road until a few near misses in the early days after James died. Find a team of people who are willing to take turns picking you up, waiting until you are finished, and returning you home. They will love being useful, and it may just save your life. I can't stress the importance of this enough.

*

Be prepared for your hormones to be out of whack for a long time. Just as with pregnancy, grief has its own set of hormones that can leave you unsettled.

My own experience was quite profound. I had stopped having regular periods and thought that I had begun menopause, but the day that James was told he had terminal cancer (at the doctors meeting at UCSF in early June), I started to bleed. All periods subsided during his illness, but another one began the day James died. On the ninth of each month after that, I started to bleed, and it became such a horrid reminder of this anniversary that I went to my gynecologist, who put me on a contraceptive pill for a few months to shift the cycle. I ceased bleeding and have never had another period. The body reacts in profound ways to the state of one's mind and heart.

*

As best you can, keep a running list of gifts/flowers as they come in. It soon becomes a giant blur and when you want to quietly acknowledge these kindnesses, it will be easier with a record in place.

*

Don't make any major decisions in the first year of mourning, if at all possible. Moving, starting new work, selling things—all of these should be put on the back burner until you have better clarity. Thank God I was reminded by many not to do anything dramatic as I was terribly scattered and desirous to run away from everything familiar. I was prevented from making a terrible mess of things by just staying put.

*

Find a place of retreat that brings you comfort. It may very well be someplace new, outside the home or your community. I benefitted from recurring visits to the monastery of New Clairvaux to be with silent monks on acres of farmland. Remote, rural settings helped me rejuvenate. All pursuits are valid.

*

"Put on your own oxygen mask first." Carol said this at every session, and it was a life saver. I had not learned how to do for me, and it was an important gift to be reminded that I had to be cared for first and foremost, especially in the early months after James's death. Even now, I remind myself to put on the personal mask when anything becomes overwhelming or when I feel myself slipping into the caretaker role for others while ignoring my own needs.

*

Pay attention to signs and dreams. There is an ability to stay connected to the dead, but we have to be receptive and open to their messages. James has blessed me with his prolific, playful greetings, but I don't feel that I have been particularly singled out for this. Other parents tell of visits from their children through nature or quirky circumstances. Be mindful and enjoy the connection when they appear. These spontaneous visits have sustained me during dark times. I do feel James close by during these often magical and unexpected encounters.

*

Plan your funeral, or at least put thought towards your wishes. What words would you like spoken, and by whom? What music played/performed/sung? What setting? Do you want a program prepared? What photos to include? Will you show pictures during the service or set up a memorial room nearby? Do you want a reception afterwards? What food to be served? While it might sound strange to plot this, I am now a huge advocate for planning ahead and putting it in writing. Leave your wishes easily accessible for those you love to use as a blueprint.

I had started to plan James's funeral months before he died as I had a sense I would not be able to do anything at the time of his death, and how right that was. When you are in shock, just putting two coherent sentences can take everything. The thought of planning and executing a memorial that will do honour to a loved one's (even your) life story feels overwhelming beyond measure. Make the memorial as personal as you would like and leave instructions as to what you desire to be included in the proceedings. Put the plans with your important end-of-life papers but not with your will as that may not be seen for weeks after your death. Let family or loved ones know where the plans are, or better yet, share them beforehand.

As I have often said, we plan a vacation more carefully than our death and funeral, and that is indeed the greatest of all journeys. Trust me, it will make it so much easier for those left behind to do what *you* would like versus making it up on the spot. The decision-making process is feeble at best after death.

Allow your family to grieve without the extra burden of uncertainty over how to remember and honour you.

*

Consider death at home. I know it sounds tough and is overwhelming, but if you have community support services, like Hospice, to help guide you, it is so comforting for the dying to be in their own home. James taught me the power of this through his determination to not be in hospital. Death is going to be messy and sad wherever it happens. This is a fact. You will be the ones left to suffer. If, through direct consultation with your doctors, you can give those at the end of their days the gift of dying at home, consider it seriously. The visitation at home was also a lovely way to connect with those who loved James and wanted to say goodbye. Having James surrounded by his story in that intimate setting made it deeply personal for all. I know this option is not always possible, but it is worth exploring and discussing with your support team.

*

There are some wonderful books available that explore dying and grief. *Grieving for Dummies* by Greg Harvey should be on your bedside table to pick up whenever you need assurance that what you are feeling is normal and you are not going mad. Many writers have been incredibly candid, telling their tales of profound loss. I include an additional reading list at the end of this book that might be helpful.

*

During the Christmas tea for families at work a few years ago, a grandmother came into the office (after asking if it was okay—"Are you up for this today?") and told me that her son had died in a tragic car accident over fifteen years ago, coming home for the holidays. Like me, she hates the song "I'll Be Home for Christmas," and we shared how getting through the holidays took every ounce of our reserve. I told her how I felt the iron wall had come down and worried it would never rise, and she confided that over time it will become cardboard (with slats), and later on, the wall might become fabric. We both wondered if a wispy lace drape might be possible and parted with a tearful hug hoping for that—perhaps one day.

After living through death, you will have remarkable people enter your life to guide and support you. Stay alert and be grateful for their insightful wisdom when they come along. You will find many of them will appear at just the right time with the message you most needed at that moment. You, too, will become a messenger to others in mourning, placed on their path at just the right time. I continue to find this truth quite remarkable.

*

Find a safe place to put your story. Write, paint, scribble—you will know what works best for you, but try to capture the essence of what you have experienced and come to learn. This is such an important part of your life and legacy, and we all need to be better about saving our stories for those who follow. Don't edit and judge yourself. Let it flow freely and then safely store it away to come out whenever you need a reminder of your loved one and your loss. You may find that over time you choose to develop these works into deeper more complex projects.

*

When you need to pack up the belongings of your loved one, do it thoughtfully and take time. Give away what you want, or not. Don't get rid of things until you feel ready to and store them carefully until you can make a decision. Avoid feeling bullied or pressured by others to act when you are not ready. There may be someone who can help you pack and store them; don't be afraid to ask for help with this.

*

As the years pass, I have found myself more capable of opening a few more drawers at a time in the "tool box" I had visualized as the safe place in which to hold all the issues I grappled with. One day you find the strength to multitask and juggle again, but the energy may never be what it once was. You may even decide that some drawers will remain closed.

This is your decision that no one can make for you. Pay attention. Be gentle and trust you are exactly where you need to be at any given moment.

*

Detached engagement is worth exploring as a tool to keep moving forward. Discover your own personal interpretation of this.

*

If you can, pay attention and be there to collect the last tear when your loved one dies. The tear may be one of sorrow or perhaps relief, we will never know, but it remains a poignant tangible of love.

*   *   *

Death has nothing to do with going away. The sun sets.
The moon sets. But they are not gone.

—Rumi

Section 5

James's Legacy

Before death takes away what you are given, give away what there is to give.

—Rumi

"Be the wind chime. Let the wind blow through you. Turn storm into song."

—James, 2000 (eight years old)

Life is short. Death is long. I have been saying this for decades as a way to explain my desire to do as much as I could in whatever time I was given on this earth. Sadly, James's story embodied this truth. When he was born, we all agreed he had a special, almost otherworldly, aura about him.

As he grew, James chose friends carefully and was an astute judge of character. He loved to be creative and had a curiosity about the metaphysical, asking thoughtful questions and dodging pettiness. He grasped that we are minuscule in the scale of the universe, and yet just our presence here on earth made us huge. James enjoyed being quiet, loved his own company yet also embraced rowdiness but only in the company of those he felt would share equally. He was intensely loyal and loving. If James was a friend, he was with you through thick and thin, 100 percent. Many wanted to be in his inner circle; few were given a chair. It was my greatest blessing to be his mother.

Our contributions of music, art and the written word provide the link to our future and past.

While we mourn the loss of James, his story and creative pursuits survive and inspire. Sharing these now is the best way for me to shed light on his spirit. Many of his writings won school awards; some here are incomplete, but they give a glimpse into his heart.

"One Minute" 1999

Don't you wish that for one short minute, a brief 60 seconds the word would stop and realize life was more than money and a snappy suit. And in those brief 60 seconds maybe someone would think twice about driving around town in their fancy new sports car, or the rich man might walk back and give the homeless man a dollar or two, and maybe, just maybe within those 60 seconds, the world will be changed.

*   *   *

"Marked by Cigarette Ashes" June 2006
(lyrics for a song)

Don't let me feel the burn
I'll ignite for all that's left,
As I spasm, twist and turn
Just watch and learn
Be happy you were right.

And now I'm falling from the sky
And I'm lighting up the night
Burning upon re-entry.
And I'm living in my mind
And I'm winning every fight.

I feel like I'm floating on air
But not very far off the ground
Could I be losing ambition this quickly?
The ashes inspire, like a bad joke
The memories threaten to fix me
The memories threaten to choke

And the vapors keep me going
And I start to drift away
And I'm killing time so slowly
That I think it's criminal.

Now I'm lighting up the night
And I'm dying through a filter
But it makes me feel alright
Able to bloom
Yet choosing to wilt.

    The chords are also provided on the adjoining page of his notebook. One day perhaps I'll find someone to piece this song together.

*   *   *

"Coastline" November 2007

It's welcomed home in wisps of fog
It comes to me in metaphors
In pairs of twos and fours
This realm of earth,
Where we belong.
My aperture is infinitely large
And this is a photo opportunity.

Like the most modest of all suns
Retrogressing into the lonesome ocean,
I too
Must return incrementally
To the asymmetrical planet
Which has,
Much to my chagrin.
Born me anew
In a world of experiments.

This equation doesn't add up
And yet I'm holding the answer.
This experiment is hands on,
Yet we were all born without limbs.

I can gaze out now,
With these new eyes
On a view that blinds me.

If you stare too long
It will seem abstract.
If you never stare at all,
How will you know it existed?

* * *

"How Do I Want to Waste My Time?" February 2009

College preparation
A step in the right direction,
Right?
If I put my best foot forward, will they call me sir, one day?
What an honor.
I could pick a suit and tie,
I could work from nine to five
But that life would be a lie
After all,
I'm just a seventeen-year-old guy.

Thirteen years (and counting)
And now with future pressures mounting
The promise land so close at hand,
Be responsible, be mature
Is this a choice? May I refuse?
Can I back out and politely excuse
Myself from the proceedings
For I have found that life is fleeting
Do I want to waste it all succeeding?

* * *

Personal Essay December 2008

This is the essay James sent with his college applications. I received it after his death.

    The portable classroom seemed too mundane a venue for such an historic moment. As I sat nervous, yet eager, staffers were laying out books and posters and shirts to be signed as if it was just another day on the job. My mother sat next to me and although we weren't talking, we shared the same level of anxiousness. I looked upwards and began to count the Styrofoam tiles that carpeted the ceiling and as I did, the door quickly creaked opened and a tall, lean man walked briskly in to the classroom.

"Where's James?" he asked with a firm but oddly warm tone.

I stood as he entered and firmly shook his outstretched hand. It was unusually soft for someone who had been working as hard as he had for the last twenty months.

"Mr. Obama," I said, "It's a pleasure.

He withdrew his hand slowly and pulled up one of the black folding chairs that my Mom and I had been sitting on. We made small talk for the first few minutes. I struggled to maintain my composure, making sure my voice was calm and my responses were eloquent and well—articulated.

In my head, I removed myself from the conversation and began to realize the enormity of the moment. I'm having a simple conversation with the next President of the United States, three days before the election.

We talked about colleges, particularly in the greater Chicago area, seeing as how that is his home turf. More chitchat followed and I found myself yet again digressing back into my own head. The true magnitude of the occasion was sinking in and I was overwhelmed by how much of an honor this was for me.

Ever since my first junior year government class, I have taken politics to heart. I vigorously followed the election from the primaries all the way through to election night, which I was lucky enough to experience firsthand, ten feet away from the stage at Grant Park.

On November fourth, Chicago was particularly alive with anticipation. As close to one million people made their way through the city to Grant Park. I found myself yet again, sitting next to my mother, except this time on a trolley outside of the Hyatt Regency. The rest of the trolley was filled with honored and political guests of the event and to my left was Steve Krofft, one of the hosts of *60 Minutes.*

Night began to fall and the trolley pulled away from the building and towards the excitement. I could already tell that I was in for an historic night. We arrived at the back end of the park, filed out of the trolley and shuffled through a row of metal detectors. My Mom and I eventually found our ourselves standing up against the barriers right next to the stage's left hand side. There was a giant screen set up which was showing *CNN* and I began to well up with exhilaration as state after state was projected to go to the calm, confident man I met only three days prior.

When the polls closed on the west coast the crowd fell silent and my mind cleared of all anticipation as everyone simply waited. Finally Wolf Blitzer looked at the camera and projected Barack Obama's victory. The crowd exploded into celebration with strangers hugging strangers and glorious praise of our next leader.

I knew I had made a wise decision and it was all thanks to the hard work of the people at *Make-A-Wish* Foundation.

Note: James told me during the college application process that he felt he'd left his essay unfinished and planned to expand and add more as time wore on. He never had that opportunity.

*   *   *

"I Think about It Now" January 2006

O great intentions,
I planned the best of interventions,
To help create a new dimension, I think about it now.

After addictions,
I started lifelong inflictions,
Distorting accurate depictions, I think about it now.

Where is
My city?
I found an adequate committee
To rain on my pity,
I don't want to think right now.

Walking on the sidewalk,
Listening to strange men talk,
A world of time without a clock, I cannot think right now.

Strange conversations,
Just to test my patience,
It causes aggravation. Thinking doesn't work.

Many passing months,
Everything at once,
Where silver spoons do bend,
Until the very end.

*   *   *

Senior Project: Goal One Final months 2009

James recorded these words to go along with photos for his PowerPoint presentation. Some of his classmates completed the presentation that was shown during the end-of-year Award Day at school. The last paragraph was read at his funeral by Gordon, head of school.

Cancer has drastically changed me. Going from an active sixteen-year-old to a cane-stricken seventeen-year-old in what feels like an instant has opened my eyes to a plethora of realizations, all of which have helped me improve my outlook on life in many different ways. Dramatic and intense change leave an impact, and in my case, that impact has allowed me to examine my life and all creation from a different perspective—one that is much more spiritual.

Immediately after my diagnosis in June of 2008, I struggled to understand the implications of my disease. I wondered how my life would change and if I would be strong enough to handle it. Gary Haugen's book, *Just Courage*, touches on some ideas that I found to be very relevant to my personal experiences throughout life. "One of the things wise and Godly people seem to have discovered about God's pathways for transformation," explains Haugen, "is that we rarely get to choose what the pathway will be" (Haugen 37). Understanding that my disease is part of an ultimate plan for my existence helps me to let go of the frustration and sadness cancer can bring. It allows me to come to terms with my situation with a positive and optimistic view. This acceptance has led to an increased amount of prayer as I find myself turning to God for guidance and help accepting my illness. One of the criteria for goal one of the Sacred Heart educational goals touches directly upon such actions. It states that students are encouraged to "open themselves to the transforming power of the Spirit of God" and that "members of the school community engage in personal and communal prayer, reflection and action." (reference?) I feel very strongly that this is a positive message. Even without being Catholic, having a place in your heart for prayer, reflection and the transforming power

311

of some larger spirit (call it God if you will) is an important quality and it is one I strive to make sure I possess. This is because it enables us to connect with ourselves and our faith, regardless of how strongly it is tied to a church.

As a result of the optimism and positive energy that I now strive to fill my life with, I have developed a new love of life as I know it. Common pleasures I once took for granted (such as mobility and painlessness) have become even more treasured and I have learned to appreciate the small things in life that make it so precious. I feel as though I am looking at life through new eyes, which is a reference that Plato refers to in his work, *The Republic*. My newfound sanguinity in regards to life relates to one of Plato's writings: I feel like a person who, as Plato wrote, "having turned from darkness to the day is dazzled by excess of light" (Plato 180). Despite having a reason to be miserable and sad, I find myself much more inclined to seek out the silver lining of my situation, for it has allowed me to see a different side of my existence; a more complete and appreciative side. After coming out of "the darkness" of my diagnosis, I feel almost "blinded" by the positive lessons I am able to take away from the experience. Another criteria for goal one states that the schools of the sacred heart strive to "affirm that there is meaning and value in life and foster a sense of hope in the individual and in the school community." (reference?) That attitude is exactly what my experience with cancer has instilled in me, and my school community continues to encourage. Because of my illness, a sense of wholeness and meaning has been directly injected into my outlook on life and my relationship with spirituality. This mindset is a large part of what goal one aims to promote and I am thankful to be in a community that supports that belief so whole-heartedly.

Trying to live a life that revolves around the positive aspects of all that encompasses it has naturally led me to be a more upbeat person. As a result of this, I am even more inspired to fight my cancer so as to ensure that I can live the rest of my life to a standard that meets my liking. Resilience is a crucial quality to possess when fighting an illness and I fight hard every day to make sure optimism gets the better of me as opposed to letting the negative side effects of cancer put a damper on my spirit. Every day, by going to school and seeing my friends and living my life, I am telling my cancer that *it* does not control me and that *I* have power over it. Walter Wink describes an analogous mind-set in Chapter Five of his book *The Powers That Be*. One of the teachings of Christ that Wink analyzes is particularly relevant to my personal experience: the concept of "turning the other cheek." The idea that "if anyone strikes you, refuse to accept that kind of treatment anymore" (Wink 101-102). This idea needs to be better developed b/c you don't convey Wink's meaning in refusing to turn the other cheek. His method in this is important as it does not involve violence! is especially inspiring to me, for I have been fighting and, in a sense, turning my other cheek to cancer for the past 9 months. It is an empowering message and it's one I need to constantly remind myself to hold close to my heart in order to have the will to keep fighting. I consider myself very lucky to be a part of the Schools of the Sacred Heart because of their commitment to spreading the message and lessons of Jesus Christ in a positive way. Another criteria for goal one states that "the school seeks to form its students in the attitudes of the heart of Jesus" (reference?), which is exactly the kind of environment I need to be in in order to guarantee that I am reminded of Jesus' teachings and how his message can fuel my strength.

Life is a gift. I belief this more whole-heartedly with each passing day because with each passing day comes a new opportunity to live fully and be content with what we have and what we can give. For me, handing over the path of my existence to a greater power has been a blessing in itself, for it allows me to live freely and without worry that my actions have too much of an effect on the ultimate outcome of life. This enables me to take each day as it comes and to make sure that I live each day with a positive attitude. I never imagined I would think to myself that cancer could be a gift (or at least transform my life for the better in some regards), but after living with it for many months I now see how it has changed me and presented a side to life that very well may have gone unnoticed and unappreciated otherwise.

By "turning the other cheek" to cancer, I have taken more away from getting cancer than I will ever let it take away from me.

*   *   *

The Round Table *is the Stuart Hall for Boys High School newspaper. James contributed stories and reviews over the years. The following special feature by Skyler Hicks (a junior student in the school) was included in the 2009 issue, one month after James died.*

The Student Teacher

One year ago, James Rowcliffe Kessler was just like most other teenage boys, with the regular flaws and weaknesses. After being diagnosed with a rare and fatal form of cancer, however, James grew into a boy that we now look to as a sort of hero.

James came to embody some of the Schools of the Sacred Heart's most desired qualities: fortitude, integrity, leadership and a deep concern for his classmates. James graduated long ago and his role at this school traveled beyond a student's normal limitations. He not only lived up to the qualities that mark the essence of our school's goals, but he provided students, faculty and administrators with a living example of being a "child of the Sacred Heart" means.

Courage

Despite spending his senior year with a strenuous burden, James did not hide from his illness. Instead, he embraced the realities of his life and took advantage of what time he still had.

He made the decision to spend much of his time at school with his classmates and teachers. "Even when he was hurt, or when he had a headache, or when he was tired, he came to school," says senior Andrew Quanci.

James's willingness to spend his final months advancing his education inspired many at the school. His AP Literature teacher Mr Farrell was especially impressed by James's persistent effort to exert all the energy he had on a given day into his studies and classroom discussions.

Integrity

As a member of the Honor Council, James constantly stepped forth and provided his unique perspective on a situation. Even now in his final weeks, he continued to make proposals on how to improve the Honor Council and the entire school.

Quanci, who was also on the Honor Council says, "He really did feel something for the preservation of this school and for what the school teaches." In these meetings, James also displayed his uncanny ability to consider the feelings of the student body as well as those in trouble.

Senior Keaton Goldsmith attests to James's consciousness: "He was very conscious of other people . . . And he was very forgiving. If most people in a room were talking about someone, he'd be the first one to play devil's advocate and stand up for that person."

In the classroom, James was always pushing for the best in himself and in others. "He would demand excellence, because he was giving excellence," explains his physics teacher Mr. Woodard.

Responsibility

James took the responsibility of being Senior Class president and provided the Student Government with leadership based on providing the example.

"He didn't use his illness as an excuse . . . James would help clean up sometimes [or do other little things] and putting that time into the school during his last couple days, months, and year, really meant a lot," says Quanci.

James's participation in the Student Government meant more "than just fulfilling a commitment, he helped out because it was something he loved [to do]," added Quanci.

Selflessness

James cared deeply for his friends and the school community as a whole. "He thought about others," says Goldsmith. "He understood that no one is absolutely perfect or absolutely bad. He understood that no one can be judged absolutely." James consistently displayed his concern for those being questioned in the Honor Council and served as a representative for both sides of the story.

The senior class bonded this year through the many hardships that they faced. Throughout it all, James was always alongside his classmates. "He was one of the people that really felt for our class. He was one of us," say Quanci.

Inside the classroom, James devoted himself to his studies. Despite his pain, he continued to attend class. "Knowing how valuable his time was, and how he was choosing to spend time with me, I stepped up my effort . . . it made me focus," says Farrell.

James took advantage of his opportunities to inspire others inside and outside of school. Junior Anthony Torrano, who was one of his closest friends, understood that at James's root, his friend "was [simply] a really nice guy." Along the back steps to the art room, James played his guitar with Torrano and many others. "James was a really good musician and artist [who] inspired me," added Torrano.

The Result

James's positive influence and contributions to our school are immeasurable. His involvement in all aspects of student life created an irreplaceable presence on our campus that will be missed. "He had a greater impact on this community than any teacher could have in an entire career," says Woodard.

James's composure and attitude throughout the past year created a model of how many of us now aspire to live. He lived more in his final year than most people in a lifetime. James understood what it meant to live and he never refused to share his knowledge. "He was the greatest teacher here [because] he taught us to live life," says Woodard.

James questioned life throughout the year in his art class with his theme, "Why do We Find Comfort in Routine?" His art became so connected to his journey with cancer," explains Mrs. Hellstom, who allowed her Adv. Art 3D class to choose the theme of "Moving Forward" as their final exam project. Outside the art room, James's classmates painted *The River of Life Reborn* along the steps as a memorial for him. His classmates chose this symbol to commemorate James and his passion for the arts.

James made our school a better place in all that he was involved in. Looking back at his life, it is easy to become overwhelmed by his body of work. However, the full and everlasting impact that he has had on our community since his death is even more impressive. "He really made me want to be a better person," says Woodard, who believes that James's life not only inspired people, but also changed the culture of this school for the better.

While he may have been a "child of the Sacred Heart" he spent his final school year teaching others, students and faculty alike. With James's passing we will have photographs and other visual aids to remind us of him, but they will not be necessary. Whether a Stuart Hall student plays catch on a baseball diamond, helps organize a school dance, or simply plays his guitar, it will be the mark that James left on this school in everyday activities that people will remember him most. His qualities gave our school life when his was running out. James is now a part of the fabric that makes up the character of Stuart Hall High School and his presence is felt every single day.

Skyler Hicks, 2009

Section 6

In Conclusion

At a loss for what to do
In the melancholy of spring
I try some hand play-
Cupping then letting flow
Rivulets of water from my eaves.

—Rengetsu

Wisdom cannot be taught; it is learned only by individual experience and being open to all things is paramount. As I ponder the notion that "Everything is one" I think of the ferryman and Siddartha's river journey and begin to understand that somehow we are connected to all things that have come before and will follow after. If I can trust in that reality, then James is always here with me and I with him. Even though it is a solitary experience, our life journey touches many and a piece of us will always remain, if even just fleetingly, with those left behind.
—Personal journal entry, 2011

Three Years Hence

And so it is now
Three years since that dreadful moment when I
Longed passionately for your peace—
To my new disposition
Of raging at the heavens because of that very outcome.

It is still fresh, as if the page has just turned
Yet I know 1095 days have evolved and the truth of time passing sits with me
My now honest, constant companion.

Are you over this?
Is the underlying message when many stop to ask
"How are you?" seeing me frail and crippled rattles them and perhaps reminds
how thin and fragile their time might be.

"Fine" is my steady response
The steps forward are being taken
Breathing hurts less and there are moments
When I can recall your smile, sorrow, grousing, smell
With a gentle joy and yes, even gratitude
That at times, miraculously, replaces the longing and hurt.

The chores of day to day are assigned new purpose
And keep me occupied.
I have moved from that place, both physically and emotionally
That on a daily basis stripped me bare.
Exposure to subtle tortures finally taking their toll.

I would still give everything
In some Faustian trade to have you back
But know it would be a futile barter.
Why would you want to return?

It is so much easier to playfully nudge and
Orchestrate from afar
Than negotiate the unplowed fields of the human condition
Where rigid landscapes are too often the norm.

You have taught me to pay attention—
Something I had quite forgotten in the mired years
And now I let days unfold for me
Rather than pushing them to fit.
"Change is constant," has become my new truth.
Simple mantras replace platitudes.

I found a small blue robin's egg
On the ground yesterday
With no nest in sight
How did it get there?
It just somehow happened, was my quiet response.

And like your death, my life and death one day

It will all just happen
Without any doing on our part,
It is.

The birds sing incessantly today
Sun and clouds have filled the sky.
Everything is different and yet nothing is different.
My personal and private place continues to bring me comfort
You are with me even when I feel most alone
And so these shared three years have been good for us
I suppose.

—*Jean Alice Rowcliffe, May 2012*

Table in Beynac, France

Section 7

Reading List

Harvey, Greg. *Grieving For Dummies*. Indiana: Wiley Publications Inc., 2007.

McNees, Pat. *Dying: A Book of Comfort*. New York: Guild America, Doubleday Direct Inc., 1996.

Finkbeiner, Ann, *After the Death of a Child: Living with Loss through the Years*. Maryland: John Hopkins University Press, 1996.

Kübler-Ross, Elisabeth. *On Death and Dying*. New York: Simon and Schuster, 1969.

Lewis, C. S. *A Grief Observed*. New York: Harper Collins Publishers, 1961.

Gunther, John. *Death Be not Proud*. New York: Harper and Row Publishers, 1949.

Remen, Rachel Naomi. *My Grandfather's Blessings: Stories of Strength Refuge and Belonging*. Putnam Penguin, 2000.

Kushner, Harold. *When Bad Things Happen to Good People*. New York: Random House Publishers, 1981.

Chodron, Pema. *When Things Fall Apart: Heart Advice for Difficult Times*. Massachusetts: Shambhala Publications Inc., 1997.

Hanh, Thich Nhat. *You Are Here*. Massachusetts: Shambhala Publishers, 2001.

Didion, Joan. *The Year of Magical Thinking*. New York: Alfred A. Knopf, 2005.

Didion, Joan. *Blue Nights*. New York: Knopf Doubleday Publisher, 2011.

Nuland, Sherwin.*How We Die*. New York: Knopf Doubleday Publisher, 1994.

McCracken, Anne, and Semel, Mary. *A Broken Heart Still Beats: After Your Child Dies*. Minnesota: Hazelden Pulishers, 1998.

Venerable Master Hsing Yun. *Letting Go: Buddhism in Every Step 39*. California: Buddha's Light Publishing, 1999.

Acknowledgements

Quote page 227
CS Lewis   A Grief Observed
1961 Harper Collins

Thank you to the following for the generous use of their photographs:
Marc Foose, Linda Privatelli, Connor and Graham Grealish

Notes

Notes

Edwards Brothers Malloy
Thorofare, NJ USA
September 3, 2013